Jack the Ripper

"Light-hearted Friend"

Richard Wallace

Introduction by Colin Wilson

To my family

First Edition 1996
Gemini Press, 33 Belmont Place, Melrose, MA 02176

Printed in the United States of America.

International Standard Book Number: 0-9627195-6-0
Library of Congress Catalog Card Number: 96-94102

I'm not a butcher,
I'm not a Yid,
Nor yet a foreign skipper,
But I'm your own light-hearted friend,
Your's truly, Jack the Ripper.

Poem received from "Jack the Ripper"

"Madness in great ones must not unwatch'd go."

Shakespeare, *Hamlet*, Act III, i, 192

TABLE OF CONTENTS

ILLUSTRATIONS AND MAPS

Illustrations

Maps

Introduction

When Richard Wallace wrote to me in the spring of 1992, asking if I would be willing to read a typescript arguing that Lewis Carroll was Jack the Ripper, my first reaction was incredulity, then amusement. During my half century as a "Ripperologist" (for I became fascinated by the case when I was about eleven) I have heard some astonishing suggestions — such as that the Whitechapel killer was a sadistic midwife, a grandson of Queen Victoria, and a homosexual boyfriend of Oscar Wilde — but this was the most staggering so far. Naturally, I lost no time in asking the author to let me see his typescript.

First, he sent me another of his books entitled *The Agony of Lewis Carroll*. Again, my first reaction was skepticism, for in the only biography I had read — by Florence Becker Lennon — he seemed one of the most gentle and charming men who ever lived. Yet when I took it off my bookshelf, it fell open at page 323, and I read that in 1936, one Dr. Paul Shilder had found that Carroll showed "oral sadistic traits of cannibalism" and created a world of "cruelty and anxiety." And on the same page, there is a reference to an anti-Freudian book containing a burlesque psychoanalytical interpretation of *Jabberwocky*. It seemed Richard Wallace was not the first to take an unconventional view of Dodgson. In his introduction to the Nonesuch *Complete Lewis Carroll* (1939), Alexander Woolcott had commented: "Indeed, everything has befallen *Alice,* except the last thing — psychoanalysis. At least the new psychologists have not explored this dream book, nor pawed over the gentle, shrinking celibate who wrote it." Clearly he had not encountered Dr. Shilder.

Now what Woolcott expresses was, on the whole, my own view of Dodgson — a shy, kindly man — although with an odd streak of religious bigotry when it came to the question of allowing dons to forego swearing allegiance to the 39 articles. So there could be no doubt that Wallace was going to have a very hard time overcoming my sales resistance to his view of Carroll as a man seething with hatred and revolt.

Now on the whole, I have to confess that his *Agony of Lewis Carroll did* fail to covert me to the view that Carroll hated his mother and harboured a deep resentment towards his father. This was not entirely the author's fault, for the truth is that there is simply too little information about Dodgson's childhood to enable us to draw any clear inferences. It is true that Carroll's birth was followed quickly by that of siblings, but — as Wallace admits — he seems to have remained the favourite. Still, in spite of my doubts, I found that I went on reading — at first for the pleasure of being amused by what seemed outrageous assertions about Dodgson's psychology, but later because I began to feel that Wallace *was* making some convincing points. Carroll stuttered badly all his life; he seemed to have an exaggerated need for security — in fact, it was this very security of his background — as a university lecturer in mathematics — that has given so many biographers the feeling that his life was as cosy and serene as one of Tolkien's hobbits. Wallace did not have to argue very hard to convince me that this was far from the whole truth, and towards the end of the book I found myself thinking: "Now all he needs is some biographical *coup de theatre*, some unexpected piece of evidence, and I shall suddenly begin to think `By God, he's right!´" But that *coup* failed to materialise. I closed the book feeling that this was a remarkable and fascinating piece of research, but that it simply lacked hard evidence.

Since there was no mention of Jack the Ripper in the book, I waited with some impatience for the arrival of the promised typescript, and as soon as it came — in the morning post — settled down to reading it in bed with my morning tea and toast.

Within half a dozen pages, I had that pleasant, comfortable sensation that I had experienced with the earlier book — the feeling that this was something I was going to enjoy. Wallace is a careful researcher, and he presents an excellent picture of the Victorian age — one of the best since Donald Rumbelow's *Complete Jack the Ripper*. And on an early page, Wallace admits engagingly that "the picture I shall be presenting is very much a psychological one... based on the symbolic meaning to be found in the details, not one depending on hard physical evidence." He then goes on to point out that most other writers, including myself, take the same approach.

What follows is as good an account of the Ripper murders — and of their social background — as any that exists. Anyone who does not have a book on Jack the Ripper on his shelf, and who wants to know about them, could not do better than read Wallace. This is also followed by an excellent survey of the various suspects. And Wallace makes the important point that most of the suspects are "gentlemen." For example, that strange character Dr. Forbes Winslow describes his suspect (whom he did not name) as "a man of good position and perhaps living in the West End of London." And since then, suspects have included the heir to the throne of England, a Cambridge tutor, and Queen Victoria's physician. If we are prepared to admit that the Ripper may have been a "gentleman," then Dodgson may certainly be classified as a suspect. He certainly — as Wallace shows — lived close enough to Whitechapel to have had the opportunity.

It is in his chapter "A Ripper Profile" that there emerges the basic difference of opinion between us. Wallace quotes me as saying that the murders were compulsive, not the result of rational choice. He goes on: "I will differ from this in the sense that they were not so compulsive as to be done without awareness. I believe they became a willed response to feelings created by the frustrations of compulsions, that all other efforts to relieve the rage had failed, that a compulsive need to seek relief in a new way pushed him to these murders."

I see Wallace's point, and it is an effective one. Given the premise that Dodgson was seething with hatred and frustration, it is perfectly possible that he might have planned to kill "gay" women (meaning women of the streets) as a kind of deliberate ritual. In fact, I foresaw such a possibility in the title of my own "Ripper novel" *Ritual in the Dark*, in which the killer is a homosexual seething with rage and frustration that dates from his childhood, and that is complicated by guilt feelings about his sexual orientation. Yet I must also admit that, looking back on the novel more than thirty years later, I am no longer convinced by my own theory. My chief criticism — which rose out of a comment by another "Ripperologist," Dan Farson — is that a homosexual would not choose to mutilate women, for the choice of victim betrays a sexual preference. And this I still feel to be one of the main objections to Wallace's theory. Lewis Carroll adored little girls and disliked little boys; that seems to betray that any suppressed sexual feelings he possessed (and I find it hard to believe that he was consciously a pedophile) were directed towards girls.

The following chapter, "Life of Motive," is the point at which most readers will find themselves either beginning to nod in agreement or tempted to hurl the book across the room. Wallace makes his own central point with typical boldness when he remarks that *The Agony of Lewis Carroll* could have been sub-titled "The Making of a Serial Killer." I have to admit that this conflicts with my own view of serial killers, which clarified as I wrote a book called *The Serial Killer* with Donald Seaman. For some odd reason, all known "serial killers" so far have been working-class in origin. A few serial killers — a very few — have been reasonably wealthy, like the Australian sex-killer Chris Wilder; but in every case I have studied so far, the childhood background has been working class. My own theory is that the kind of murderous "resentment" that can lead to the serial murder originates in the killer's childhood, usually in emotional starvation or in downright abuse, poverty and misery, which produces the feeling that the world is a jungle in which you grab what you can. A child with a middle-class or upper-class background may feel angry and frustrated, but he never quite has that feeling of being abandoned-to-sink that springs out of dirt and degradation.

Now the nub of Wallace's argument is that a middle class child — like Dodgson — *could* generate such hatred and resentment under the right — or rather wrong — conditions. He suggests that Dodgson was a quiet little boy, dominated by his clergyman father and his thoroughly Victorian mother, and forced into a kind of straitjacket that left him emotionally crippled and unfitted for life. This is a plausible view; even Professor Harry Morgan Ayres argues in *Carroll's Alice* that the Alice books are a satire on education and its distortion of the natural child. Wallace goes on to suggest that at Rugby school, Dodgson became a victim of the "fagging" system, which often involved homosexual rape. And here I can agree that the remark made by Eric Lindon in *Sylvie and Bruno*: "Years ago I offered myself as a *slave* - as a *"Confidential slave,"* I think it's called..." seems to conceal some odd memory of sexual humiliation ; its very gratuitousness suggests a hidden significance. I am also much intrigued by that curious illustration — drawn by Dodgson — to *The Rectory Umbrella*, showing a smiling bearded man who wears what seems to be a girl's dress and shoes, and whose legs are too shapely for a male — as well as by the picture of the distinctly feminine "knight" who is about to slay the Jabberwock. These, I must admit, suggest to me that perhaps the nature of Carroll's sexual "oddity" might have been transvestism. And this admission reveals the extent to which I have come to accept Wallace's thesis that there *was* something very odd about Dodgson. Still, I find it impossible to take that final step and agree that his "secret life" might have involved disemboweling prostitutes.

Now we come to what, for most readers, will be the major stumbling block to accepting Wallace's theory: his insistence that the vital clues are concealed in anagrams. Literary critics have been suspicious — not to say contemptuous — of anagrams ever since Ignatius Donnelly's *The Great Cryptogram: Francis Bacon's Cipher in the So-Called Shakespeare Plays* (published, oddly enough, in the year of the Ripper murders). Donnelly claimed that the plays of Shakespeare were written by Bacon — who was also a cipher expert — and that encoded in them are anagrams that admit his authorship. He inspired dozens of cranks to seek out anagrams in Shakespeare's plays. The Catholic prelate Ronald Knox satirised the whole tendency in an essay "On the Authorship of *In Memoriam*," which claimed to discover anagrams in the poem which proved that it was written not by Tennyson but by Queen Victoria — anagrams like "Queenie, Alf's pen-poet."

But Donnelly *did* have a valid point: that Bacon was a cipher expert. I do not believe that there is the slightest chance that Bacon was Shakespeare — their characters are too different — but have to concede that *if* Bacon had written Shakespeare's plays, nothing is more likely than that he would have been unable to resist the temptation to introduce ciphers and anagrams that revealed his authorship.

Now I agree that the title: *The Hunting of the Snark: An Agony in Eight Fits* certainly sounds as if it might conceal an anagram. But I find it difficult to accept as one possible "decoding": "Hunt the King of Hearts, a non-gay in fine tights," even when a consultation of the relevant chapter in *Alice* reveals that the King of Hearts *is* dressed in "fine tights." As far as I know, "gay" as a synonym for homosexual was simply not used in the Victorian era — or indeed, much before our own time. Wallace is fair enough to point out that, in Carroll's time, "gay" referred to a lady of loose morals.

Yet having said this, I have to acknowledge that Wallace is obviously correct when he makes the point that Carroll, a mathematician who was devoted to puzzles, also loved anagrams, and that if he had a secret, it would almost certainly be concealed in his "nonsense" verse, and in a title like *The Hunting of the Snark* or *Phantasmagoria*. The major question here is how we decide which anagrams are plausible, and which simply go too far. And where anagrams are concerned, there is no obvious criterion.

All this must be left to the critical sense of the individual reader. I have no doubt that reactions to this book will range from scornful dismissal to the conviction that Wallace is a psychologist of genius. My own view is somewhere midway between the two. Most books on Jack the Ripper demand a certain suspension of disbelief. The most widely known, Stephen Knight's *Jack the Ripper: The Final Solution*, asks us to believe that Queen Victoria's grandson, the Duke of Clarence, secretly married an artist's model, and that the murders were a conspiracy of Freemasons, led by Sir William Gull, to suppress this secret. *The Ripper Legacy* by Martin Howells and Keith Skinner, suggests that Jack the Ripper was an unsuccessful barrister — Montague Druitt — who was murdered by a clique of Cambridge homosexuals to prevent him from disgracing their secret society. Aleister Crowley believed that Jack the Ripper was a black magician who committed the murders as part of a magical ritual to gain godlike powers. In this company, Richard Wallace's theory seems almost conservative and respectable. It is certainly plausible and totally original. For all my disagreements on xi

individual points, I have to doff my hat to Mr. Wallace and acknowledge that he has totally succeeded in the modest aim he set for himself: to introduce Lewis Carroll as a possible suspect for the Ripper murders.

Whom do I believe was the Whitechapel killer? I am inclined to believe that he was no one that you or I have ever heard of. My own "psychological portrait" would be a native of the East End of London, a man of high dominance and a heavy drinker, who committed the murders when he had been drinking heavily. But I must admit that virtually everyone who has written about Jack the Ripper takes a different view, and that the majority of Ripperologists believe, as Wallace does, that he was a "gentleman" with a psychotic hatred of prostitutes.

After reading Richard Wallace's two books, I was so intrigued that I asked him to tell me something about himself. The reply was as follows:

Personal
I'm fifty-four years old, spent twenty-five years in data processing as a computer programmer, systems analyst, and manager, "retired" when the parent company of the ... subsidiary I headed was purchased. Seeking something more interesting after [experiencing two] earlier mergers, I returned to school to take up social work, the goal being to become a therapist for children and their families. I did this in 1988, became interested [in Lewis Carroll] at the time, began research in 1988 and finished the two books before beginning work as a therapist in January 1991. I have since been providing therapy to severely sexually and physically abused children, with a focus being the release of rage in therapeutically violent but safe ways until the need for violence subsides and alternative releases can be taught. As you probably know, training as a therapist involves the use of feelings raised in the self by what the patient presents to help diagnose feelings in the patient. It was those "diagnostic" feelings that led me to the books, while I think it was programming and systems analysis that supported the simultaneous minute focus yet global view required to see and solve anagrams (along with Carroll's "sound and sense" explained in *Alice's Adventures*).

I have been married for thirty-one years and have three grown children.

Lewis Carroll:
I had little interest in Lewis Carroll as a child, do recall enjoying my mother's animated rendition of "Off with their

heads!" It was while in school titling a paper on a psychological topic "Through the Looking-Glass" that I thought I should read the book by the same title to determine if someone had been there before me. In a way Carroll had. Feelings of unaccounted-for rage emerged in the reading and examination of his "children's" books and biographical material, rage not adequately accounted for. In a serendipitous discovery, I suddenly realized that the title of the mock epic poem "The Hunting of the Snark: An Agony in Eight Fits" was an anagram; using Carroll's words, "It came to me as if in a dream." I just continued to pursue that notion in other areas of his works and *The Agony* evolved. Not satisfied that all the rage had been identified, that writing smut in secret was not an adequate release for the rage, in fact only fueled it, I dabbled for three months with the thought that he might be Jack the Ripper, finally traveled to England for research after discovering material in the *Sylvie* works. The "Jabberwocky" anagram as a profound statement of rage had also stuck with me. So, while I really had no interest in Carroll for a lifetime, I now have an entirely different appreciation for the man and his ability to "weave a tale."

Whatever the final verdict of you, the reader, on this controversial theory, I am certain that you will share with me an appreciation of the ingenious Richard Wallace, and *his* ability to weave a tale.

Colin Wilson

Author's Preface

After readying *The Agony of Lewis Carroll* for publication in 1990, I had hoped that I could and would leave what had been a difficult research and writing task and resume my newly found career in social work. I had hoped that others, but not I, would continue the study of Carroll's life and works. Little did I realize that however much I wished to leave the inner world and life of Lewis Carroll, I would not be able to do so.

I continued to experience a nagging doubt, that the whole story of Charles Lutwidge Dodgson's struggle with life still had not been told, that the rage — what seemed unbridled rage — which continued to manifest itself into his sixth decade of life, had not sated, was still seething, seeking relief. Questions emerged that just would not go away. Was it possible that hiding all the expressions of anger I had found in his works did not, in the end, provide adequate physical or psychic release from his torment? What would such a hater of women, of mothers, and most secretly, of preadolescent girls, do to relieve what seemed an explosive rage, but one which an extraordinarily controlled man had seemingly managed to keep in check? How could such an attack, hidden so deeply in his books that no one could find it in his lifetime of publishing, really satisfy if its intended targets were unaware of it? Would it become compulsively necessary to openly attack surrogates for the very women to whom he avowed a closeness? Could he have physically attacked women? Was the unthinkable possible, that further research into the life of Lewis Carroll could provide a solution to the riddle of Jack the Ripper? Could they be one and the same person?

On just that thin thread of feeling I wavered for months, ambivalent about taking on the task of staying inside this very disturbed man, concerned that I had already done enough to the legendary author and his works, concerned that I was not up to what I knew would be a very draining effort, concerned that I was treading too far beyond the safety of the real world, too deeply into madness. I had thought the British Broadcasting solution which appeared on American television in 1988 had "credibility" and certainly had had far more resources applied to it that I could muster. After a month I abandoned the effort, then took it up again two months later as feelings continued to linger.

Following a full year's intense effort, a manuscript emerged, and it was not until it was nearly finished, not until all the many puzzle pieces of fact, fiction, symbolism, and coincidence had been assembled into a whole, not until the first book was by now in print, that even I became convinced that what I had found was quite complete, very possibly true, and worthy of being presented for public scrutiny.

I already knew that "proving" a hypothesis regarding a one-hundred-year-old crime was nearly impossible. And by every measure my "solution" seemed preposterous. I also felt strongly that something was owed to a "number" of women (no one really knows how many), who were nameless except for the notoriety of their killer and the manner of their deaths, and who cry somewhere for justice, perhaps just to know who struck them down, or why. But the primary motivation behind the telling of this story is my belief that it is compellingly true and that in its truth I continue my study of child abuse, hypocrisy, alienation, and the enormous rage which all three create in their victims. While I had believed that *The Agony of Lewis Carroll* defined the destruction of a young boy as total, it is only in this work that I really came to know how total it was.

My thanks go to my family, again, as with the first book, but especially to my wife, who continued her still patient acceptance of what was driving me to this effort and its intrusion on our lives together. And I must thank my many friends again for providing me with periodic relief from the task, an escape from a world of madness, an often and much needed touching of the real world of gentleness they offer, and, of course, for their encouragement. I must mention especially my brother Allen; Robbie Tourse, Ph.D; Jennifer Locke, Esq.; Barbara Blum, LICSW; Barry Melnick, Ph.D; Donna Ferrullo, Esq.; and Doreen Hardy, LICSW.

Thanks are due the library and staff at Boston College, for their funders and preservers of the Burns Collection of rare books, to the staff of the British Library in London and Colindale, the library at Christ Church, Oxford, the Public Records Office in Kew, and the Records Office at Guildhall, London, for providing me access to original material and for not demanding to know what I was doing.

A deep debt of gratitude is due people whom I never met, whom I came to know only in their books — the fraternity of "Ripperologists" — especially Colin Wilson, Donald Rumbelow, the late Stephen Knight, Daniel Farson, Martin Howells and Keith Skinner, Robin Odell, Philip Sugden, and many others. Without their published writings, most of what has been lost in its original form would have been unavailable to me. So, too, would their thoughts and analyses, which became very much my starting point.

Colin Wilson, who kindly responded to my request that he read the typescript by writing an introduction to support the presentation of this case, has been a lifetime pursuer of the Ripper. He still judges the crimes as unsolved, has suggested that investigators should stop trying to fit the profile of a murderer and mutilator to their suspect, that they should instead find a person who possesses the proper profile and investigate the possibility that he could be the infamous killer. I think I have done that.

Perhaps strangely, I must thank my subject and suspect, Charles Lutwidge Dodgson, who wrote down so much of his experiences from which we can learn. For without his enormous body of literature, however much he may have used it for his own purposes, I would have nothing, and his life of inner torment and turmoil would have been lost. If you come to accept him as Jack the Ripper, I hope you also come to understand the terrible and totally destroying ordeal that he must have experienced in his early life that would lead him to such atrocity at his by then fifty-sixth year.

Lastly, I must acknowledge the sustaining presence of God in my life during this very difficult period when I became totally immersed in the exploration of the darkest side of the human condition.

Richard Wallace

Alice Holding the Baby Boy

Source: *Alice's Adventures in Wonderland*, Chapter VI.

Prologue

This is a story of Jack the Ripper. I say "a story" because there have been many, and this may become known as just another. On the other hand, you may come to feel as I do, that this version, however bizarre, is very close to, if not the true one. In writing of these crimes in the *Pall Mall Gazette* in December 1888, the Earl of Crawford Balcarres noted:

> ´In endeavoring to sift a mystery like this, one cannot afford to throw aside any theory, however extravagant, without careful examination, because the truth might, after all, lie in the most unlikely one.´ [1]

Readers would do well to recall the earl's advice as this presentation unfolds.

My telling of this story will focus primarily on the crimes themselves, a detailed examination of the evidence available, and a single and historically a most unlikely suspect — Charles Lutwidge Dodgson — known far better by his pseudonym Lewis Carroll, under which he wrote *Alice's Adventures in Wonderland* and a whole body of nonsense and children's literature.

This book is also a sequel, an unexpected sequel, to my first study of the troubled writer titled *The Agony of Lewis Carroll*, a psychobiography published in 1990. Like that book, I have written this one in the first person because it represents a continuation of the journey on which I invited readers to accompany me, a journey into another's painful inner life. For those not up to tackling the first book, a summary of relevant material appears in chapter 3. There are many references to that work in this one. The earlier work also contains two rather technical appendices pertinent to this book, one of which discusses the psychological origins of rage, especially murderous rage, the second of which discusses sexual perversions as expressions of rage.

The Investigatory Setting

Before setting the Victorian London stage on which these notorious crimes took place, a word is in order regarding the modern stage on which this investigation proceeded. The sources for my initial research on Jack the Ripper were the several books available in local libraries, but not too available as many of them have "disappeared" over the years. Eventually a trip to London was necessary as it became apparent that close-to-original documents in the police files needed to be examined so that my own "editing" could be done. These were found on microfilm at the Public Records Office in Kew, outside of London proper, and the offices in Guildhall. Lastly, in order to determine what Charles Dodgson might have known about the murders from the publications of the day and to obtain a flavor for the atmosphere generated by the murderous spree, the microfilm newspaper records at Colindale, part of the British Library collection, were examined.

Perhaps the most important source documents in this entire research project were the original handwritten diaries of Charles Dodgson, a gift from the Dodgson estate, lying in the Manuscript Collection of the British Library. For it was in these that I saw the depth of emotion which had been recorded and never really reflected in the heavily edited version published by Roger Green, *The Diaries of Lewis Carroll*. Also buried in the diaries was other unpublished material I thought might be useful and relevant. In addition to these diaries, to which I was given ready access, I examined nearly one hundred other books, several on Jack the Ripper which were unavailable locally, but more importantly a broad array of material that ranged from Dodgson's father's published sermons and many of the works on Lewis Carroll which have been published in Britain, to the more access-restricted volumes on sexual pathology and Victorian pornography.

Unable to locate the diaries of Dodgson's friend Thomas Vere Bayne, which I presumed had been published, I traveled to Christ Church, Oxford, hoping on hope I could get into the library to inquire about them. Much to my amazement, within fifteen minutes of voicing my request to the "bull-dog" on duty at the gate at Christ Church, I was sitting in the library with the four extant volumes of the hand-written diaries in my lap.

Throughout all of this investigation I feared someone would challenge the purpose of my research effort and inhibit it. No one did; perhaps it was an unnecessary concern.

Efforts to make contact with Scotland Yard and the London Police Department as a "Ripper researcher" were unsuccessful beyond the courtesy of providing me information regarding the nature and location of the filmed material and, of course, access to the material they did have.   While disappointed, as I would have liked their critical review of my preliminary case and the doors that might have opened if they were favorably impressed, I came to understand that the century-old old crime was not as high on their agenda as it was on mine.

With the cooperation of the British Library and the Public Records Office I did return home with facsimile copies of selected pages from Dodgson's diaries for the period preceding, during, and following the Ripper murders and facsimiles of several "Ripper" letters from the microfilm, letters I thought for my own reasons might have been authentic. Chapter 12 reflects the results of an analysis performed by a forensic handwriting specialist and licensed graphologist recommended by the Masssachusetts State Police.

That describes pretty much the environment in which the research took place. So much original Ripper material has been lost, either through lack of attention and protection, damage or loss during World War II, or pilferage by souvenir-gathering researchers before things were placed on film, the published works of others became the primary source of data. While the Black Museum in London no doubt houses material that might have been useful, I did not attempt to gain access, which I understand is somewhat limited to the law enforcement community, of which I am not a member.

Finally, as readers shall see, much additional material comes from my own research into what I believe was Dodgson's unique method of communication hidden in his published books and poems.

The Victorian Setting

These murders occurred in a society which was in the middle of enormous social and economic change and the pressures such forces create. The age of science and research was thriving by the 1850's. Nowhere was this more evident than in the emerging studies of man as an evolving species which would begin then and which continue today. Scientific investigation and theories were challenging fundamental religious beliefs regarding man and God, indeed, even the existence of God.   Man as a created creature was becoming man *the* creating creature, the center of focus at the top of the evolutionary scale. The perceived need for a God to explain things was being questioned in new ways with new theories and evidence. Religious certainties were disappearing along with the comforts that such certainties about ultimate things can create.

The Industrial Revolution was well underway, evidenced not only by the growth of technology but by the enormous economic potential created by that early technology, and the building of an extensive rail system and manufacturing processes. The more sinister depersonalization and alienation fostered by the new economy were just being recognized. Along with those changes came migration of workers to the cities, increased demand for cheap labor, and increased disparity between the rich and poor. Foreign unrest brought a large number of immigrants to England where they crowded sections of London. Socialism was birthing and its demands for greater equity in the distribution of wealth and power were pressuring the entire social fabric of a nation steeped in monarchical tradition, an entitled upper class, and inherited privilege. By 1888, in the fifty-first year of the reign of Queen Victoria, unrest was clearly evident in London.

Throughout it all the British lady and gentleman were expected to retain reserve and decorum, with the greatest social sin being public disclosure that reserve and decorum had been privately compromised. The hypocrisy of the period was clearly evident in the importance given to appearances over substance, of facade over reality. The social age demanded the development of a split personality, a person who could isolate his private thoughts and feelings and the behavior they create from his public image, of his avowed moral code with his practiced moral code, be it in sexual, economic, or political affairs. While there had long been a "social mask" which people used in public, in this age its maintenance was raised to high art (and not just a little humor) among an increasing number of the growing population. In reality, the very historical foundations of society and all that was good and acceptable, based as it was in the upper class mores, was becoming exposed as a facade.

It was an age when an increasing population of comfortably rich, most often educated at the best schools, were bored stiff, had nothing to do, and kept themselves busy in trivial pursuits, often characterized by self-indulgence. This was especially true of women who were virtually excluded from affairs, mere ornaments to support the social needs of their husbands, engaged full time in facade maintenance, and employable as governesses in the best circumstances, sweat-shop laborers and prostitutes in the worst.

The murders by "Jack the Ripper" occurred in the East End of London, the most crowded, poorest, and neglected section of the city. Though barely three square miles in its very core, it was filled with over

900,000 inhabitants, over half of them immigrants, called "foreigners" (the Victorian euphemism for "Jews"), 80,000 artisans who earned barely £ 1 per week, and numerous street vendors. Over half of the children died before the age of five. [2]

Police accounts differ with some other published reports, no doubt intended to paint a picture favorable to the establishment that tolerated it. The records indicate that the East End contained 233 Common Lodging Houses which housed 8,530 people. Sixty two of the houses were known to be brothels. [3] It was estimated that there were 1,200 prostitutes operating in one small area, soliciting in the streets, and, if they had no room, finding a dark corner to earn their pittance. One church official claimed that the number of prostitutes operating in all of London approached 80,000, but he was dismissed with the claim that it was "not more than" 8,000. [4]

The Common Lodging Houses were inhabited by structured classes among the poor, with prostitutes, thieves, and tramps pretty much isolated from the more respectable. In many cases, particularly among the alienated, the rent or doss was paid daily, the tenants doing whatever was necessary to get the few cents required to keep their room. Inhabitants often shared quarters with large numbers of unrelated people even if many of them attempted to maintain all the airs of propriety in the midst of their poverty. A common kitchen served to provide a place to socialize or fight as food was prepared and shared to varying degrees. Brawls could even break out over the ownership rights to a piece of soap. Lacking the rent, the night was spent in the street.

Partly as a result of the public outcry which emerged during the Ripper's spree and the efforts of the crusading Reverend Samuel Barnett, new barrack-like housing was built to replace many of the Common Lodging Houses. [5] These still stand today and are quite attractive from the outside. Somehow they escaped the blitz of World War II, though nearby streets were not so fortunate.

When the Home Secretary initiated an attempt to clear the area of prostitution during the time of these murders, he was met with the very real objection voiced by his police commissioner Sir Charles Warren. He protested that until the demand for prostitution were reduced, he could do little about the supply. [6] Much of that demand came from West Enders whose purse or wish for anonymity kept them from the high-class prostitutes in their own area. This, too, would become a problem in the investigation of the Ripper murders as there was significant trafficking by outsiders, well-dressed outsiders, in and out of the neighborhood. The sad fact is that Victorian society did not have a work alternative for the poor, so there was little motivation to eliminate this source of income while aggravating those with the money and inclination to pay.

A community filled with Jews, the East End naturally attracted and contained a large number of slaughtermen qualified to perform the appropriate rituals in the preparation of the animals and a large number of slaughterhouses in which the activities were undertaken. This also inhibited the investigation during the spree of murders as it was not at all uncommon to see men walking in the streets with blood on their hands and clothes.

While police records and news accounts reflect there was a police presence patrolling in the East End, as is true in neglected areas, the number of men compared to the population and number of crimes were relatively few and there was obviously a great deal being overlooked. Gangs of young punks roamed the streets and pretty much had their way. Investigations into violence were cursory unless a perpetrator was captured quickly. Police often patrolled in pairs for their own protection; they would come to do so in makeshift rubber-soled shoes contrived by attaching strips of bicycle tires to their soles. All of this represented an attempt to permit police to sneak up on the Ripper and catch him in the act. In some areas the morgue consisted of a shed where bodies were left to rot, unburied for days, the stench tolerated by poor neighbors whose complaints fell on deaf ears.

As we move to the murders themselves, we can gain a sense of the flavor of the period by quoting a letter written by Socialist and wit George Bernard Shaw to the *Star* on 24 September 1888, during the height of Ripper mania. It reflects the changes that were quickly taking place during the period in which Jack owned the East End and of the real panic he was creating in the establishment. Commenting that the Whitechapel murderer had been more successful in calling attention to social issues than the Socialist organizations to which he belonged had been, Shaw writes:

> Less than a year ago [at the time of the riot in Trafalgar Square popularly called "Bloody Sunday"] the West End press were literally clamouring for the blood of the people — hounding Sir Charles Warren to thrash and muzzle the scum who dared to complain that they were starving — heaping insult and reckless calumny upon those who interceded for the victims — applauding to the skies the open class bias of the magistrates and judges who zealously did their worst in the criminal proceedings which followed, behaving, in short, as the

propertied class always does behave when the workers throw it into a frenzy of terror by venturing to show their teeth.

[After referencing that £78,000 had been raised for the poor during the dock strikes of 1886] . . . Indeed if the habits of Duchesses only admitted of their being decoyed into Whitechapel backyards, a single experiment in slaughterhouse anatomy on an aristocratic victim might fetch in a round half million and save the necessity of sacrificing [what was then thought to be] four women of the people. [7]

Tempers were strung tight. The police and establishment were furious. A popular antiestablishment hero was being born. A legend in criminal atrocity was already beginning to emerge.

Chapter 1

The Murders

It is hardly an understatement to suggest that "Jack the Ripper" has become the foremost legendary figure in the folklore of crime. Nearly everyone knows that Jack murdered a number of women, savagely, in London, a long time ago, and that he was never captured. In many ways it hardly seems necessary to describe what happened in excruciating, sequential detail. Yet, of course, the story must be told and told in adequate detail to glean the clues that do exist in the accounts that have come down from original material long since lost from neglect, wars, and souvenir-hunters. What follows is a compilation of material taken from previously published books, newspapers of the day and records in the police files. All other sources notwithstanding, the superb investigatory work performed by a tireless Frederick George Abberline and Chief Inspector Donald P. Swanson, both of Scotland Yard, as they coordinated an extraordinarily frustrating investigation with never the satisfaction of capture cannot go unacknowledged. However, the primary published sources are the works of Colin Wilson and Robin Odell, Martin Howells and Keith Skinner, Stephen Knight, and Donald Rumbelow. Since very little source material is identified in these works, I have provided citations only for material which seemed unique to each author; much of what they have written has become part of the "lore." It would not be until 1994, three years after this work was "completed," that I would have access to Philip Sugden's detailed and well annotated work *The Complete History of Jack the Ripper*. A few changes became necessary (and welcome) based on the thoroughness of his research and access to original documents which I did not have. Since this book is structured to focus on certain aspects of the case in each chapter, some of the detail and its analysis is left for its appropriate place. Likewise, much local color is omitted entirely, for the fact is that no viable local suspect was ever apprehended for the crimes. So, much of the detail presented in other versions is of interest in providing flavor but not substantial to solving the mystery one hundred years later. This sorting and omitting was done only with great care, however. Nothing has knowingly been omitted which I believe either supports or refutes the case I will be making regarding Charles Dodgson. I am much indebted to Colin Wilson, Robin Odell, Donald Rumbelow, and Philip Sugden both for the detail their works provide and for their expert evaluative judgements that despite the assertions to the contrary by several other writers and researchers, the Ripper mystery is still unsolved.

Still unsolved when *The Diary of Jack the Ripper* was published in 1993 and identified James Maybrick as its author and perpetrator of the Ripper attacks? There are numerous reasons — from an inappropriate "profile" of Maybrick to the questionable authenticity of the handwriting, the sudden appearance of this document from nowhere, to its appearance of having been written extensively in single sessions — to disparage this diary as a fabrication (although the work itself appears sincere and well done). It could certainly appear self-serving to do so; I will leave that to others and history and proceed to present a compelling profile and circumstantial case.

The primary reason for a detailed description of the murders is that the solution I shall be presenting is very much a psychological one. It is based on the symbolic meaning to be found in the details, not one depending on hard, physical evidence. There are no fingerprints, blood, semen or hair samples which can be examined using sophisticated laboratory techniques. In fact, as one reviews the literature on Jack the Ripper, one reaches a startling conclusion. As each writer in turn either dismisses all historical suspects, one by one, as Wilson, Odell, Rumbelow, and Sugden do, or makes his case for his own suspect, whatever physical evidence was gathered at the time plays virtually no role in the argument. For there really existed little more usable evidence than murdered and mutilated bodies, a missing body part that arrived in the mail, and taunting letters by the thousands, some very few of which were believed to be from the Ripper. It was Stephen Knight who really began to see symbolic patterns in the murders, patterns we will find constitute important evidence even if Knight and I arrive at very different conclusions. For these patterns and the symbolism surrounding them, the relationship between those symbols and the symbols important in our suspect's life become crucial. Finally, in combining this meaning with motive, knowledge, opportunity and a wealth of coincidence, we find a strong case that Charles Lutwidge Dodgson, a.k.a. Lewis Carroll, should have another alias attached to his name, that of Jack the Ripper.

A map of the East End of London is provided on page 237 in chapter 14 which examines more fully the geography of the crimes. The locations of the murders are marked so that readers can follow the location of victims and make note of the very small geographic area in question. It is here where Jack's audacity helped create the legend as he moved about the shadows with impunity despite what was thought to be a tight and closing police net.

London was not at all prepared for what was about to happen in the spring of 1888, least of all the police. Department morale was poor, the upper echelons were overwhelmed by the politically based reorganization that had taken place after the city police labor actions of the early 1880s. General Charles Warren, a much respected military man based on his successes in the colonies, had been made commissioner in order to restore a soldier's discipline to the force as part of a strategy to confront increasing Socialist unrest. It was a military style squashing of what became riots in Trafalgar Square in 1886 that demonstrated the extent to which a domestic police force had distanced itself from the people it exists to protect and whose trust is required to be effective. Pay was low; morale was lower. And the East End would prove to be tougher duty than normal for the hundreds of police who would eventually be thrown into the breech to find a single monster who became a taunting embarrassment to the establishment.

On 3 April 1888, in that area of the city given to extreme poverty, overcrowding, neglect, and the violence these ills spawn, forty-five-year-old Emma Smith was attacked and beaten, an ear nearly removed, by what she said were three men (or four, by some accounts), on Osborne Street, Spitalfields. She made her way a quarter of a mile back to her apartment on George Street, most likely hoping she could treat herself; then, accompanied by a friend, she walked about a half a mile to the London Hospital. If she passed any policemen over that journey, she did not seek his assistance. It was only at the hospital that the extent of her injuries were determined for she had placed her shawl between her legs to absorb the flow of blood coming from massive injuries to her vagina. An unidentified blunt instrument so large that it tore the vagina walls had been used to violate her. She died the following day of peritonitis. The police were notified on 6 April, in time for the post-mortem. Only the *Times* mentioned the death as part of its routine of reporting autopsy results. A cursory investigation found nothing.

Changing patterns in the sequence of murders has been the reason for historically excluding this one and the next from the Ripper's spree, just as it tends to exclude the later ones. But, as we shall see, there may have been reasons for the change in pattern, and its evolution should be noted.

This murder involved three or four men who appear to have held their victim and struggled to hold her, not for purposes of rape by one or more of them, but for purposes of violating her with an instrument, a substitute for the penis, a symbolic penis. And the substitute was so large as to take on the distorted dimensions found in the pornography of the Marquis De Sade as well as that pouring forth from the French and English underworld, where the instrument of penetration, whatever it might be, was invariably of outlandish, impossible physical dimensions. This pain-inducing distortion is an essential ingredient of the pornographer's fantasies regarding his power (but founded in feelings of powerlessness) and his physical endowments. Whatever other motive existed in the violation of Emma Smith, the desire to inflict conscious pain was present. There appeared to be no effort to make her unconscious before the violation. We'll never know what stopped the attack, whether it was "finished" with what was done or whether attackers, fearful of detection, abandoned the injured woman before other atrocities could be committed.

This modus operandi would later give some justification to the notion that the murders were the work of "High Rip" gangs who extorted money (which could never be more than a few cents) from prostitutes with some regularity and impunity. Such an attack as this combined with no effort on her part to seek the aid of police could mark it as an act of retribution or intimidation for other prostitutes to see. Perhaps Emma was or believed she was being attacked by such a gang and acted accordingly.

Writers comment that this murder was typical of what was a regular occurrence in Whitechapel, but this does not jibe in some ways with the attention it would eventually receive, isolated as the "first" in retrospect and even appearing in Queen Victoria's encrypted messages as the first. [1]   As neglected as this murder was because of *where* it took place, the filthy East End, it eventually would be treated as somewhat qualitatively different from other East End murders, most of which were based on emotional outbursts involving property, jealousies, or long-standing domestic wrangling.

There would not be another attack of this type or severity (not otherwise explained) until 6 August 1888 (for some reason some date it the 7th) when thirty-nine-year-old Martha Tabram (a.k.a. Turner) was found stabbed thirty-nine times in her throat, breast and stomach with what appeared to be two different instruments, a bayonet and (primarily) a short knife. This murder occurred in George's Yard, one street east of Osborne Street. A friend of the victim reported having been with her in the company of two soldiers just before she was found, but several lineups involving men from the units stationed at the nearby Tower of London failed to produce any identification or a suspect lacking an alibi. [2]   Whether Martha's friend refused to identify men she recognized has been hypothesized but is not known. Doing so would certainly have put her own life and safety at risk or harmed future business prospects for herself or fellow prostitutes from the steady source of customers the garrison provided.

The foreman at the Coroner's Inquest criticized the lack of success resulting from the police investigation, claiming that the East End was being neglected in a way that would not have been tolerated if this and the Smith murder (already being connected) had taken place in the West End. The *Daily News*, perhaps still reticent in acknowledging the possibility of such atrocity having been perpetrated by an English gentleman, headlined a brief story with "Supposed Murder in Whitechapel," apparently suspecting the victim of gross incompetence in a bungled effort to commit suicide. [3]   The *Times* dutifully and routinely reported the results of the inquest. If there was any significant police effort to solve the crime, it certainly was not the result of public interest or pressure.

The presence of two instruments is a mystery. At the time it raised the question of whether there was a single attacker who might have been ambidextrous, [4] perhaps wielding the weapons simultaneously at some point in a frenzied attack. Or there could have been two or more participants, each attacking in sequence with a different instrument, a sharing by two participants based on some mutual commitment to the task. It is unlikely that two would be attacking simultaneously since the wounds were to the front of the body and would have put the attackers at risk of injuring one another.

If this was a Ripper murder, it was markedly different from the previous one. The object was obviously murder, and the stabbing continued for some time after the attacker must have known that the victim was mortally wounded, if not already dead. The killer had brought traditional cutting and stabbing weapons to the scene. It was a safer affair, one that reduced struggle and the chance of the victim crying out or identifying participants. It also kept the blood contained within the clothing, off of the murderer, as all of the clothing was found still in place. We have no way of knowing the sequence in which the stab wounds were made, whether the infliction of conscious pain was a dynamic (which would have required a muffling of cries), or whether the attack was still lacking in the "organization" that would become so evident in the murders still to come.

In both of these cases, and in those to follow, the absence of robbery in the traditional sense as a motive is clear. All of the victims were of the lowest economic class, prostituting themselves for the three or four cents required for a night's lodging — the doss — something to eat or drink, the extravagance of something pretty for themselves or to improve their possibilities in attracting the next customer. These were abjectly poor women, worn out and weakened from the hard lives that brought them to their current situation and occupations.

Things changed again just twenty-four days later with the murder of forty-two year old Mary Ann Nichols on 31 August. Seen at 2:30 A.M. on Osborne Street right near where Emma Smith had been found, a little over an hour later her still warm and mutilated body was discovered in Buck's Row (now Durwood Street), a secluded passageway nearly a half mile east of Osborne Street.

On his way to work at 3:40 A.M. George Cross came upon what he thought was a bundle, but which, upon investigation in the dim light coming from the end of the street, was a woman, perhaps unconscious from rape or drink. She was lying on her back with her skirt up nearly to her waist. He summoned a passerby, John Paul, to help him raise her. Paul searched for a heartbeat and, sensing life, rearranged her clothing for the sake of modesty. They both left to search for a policeman and raised John Neil, who had been walking that beat just minutes before and who had heard nothing. With his bull's lamp, they were now able to see that there was a pool of blood beneath the body and that her throat was cut. Her hands were cold, but the upper arms were still warm. They now fetched a local doctor, Dr. Ralph Llewellyn (he would be busy the rest of the year), who examined the two severe cuts in the neck, one four inches long starting beneath the left ear, one eight inches long running below and parallel to the first, ending under the right ear. The cuts severed everything back to the vertebra, which was also damaged by the depth and force of the strokes. The extent of the bleeding was now evident in the clothing and in the small pool of blood on the ground. The doctor sent for the ambulance to take her to the mortuary (such as it was - a shed next to a workhouse) while a bucket of water was used to disperse the blood on the ground. The on-scene investigatory process during these early murders was little more than what one would do for a dog struck down by a truck.

Indicative of the quality of postmortem facilities and process in the East End, the body was stripped by two untrained paupers from the workhouse next door with a policeman present to inventory the clothing as it was removed, according to Rumbelow, but not according to Francis Camps in his *The Investigation of Murder*, who also indicates that the body was washed before any investigatory activity took place, even before the postmortem doctor arrived. At the inquest the two men were emphatic in their assertion that they had been told specifically to remove the clothes and wash the body. [5] It was only after this that the extent of the mutilations to her lower body became evident. Dr. Llewellyn was called back to reexamine the body. He found signs of struggle-wounds on her throat and face, cuts across the abdomen, and several deep wounds from the center of the rib cage down the right side and under the pelvis and through the stomach area. The vagina had been stabbed twice. Rumbelow describes the abdominal wounds as the result of a downward thrust, [6] but Farson, quoting the *Star*, has two vicious cuts being made in an upward direction, one along the right side, the other up the center. [7] The *Times* account is the same as the *Star*, most likely because both were drawing from the Central News Agency.

Tracking down labels sewn to her clothing, police soon identified her as Mary Ann Nichols, a poor prostitute who had been moved from workhouse to workhouse, finally landing in Lambeth Workhouse in lower Whitechapel. She was married but had not seen her husband for six or seven years since he had abandoned her because of her drinking. At the time of her murder, she was living on Thrawl Street, which, with Flower & Dean and Fashion Streets, formed a three-block square of heavily populated lodging houses.

Police determined that she had been murdered where she was found, that none of several neighbors who considered themselves light sleepers had heard an outcry or any other noise, and that there appeared neither motive nor suspect.

The newspapers were now on the scene with the *Times* headlines reading "A REVOLTING MURDER. ANOTHER WOMAN FOUND HORRIBLY MUTILATED IN WHITECHAPEL. GHASTLY CRIMES BY A MANIAC." They would continue to follow the story for four days, finally printing interviews with Whitechapel locals.

By 5 September the *Times* was reporting problems in the upper echelons of the Police Department, referencing back to the riots in Trafalgar Square in 1887. Everything was hush-hush, however, as Sir Robert Anderson, newly appointed to replace the controversial James Monro, and the man really in charge of the day-to-day operation of the department, was reported to be off to the Continent for a promised vacation before beginning his duties.

Although not supported historically by other writers, Detective Frederick George Abberline, the Scotland Yard investigator assigned throughout the Ripper murders and whose summaries appear in the records, felt that Nichols' throat had been cut after the mutilations. [8]

This would imply that the infliction of conscious pain may have been a dynamic in the attack. It would also explain the relatively small amount of blood found at the scene, most of which had absorbed into her skirts. Dr. Llewellyn disagreed, [9] although somewhat inconsistently since he acknowledged that most of the blood had been lost from the abdomen where it had settled. For him the cut throat explained the absence of any scream. [10]   As Rumbelow came to believe regarding this and subsequent murders, however, strangulation prior to cutting was likely; it would have prevented any cry as well as the forceful spattering of heart-pumped blood from the throats when cut, bleeding the killer would otherwise have had some difficulty avoiding. A second police suspicion was that the attack was made from behind, a belief which continues to carry great weight today although Sugden places the murderer strangling his victims from the front and lowering them to the ground before cutting their throats. The *Times* reported on the 3 October 1888, that police were already associating this latest murder with the first two; they had occurred within two hundred yards of one another.

The modus operandi is different again from the prior attacks. Organization appears to be entering into them; strangulation, a pattern of near-beheading (not necessarily to induce death, but for psychic or perhaps for symbolic purposes) that would continue, and an increasing focus on the destruction of the abdomen and internal organs.   This murder could clearly have been committed by one person, and the killer had at least enough anatomical knowledge to efficiently destroy the vital organs, both opinions held by Dr. Llewellyn. [11]   The bruises on the face and neck suggest perhaps some effort to struggle against something or at least rough handling by the murderer. An attack from behind, presumably after solicitation for sexual activity, would have provided the element of surprise, and made a relatively weak victim defenseless. It would also have kept the killer positioned away from the bleeding.

By 7 September the newspapers were quiet again.

But on the 8th, the *Pall Mall Gazette* wrote:

HORROR UPON HORROR.   WHITECHAPEL IS PANIC-STRICKEN AT ANOTHER FIENDISH CRIME.   A FOURTH VICTIM OF THE MANIAC.

London lies to-day under the spell of a great terror. A nameless reprobate — half beast, half man — is at large, who is daily gratifying his murderous instincts on the most miserable and defenceless classes of the community. There can be no shadow of a doubt now that our original theory was correct, and that the Whitechapel murderer, who has now four, if not five, victims to his knife, is one man, and that man a murderous maniac. . . . Hideous malice, deadly cunning, insatiable thirst for blood — all these are the marks of the mad homicide. The ghoul-like creature who stalks through the streets of London, striking down his victim like a Pawnee Indian, is simply drunk with blood, and he will have more. . . . [12]

At about 6:00 A.M. forty-five-year-old Anne Chapman (a.k.a. Siffy) had been found in the rear of 29 Hanbury Street, a half a mile north of Buck's Row, just a block away from Christ Church, Spitalfields, and two blocks from her lodging on Dorset Street. She was a widow with two children who had long since been removed from her care. A friend had seen her a little after 2:00 A.M. in front of the house with a slim "foreign" looking man over forty years of age. Not a resident of the house, she most likely entered the backyard through the front-to-back hallway characteristic to that type of structure. It was frequent for prostitutes to find quickly an out-of-the-way place for the few minutes it took to satisfy their customer. The inquest would determine that it was the habit of the landlord to keep both front and back doors open at all hours for the convenience of tenants, but, perhaps more cynically, to insure tenants could pay the rent.

Anne had left her landlord at Dorset Street just hours before, decked out in her new hat, telling him not to let her room, that she would be back shortly with the money for the doss. Perhaps a meeting had been prearranged.

Inspector Joseph Chandler reported:

I. . . found a woman lying on her back, dead, left arm resting on left breast, legs drawn up, abducted, small intestines and a flap of the abdomen lying on right side above right shoulder, attached by a cord with the rest of the intestines inside the body; two flaps of skin from the lower part of the abdomen lying in a large quantity of blood above the left shoulder; throat cut deeply from left and back in a jagged manner right around the throat. [13]

Her wounds were so severe, with new and disturbing details to come, that women and boys would be removed from the inquest before Dr. Bagster Phillips, the Police Department's examining physician on several of the murders, was allowed to continue his testimony. Only the *Lancet* would publish them in detail some months later. Anne's throat had been cut in the same fashion as had Nichols'. Two separate cuts had virtually removed her head from her body in an act which Dr. Phillips considered as evidence that beheading was deliberately intended. [14] There were recent marks on her face and neck, signs of some struggle or pressure having been applied.

> The abdomen had been entirely laid open; the intestines, severed from their mesenteric attachment, had been lifted out of the body, and placed on the shoulder of the corpse; whilst from the pelvis the uterus and its appendages with the upper portion of the vagina and the posterior two thirds of the bladder, had been entirely removed. No trace of these parts could be found. . . . [15]

Inspector Chandler, who had taken the first call, supervised the on-scene investigation with great care, despite the crowd of onlookers who had gathered by the time of his arrival. He was taken by another curiosity that would come to be seen as having symbolic meaning, the nearly ritualistic arrangement of combs (but not coins and rings as reported by some) by her feet. Her rings appear to have been wrenched from her fingers and removed from the scene. In his report for the day Chandler asked that Inspector Abberline be assigned to the case. In the meantime, residents of 29 Hanbury Street began charging a penny for a view of "where it happened."

> . . . malignant insanity, . . . a monster is abroad. . . [defying] all rules of nature. . . utter absence of a moral sense with the most finished cunning in the adaptation of means to ends. . . suggests a mind completely off its balance — that is quite undershaped on one side.
>
> The police have to find for us one of the most extraordinary monsters known to the history of mental and spiritual disease, a monster whose skull will have to be cast for all the surgical museums of the world. No other theory is admissible. [16]

So wrote the *Daily News* on 10 September.

The body was shipped off to the "mortuary" for the postmortem. As had been done in the Nichols case, the body was stripped and washed before any investigatory officers were present thereby preventing Dr.

Phillips from establishing any sequence in the butchery. [17] In fact, it was only there that the extent of the neck injuries were really noticed, as Chapman's head nearly came off when a handkerchief wound tightly around her neck was removed. He complained about the facilities as being a "shed," giving the lie to the misuse of "mortuary" and "mortuary attendants" used thus far in the reports. The West End was slowly becoming aware of life and its amenities in the East End.

A water-soaked leather apron had been found a few feet away from the body, immediately making "Leather Apron" John Pizer a suspect. He was a leather worker and known woman hater, with a reputation of harassing prostitutes; his name had come up in the investigation of the Nichols murder. But he was found to have been hiding for his own safety from both public and police in the home of relatives when this murder was committed. Police would later determine that he had solid alibis for both murders. The apron would be discovered to belong to a neighbor of 29 Hanbury Street; she had washed it for her son and hung it out to dry the previous Thursday.

A neighbor had heard a cry of "No!" followed by a bump, then silence about an hour before Chapman's body was found. Cries in the middle of the night were so common that they were universally ignored unless repeated.

The *Times* of 10 September called for a £500 reward for the capture of the "Man Monster." The police were befuddled. Crowds were in the streets and gathered around the police station looking for any word of progress in the investigation and eying any suspects that were brought in for questioning. Vigilance committees were formed, the most prominent and durable headed by George Lusk, who sent a lengthy letter to Queen Victoria seeking the posting of a reward endorsed by the Crown. Police presence was increased significantly, so much so that the organized criminal element began assisting in the search in order to remove the pressure and interference with their activities. With the local rumor mill unable to identify a suspect, suspicions began to form that he was not from inside the community at all. The press began to write about every "petty" crime that occurred in Whitechapel and called for more funding for civic improvements. At the same time, they began to refer to the "good citizens" of the East End, suggesting that not all of them were given to crime and prostitution, that they deserved protection from what was happening in their neighborhoods.

Socialist George Bernard Shaw would not lose the opportunity provided by these murders and the disarray in which the authorities found themselves to point out the inequity and hypocrisy of Victorian society or the apparent failure of Christianity. He is believed to have written (they are in his *Collected Letters*) two letters during September: one from "JC" (Jesus Christ), the second from "Shendar Brwa," which is a not-too-subtle anagram for "Bernard Shaw," although it would also allow for a prophetic anagram regarding Sir Charles Warren's tenure at the head of the Police Department — "Warren bash'd." Neither letter was published by the papers. But a more serious one was printed on 24 September in the *Star*, a portion of which has already been quoted:

> ... Whilst we conventional Social Democrats were wasting our time on education, agitation and organisation, some independent genius has taken the matter in hand, and by simply murdering and disemboweling four women, converted the proprietary press to an inept sort of communism. The moral is a pretty one. ... "Humanity, political science, economics, and religion... are all rot; the one argument that touches your lady and gentleman is the knife." [18]

The government and the Church of England as the official presence of Christianity were beginning to experience public ridicule by the wits of the day. The full torrent of letters from the public would follow.

Wynne Baxter, supervising the inquest, would conclude on 29 September with the assertion that he believed some anatomical knowledge was required to be able to locate and remove the missing organs quickly and cleanly. He also felt that the removal and possession of the uterus was the underlying motive for this murder and that there was a market for such organs.

Adding to the bizarre events accompanying this series of crimes, he had been told by a Dr. Thomas Openshaw of the London Hospital Museum that an American had sought preserved uteri in good condition from him and another hospital. He was offering £20 apiece and claimed he intended to provide one with each copy of a book he was writing. (We'll learn later that during this period Dodgson was working on a book which contains suspected Ripper disclosures.) Of course this made the papers, which just added to the fear and to the themes that would appear later in letters "from" the Ripper.

We can see a number of changes in this murder. The focus on abdominal destruction has increased; organ removal and possession has been added to organ destruction. Handling of the inner organs has replaced the more sanitized cutting of the abdominal wall and the even more distant stabbing through garments. The ability of the murderer to tolerate the gore is becoming more evident. The acts are becoming more symbolic, more ritualized, both in the laying out of the body, the arrangement of combs, and the fixing of the intestines to the victim's shoulder. The effort to remove the head appears more motivated and intense.

Things quieted down for nearly three weeks. In many ways it was more quiet than one would wish, as it reflected also that no reportable progress was made in the investigation. Then, among the letters received at the Central News Office, one caught the eye of the police as possibly authentic. It was a taunting letter that disparaged the current theories and predicted the nature of future mutilation. Written in the perfect penmanship of a Victorian schoolboy, it was signed "Jack the Ripper" and was followed by a post script ". . . don't mind me using the trade name. . . ." It would be the name that stuck. The detailed analysis of this and other letters is left for chapter 4, in which both authenticity and communication style are evaluated. But its arrival and its later publication under the belief that it was authentic and might stir someone with knowledge as to the letter's authorship to come forth just served to increase the growing panic and circus atmosphere.

One day after the Chapman inquest was closed, if it were possible to increase the audacity and atrocity of these crimes, the Ripper found a way. For now, on the same night, there were two murders, what later came to be known as the "double event."

At 1:00 A.M. on Sunday morning, as Louis Diemschutz was bringing his horse-drawn cart up a narrow court leading from Berner Street, his pony shied away from a presence in the darkness. Climbing down from the seat to investigate, he found the body of a woman he thought might be either dead or drunk. He ran up the path to the International Working Men's Educational Club, still going strong with dancing and singing after an evening of debate, to find a light and assistance. When they returned, they found that the woman's throat had been savagely cut, with blood still coming from the wounds and puddling on the pavement. Her bloodied right hand rested on her chest; her left hand was still clutching a small quantity of cachous (breath mints) wrapped in tissue. He quickly gained the attention of patrolling policemen who sealed off the entire area after raising Dr. Bagster Phillips, who examined the still warm body and declared the woman deceased. A thorough sweep of the area was undertaken immediately by a squad of policemen. Each club member was examined and questioned, intrusively, they felt (they were foreigners and Socialists), and each room in the area searched, under the belief that the murderer could scarcely have escaped, indeed must have been interrupted by the approach of

Diemschutz, may even have been what the pony shied away from. The search revealed nothing. They would later learn that the victim was Elizabeth Stride, a known prostitute and heavy drinker, who had long since left her husband and until just days before had been living with a Michael Kidney on Fashion Street.

While this investigation was going on, another search was also under way. For scarcely a half mile further east, in Mitre Square, a secluded court off of Mitre Street, the body of another woman had been discovered at 1:30, less than fifteen minutes after a policeman on his rounds had found the area vacant. This woman not only had her throat cut in what was now the all too familiar manner, but her face was horribly mutilated and she had been disemboweled, her abdomen opened from the rectum to the breastbone. Drs. Frederick Brown and George Sequeira were on the scene immediately, quickly enough to find that this body, too, was still warm.

Mitre Square was under the police jurisdiction of the London Police Department, not Scotland Yard, so an entirely new police force was mobilized. A dragnet of the surrounding area was begun, with squads of police swarming from house to house, apartment to apartment in search of a suspect still believed close by. Around the corner and up on Goulston Street, inside a ground-floor hallway, a piece of apron was found, stained as if it had been used to wipe a knife. This would be later found to match a missing piece of apron worn by the victim. The sink in the hallway was still wet with blood, the killer apparently having stopped to wash his hands.

But most curious of all was a message written in chalk on the hallway wall, a message which could only have been placed there recently as tenants would have accidentally scuffed or intentionally removed it in passing. Written in a good schoolboy hand, it read: "The Juwes are the men that will not be blamed for nothing." Commissioner Warren was called to view this area filled with evidence. When he arrived, he expressed immediate concern regarding the potential for anti-Semitic hysteria such a message might inflame. Despite the protestations of other police officers that the message must be saved as evidence, that the area could be cordoned off so that it would not be seen, that the message could be covered, that just the inflammatory word could be erased, that he should wait just the hour before daylight so that it could be photographed, Warren is said to have erased it quickly himself, but not before it was hastily written down. There would be discussion at the inquest regarding its exact wording, the placement of the first *not* and the spelling of *Juwes*, and questions by later writers regarding its meaning. It would be Stephen Knight who hypothesized a Masonic meaning in the word *Juwes*. Records of the time reflect by the absence of comment that it had no meaning, or, in Knight's scenario, any meaning should be kept a part of the Masonic secret. Discussion of the message is left for chapter 5.

The postmortems for the victims revealed repetitions in the pattern along with new atrocities. Elizabeth Stride was found to have a scarf wound tightly around her neck, with the cut running just below it, all the way to the backbone. She was believed to have been drawn down from behind and murdered while lying on the ground. A round-ended knife found on Whitechapel Road earlier in the evening, with a blood-filled handkerchief wrapped around the handle, was dismissed as the murder weapon because it lacked the point evident in the cuts. It was clear that this murder had required less than five minutes to execute and was most likely interrupted.

The victim at Mitre Square was identified as Catherine Eddowes (a.k.a. Beddowes, a.k.a. Kate Kelly), a prostitute separated from her husband and living with a man named Kelly. She had been in police custody at Bishopsgate Station for the entire evening after having been found on the street, drunk, unable to stand. By midnight she was agitating to be released and she headed off toward Houndsditch and Aldgate at 1:00 A.M., just thirty minutes before her body was found. She, too, had a scarf tied tightly around her neck, appeared to have been brought down from behind, and her head nearly severed while she lay on the ground. The mutilations to her abdomen, inflicted after her throat had been cut, consisted of several jagged strokes, one of which cut deeply into her liver. As in the mutilation of Chapman, the intestines had been pulled out and placed on her right shoulder in a ritual fashion. A detached portion of intestine had been placed between her body and left arm. At the inquest that followed, the word *placed* was reemphasized under questioning; there was design to the arrangement. The left kidney and the uterus had been removed and were missing. Dr. Brown's report indicates that the abdomen was opened with an upward cut, from the rectum to the breastbone. It would seem that the knife took on more precisely the symbolism of the penis in anal, not vaginal penetration. Unlike the others, the attack on the abdomen most likely was done while the killer was kneeling in front of the body, possibly throttling it, not on the right side, as had occurred with earlier mutilation victims.

But now something new was done. The victim's face had been mutilated in a bizarre way, one that reflected the symmetry of a clown's makeup. The eyelids were cut with the tip of the knife. Her nose was cut from the bridge down through the left cheek as if there were an effort to sever it completely and its tip was removed. Her ear lobe was cut off. Under each eye the tip of the knife had been used to make a cut which left a triangular flap of flesh. The mouth and lips were cut.

The next morning and days that followed were filled with nothing less than hysteria and panic in really all quarters. It began with the receipt of a "Dear Boss" postcard from "Jack the Ripper," which referenced the murders just committed, was believed to be authentic, had been posted on the day the first newspaper accounts appeared (1 October 1888), and its writer thanked the police for holding back the previous letter, whose existence they had not publicly acknowledged until 2 October. Both the card and earlier letter made their way to the newspapers and within days were reproduced (and incorporated into police posters) asking anyone who recognized the handwriting to come forward.

There were more calls that the Crown post a reward, a request still denied, although the City of London posted one immediately. Crowds filled the streets; a demonstration by over one thousand people formed, seeking improvement in conditions and police action. Women in the West End were beginning to feel at risk and made conscious efforts to avoid going out at night.

The upper echelons of Scotland Yard were clearly under great pressure. Queen Victoria herself was making suggestions on how the investigation should proceed, asking whether sailing ships had been checked, whether lighting was adequate, suggesting that the Ripper might be using the trains for his escape. [19] Commissioner Warren began defending his actions in the press. He denied that he had transferred inexperienced police onto the case, declared in fact that all available men had been assigned. But the press bellowed "War on Warren!" and called for his resignation. On 1 October the *Daily News* wrote an indictment dripping with sarcasm:

> ... [The murderer, covered with blood] was observed by no one, and especially by no member of that Force which is supposed to have eyes for a sleeping world. It is impossible to avoid the depressing conviction that the Police are about to fail once more, as they have failed with CHAPMAN, as they have failed with NICHOLLS, as they have failed with TABRAM, as they have failed with SMITH, as they are failing with the unknown victim whose limbs apparently are being scattered broadcast over the metropolis, from Pimlico to Newington [referencing the remains of a body found in various locations around London].

The Police have done nothing, they have thought of nothing, and in their detective capacity they have shown themselves distinctly inferior to the bloodhounds [who had tracked a child-murderer elsewhere in the provinces]. . . . None of the accepted apologies. . . will cover their repeated failure. . . . [Despite an increase in numbers on the beat] the policeman tramps slowly by, as he tramped before, and to those who have an interest in the calculation his returning tread may be timed with the same certainty as the movement of a planetary body. . . . The gallant soldier [Warren] who is at the head of it will never be able to tell us what [is wrong with the department's organization and strategy]. . . . [20]

Warren now added another embarrassment to what was already a bad situation. He acceded to suggestions, to the point of personally getting involved in their acquisition and testing, that two champion bloodhounds be made available to the police for purposes of tracking the killer, if not now, in the future. The tests, conducted under perfect conditions at Hyde and Regents Parks, with Warren as the "scent" on two occasions, were embarrassingly unsuccessful and became the source of some much deserved ridicule. For it pointed out how little he knew about the East End, which was filled with slaughterhouses, the movement of blood-covered workers and carcasses around the city, and the enormous press of people on the streets, which made success by even the best of dogs highly unlikely.

Harry Furniss, an enterprising journalist and illustrator (remember the name: he was Charles Dodgson's illustrator for *Sylvie and Bruno* during this period) would describe the events of the evening in *Famous Crimes*:

Like a prowling tiger seeking its prey. . . when he vanished from Berner Street [the killer] stole silently into the City, with his soul athirst for blood, and his long knife adrip, seeking for another victim on whom he might glut his fiendish appetite. [21]

It was during this period that the theory emerged that there might be two murderers. For there was barely time to move from Berner Street to Mitre Square and commit a murder, organ removal, and mutilations that took at least seven or eight minutes (as the doctors believed), and then disappear outside of the net that had been formed. By the time of the inquest, two suspicious incidents had been unearthed.

Elizabeth Stride had been seen at 12:45 A.M. in the company of a man about thirty years of age, between five feet, five inches and five feet, eight inches, mustached, respectably dressed with a peaked cap and a parcel wrapped in newspaper. He had forced her to lie down and suddenly shouted "Lipski," an anti-Semitic epithet, seemingly in the direction of a somewhat taller man observing the scene as he smoked a pipe across the street. The witness, a Jew named Israel Schwartz, fearing that he was in danger, ran from the area, followed by the man with the pipe, who apparently turned in another direction by the time Schwartz reached the railroad arch. A man of similar physical charac-teristics, looking something like a sailor, was seen in the Mitre Square area at 1:35 A.M., just moments before Eddowes was murdered. [22] There was some concern that perhaps the call had been a signal for the second man to head off in search of a second victim in order to create what would appear to be two murders committed simultaneously at an agreed-upon time.

There also emerged some concern that a "black magician" was involved, able to disappear and spirit himself across the city.

A William Marshall testified that he had seen Stride with a man earlier in the evening, at 11:45 P.M., on Berner Street. He was well dressed, middle aged, about five feet, six inches, stout, with a peaked cap, and the appearance of a clerk, mild mannered and educated. He heard him say, "`You could say anything but your prayers.´" [23]   This would lend support to the notion that there was a religious fanatic at work, "down on whores," or, failing to convert them, bent on sending them to the eternal damnation he had warned them to avoid.

Three days before, at the Three Tuns Hotel in Aldgate, just off of Mitre Square, a man fitting these descriptions — well dressed in black, with a black bag — was reported to have inquired at what time the women left the bar for the evening and the route they took when they left. [24]   This "black bag" entered the lore and continued the suspicion that the Ripper was a medical man, a notion reinforced by published inquest findings that the removal of organs required anatomical knowl-edge such as a doctor would possess.

Through it all, letters poured in at the rate of one thousand two hundred per day, each requiring some analysis and some follow-up, most of them to be discarded.

As if to assert emphatically that things were not yet finished, the Ripper sent a gift to George Lusk, head of the Vigilance Committee on 16 October. It was a letter "from Hell" accompanied by a small box which contained what later came to be believed was half of Catherine

Eddowes missing kidney. The letter claimed its writer had fried and eaten the remainder.

   An uneasy calm seemed to settle in as October passed without another visit from the Ripper. November started off quietly and the city prepared itself for Lord Mayor's Day, complete with parade, on 9 November. Innocuously enough, at 10:45 A.M. Thomas Boyer, assistant to the lodging-house keeper John McCarthy, approached the apartment of twenty-four-year-old Mary Jane Kelly (a.k.a. Mary Ann and Marie Jeannette) at 13 Miller Court, a secluded courtyard off of Dorset Street, to collect thirty-five shillings of back rent. She had been living with her common-law husband Joseph Barnett, who had abandoned her when she invited a prostitute friend to live in the household and perhaps also because of her drinking. She was now living alone. Receiving no response to the knock at her door and finding it locked, Boyer went to the window, reached through the broken pane, pushed back the curtain to see if there was any sign of life, and was confronted with what appeared to be a pile of human flesh on the table by the window, a body on the bed, blood on the floor, and no sign of life. He ran for McCarthy, who came and verified the scene, and then he ran for the police. [25] While he, Inspector Abberline, and three doctors merged on the scene, even scarcely before a crowd had begun to form, a cryptic message went out by telegraph to all area police stations: "The woman is simply cut to pieces." [26]   The only policeman called who did not appear was Commissioner Warren; it was still a department secret that he had tendered his resignation on the 8 November. [27]

   After the doctors determined from the window that the woman was dead, that no life-saving assistance would be required, and with the door apparently locked, police cordoned off the area and waited for word from their supervisors on how to proceed.   They waited for the now-decimated and confused leadership to gather itself.   Warren's bloodhounds were called, but never came. By 1:30 P.M., a crowd of thousands had gathered round, no longer interested in the parade festivities. Superintendent Arnold finally took charge, and the window was removed to provide a better view and access to the room. The sight on entering was one of pure carnage.

   Descriptions vary and were embellished over time. Detective Dew would write in memoirs that he slipped and fell in the slimy gore. [28] Newspapers wrote that it was nearly impossible to tell that the victim was a human being. Others indicate that pieces of flesh had been hung from nails in the wall as if for display; this is not true. What is clear from descriptions and the photograph that was taken and has been published in several books, one of the clearest in Sugden's, is that a frenzy of mutilation and butchery had taken place. Perhaps the most telling evidence of the extent of the Ripper's work lies in the postmortem report in the Metropolitan Police files. While it runs for pages, the handwriting deteriorates until it is nearly indecipherable.

Drawing from composite material, the body was lying on its back on the bed, naked except for the remains of an undergarment; a large pool of blood congealed on the floor beneath the mattress. In all likelihood, she had been smothered before her throat was cut, although loss of blood from the throat wound was judged the cause of death. The head was nearly severed from the body, as was the left arm, which, nevertheless, had the hand stuffed into the abdominal cavity. The face was totally mutilated except for the eyes, which were untouched. The nose and ears were removed, the mouth cut to pieces. Internal organs were placed in various places, some under the head, some by the feet. The breasts, along with large pieces of flesh from the thighs which had been carved to the bone were placed on the table by the window. Large portions of the legs had been skinned. The heart had been removed (and would never be found after a thorough reconstruction of the corpse), and there was damage to the lungs, but the description in the postmortem was indecipherable. There were savage knife wounds to the rectum and vagina. There was blood covering the bed and spots on the wall caused by spurting from the severed arteries.

There had been a large fire in the fireplace, hot enough to melt the spout on the kettle. It has been theorized that the fire was for light (although a candle on the table had not been used) or warmth (it was November). The latter explanation is the likely one given the more recent thinking that the murderer was naked during the attack and orgy which followed. [29]   There has been some hypothesis that the attacker had gained access to the apartment disguised as a woman. The ashes revealed that some woman's clothing had been burned, yet Kelly's clothes were neatly folded on the bedside chair. What else was burned to create such a fire is a mystery. It was later determined that the key to the room had been lost ten days earlier, that the murderer reached in the broken window to lift the gravity latch, which fell and locked the door every time it was closed.

Except for a single cry of "Murder" heard by the tenants in the apartment above just before 4:00 A.M., about the time the postmortem determined death had occurred, there were no other sounds. The investigation determined that men had been seen in the area earlier in the evening, some with Kelly. They all have the same general description as with the other murders — a man in his thirties, five feet, six to eight inches, "Jewish" looking, well dressed, some carrying a black bag. Police were of the opinion that the killer had been with his victim at least two hours.

The pattern in this crime, or change in pattern must be noted. Mutilation and a lingering, most likely a wallowing or merging with the warm, mutilated remains took place. This was the first murder committed in the light. It followed the only murder in which the killer throttled his victim. The results of the carnage were laid out, nearly with a prideful "Look what I can do!" or perhaps a climactic anguished cry for relief "What more can I do?" There is another destruction of the nose, this time complete removal. And the heart was removed this time, not the sexual organs.

Marie Kelly was buried in a nice casket, the expenses paid for by an anonymous donor (later identified as an elderly clerk in the local church), but donations requested for a grave marker did not raise enough to provide one. [30]

Things quieted down after this murder. It was as if it were the crescendo and finale combined; nothing more could top it. If it was the Ripper's intention to send a message to the establishment, they heard it. The police and others came to believe that no one could sustain being in that room for the two or so hours involved and not have gone mad, nor could he have avoided a remorse so strong that suicide would be the only relief. The glut of frenzy had done the Ripper in, must have done him in. The investigations went on, but quietly, without fanfare. Marie Kelly became the last of what investigators and most writers consider the "certain" Ripper murders.

Forty-two days later, on 20 December, Rose Mylett (a.k.a. "Drunken Liz") was found strangled in the Poplar district, about two miles due east of Whitechapel. The news reports returned to the style evident in Emma Smith's murder, using the word "supposed" regarding whether she had been murdered or not. With blood oozing from her nostrils, they claimed she had died from excessive drink, and with a tight collar the cause of marks on the neck, suggesting that she had not been strangled. All this was in spite of the postmortem which judged that some of the marks appeared to be signs of a struggle and that something, probably a cord, had been twisted tightly around her neck from behind. There were no signs of knife wounds. The papers did make note that the area was at that time significantly less protected and its people more exposed than Whitechapel, which was still subject to heavy police patrols. It could have played into fears that the Ripper would move out of Whitechapel for his own safety, but did not, evidence that everyone really thought he was finished.

On 31 December, the body of an unsuccessful lawyer by the name of Montague Druitt was pulled from the Thames, the apparent victim of a suicide. A note that was believed to confirm that conclusion was later found in his rooms by his brother, and suicide became the official cause of death. In the minds of the many police (but not Abberline) Druitt came to represent the outcome of the Miller Court glut and has been a continuing Ripper suspect from the time he appeared in the notes belonging to Sir Melville Macnaghten, to the works of Dan Farson and Tom Cullen, and most lately by Howells and Skinner. Chapter 15 is devoted to an examination of the material surrounding Druitt.

On July 17, 1889, Alice McKenzie, a heavy drinker but perhaps not a prostitute, was found murdered in Castle Alley, and for a while there was concern that the Ripper was back, that he had not died as was believed. Alice's throat had been cut savagely, but not with the long, deep, severing strokes. Her dress had been raised above her waist and her abdomen mutilated, but not enough to open the cavity wall. Her genitals had been stabbed. Dr. Bond, asked to provide a second opinion in the postmortem by now-Commissioner Anderson, concluded that despite differences, the murder was the work of the Ripper.

> ... I see in this murder evidence of similar design to the former Whitechapel murders [in modus operandi] [with] each mutilation indicating sexual thoughts and a desire to mutilate the abdomen and sexual organs. [31]

Dr. Bagster Phillips, who had performed the postmortem, disagreed, however, seeing significant differences in technique, enough, in his opinion, to eliminate this as a Ripper murder.

The then head of the Vigilance Committee began to stir for more protection for the people of the East End. There had been a slow and gradual decline in police attention as all levels of authority came to believe that the Ripper was dead, the spree over.

On the first anniversary of Annie Chapman's murder, 8 September 1889, a woman, never identified, was dismembered, with only the trunk found two days later beneath the tracks at Pinchin Street, near Berner Street. This, too, is not considered a Ripper murder because there was no mutilation or organ removal, evidence did not show that death was by cutting of the throat, and the body had been moved from where the dismemberment had taken place. While the abdomen had been stabbed, it appeared to be either an accidental slip or the action of someone who had changed his mind. All aspects of this murder reflected a completely different modus operandi. The missing parts were never found. The

Metropolitan Police file indicates that the body appeared to have been washed. [32]

There would not be another Ripper-like murder until 13 February 1891, when Frances Coles was found, still breathing, under the arch at Swallow Gardens, near the entrance to the Tower of London. She died shortly thereafter, unable to talk from the severe throat wound and furtive mutilation of her lower abdomen. The policeman who found her, wearing rubber-soled boots on his first night patrolling alone, most likely surprised the killer. He later felt he had run past him just before he spotted the body and regretted for the rest of his life that he hadn't given chase rather than proceed forward on his beat, only to find the woman a moment later. When a man by the name of Saddler, who was known to have been with Coles earlier in the evening, returned to the lodging house at 3:00 A.M., his hands covered with blood, the police believed they had finally caught the Ripper. But when the sailor was brought before the judge, with excellent character witnesses from his ship captain and mates, he was freed for a lack of evidence.

Indicative of the public's craving for sensation and their "Ripper cult" celebration of what they perceived as the Ripper's continuing insult of authority, one newspaper reported this scene following the murder of Frances Coles.

> `The night following the murder groups of roughs and even young boys and girls gathered near the scene of the crime [to view the spot where the body had been found].
>
> [They] . . . laughed, joked and swore as they searched the spot for traces of the victim's blood. A loud-thumping piano-organ was dragged to the spot and struck up a tune. The roughs and girls danced, the former bawling improvised choruses about "Jack."´ [33]

This was the last of the murders which have been even remotely connected to the Ripper. Inspector Abberline, the most consistent presence in the investigation, retired in just two years. He never appears to have had a suspect, and he never appears to have accepted the theories that held sway for so long until writers began opening up alternatives fifty years later. If he ever had an opinion, he never wrote it for public consumption.

From the standpoint of the period in question, Jack the Ripper appeared from nowhere, released an enormous pent-up rage, and just vanished, a scar on a society and an era that prided itself in its upright-ness even while it hid its sins. Yet he has lingered in the imagination and lore for a hundred years, perhaps the most notorious of all criminals.

Chapter 2

The Ripper Profile

Given the nature of these crimes, what kind of a person should we be seeking? Certainly the police of Victorian London were seeing something quite outside their experience. There were murders — many of them in the East End. There had been about two hundred in 1888. There were "lunatics;" but there were not murders on the scale of these. Something new was happening in a society that, while it tolerated the socioeconomic obscenity that was the East End and the moral hypocrisy in the West End, did not tolerate personal excess unless it was done "with discretion." Jack the Ripper was not discreet; he tarnished the image of the English gentleman.

True to an age that gave birth to the Darwinian view of man's kinship with the ape, the suspects who first caught the attention of the police, press, and public were low on society's evolutionary scale. They were "low-lifes" like bootmaker John Pizer, a.k.a. "Leather Apron" and a known woman hater and abuser, or "foreigners," the Victorian euphemism for Jews, slaughtermen, and sailors. A proper Christian Englishman would not be capable of such atrocity.

Then, after the murder and mutilation of Annie Chapman, there appeared to emerge a sense that some medical sophistication was evident, along with a possible literary flair as evidenced by the taunting communications. Potentially demented medical students or doctors joined the list of possible suspects. Finally, from the standpoint of police records, we end with Macnaghten's three, focusing really on one, Montague Druitt, the "sexually insane" moderately successful young lawyer whose body was found in the Thames. Or, consistent with the belief that the killer was insane and could not have endured beyond the carnage at Millers Court, perhaps it became easy to believe that the spree was over with the death of a credible suspect. Then again, there may have been an underlying belief that it might be prudent to decrease the intensity of the investigation and inherent notoriety that had been created in the chaos of the fall of 1888 in the hopes that the killer, if indeed he still lived, would just disappear and bother London no longer. Maybe he had fled England after all.

As one hundred years have passed, the literature has moved "up" the evolutionary ladder, to include not only a continued interest in Druitt (which began with Macnaughton and was popularized by Tom

Cullen and Dan Farson), but one in Sir William Gull, eminent Physician-in-Ordinary to the Throne; artist Walter Sickert; the upper echelon of the Masons; J. K. Stephen, homosexual poet and tutor to the Duke of Clarence (Albert, eldest son of the Prince of Wales); and even the duke himself. The 1987 book by Howells and Skinner focuses back on Montague Druitt as a homosexual acting out his rage at his mother, but also as a scapegoat, himself murdered to protect a secret society of powerful homosexuals known as the "Apostles," to which he belonged.

In his 1992 work *Murder & Madness: the Secret Life of Jack the Ripper* David Abrahamsen extends Michael Harrison's thesis of 1972. Abrahamsen suggests that Prince Eddy and his tutor friend James K. Stephen committed the murders in tandem as outlets for their homosexual rage. While some of his psychological analysis supports my thesis regarding my suspects, his case against these two is unconvincing and often seems to demand a leap of faith in lieu of evidence regarding the depth of their misogynistic feelings and their propensity to murder and mutilation.

While psychological theory as a systematic science was yet to take form in the person and work of Sigmund Freud, it is amazing as one goes through the opinions of "experts" of the day, some of whom were quite rejected, to find that the psychological profile assigned to the Ripper coincides closely with current theory. For we find a recognition that the seeds of homicidal rage are laid at all levels of society and not just with those possessing "primitive" or unusual cranial features. What we see in their profile, as yet undeveloped in theory, was a suspect who had somehow, in some way, undergone an early destruction of "self," and whose inner rage at that experience and its impact on his adult life, long dormant, being held in check only with enormous effort or being discharged in less violent ways, finally erupted. But quite beyond their theory that an uncontrollable, perhaps an out-of-awareness, frenzied, schizophrenic or epileptic attack was involved, they had not yet met the modern psychopath, able to travel between two quite different worlds with a degree of lucidity not dreamed of.

One of the interesting Victorian participants in Ripper profile development, although he never organized his thoughts into memoirs, was Dr. L. Forbes Winslow. [1] His father had founded an asylum for the insane in Hammersmith, and he followed in the parental footsteps, gained his degree in medicine in 1869, and spent his life working with the mentally ill. The senior Winslow had been active in the development of the "insanity defense" in English law, and the son completed his own thesis on the subject as part of his degree requirements. Considered an outsider by the police during the investigation, in part due to the fact that his opinions often ran counter to current "psychological" thinking, his rather persistent efforts to intrude on their efforts, his "bizarre" suggestions, and the belief that he was seeking notoriety, Winslow was very much ignored at the time. In addition to offering unsolicited advice to Scotland Yard, he was interviewed by the press and often quoted. He would later take credit for the cessation of the murders based on his belief that his private efforts and public statements were increasing the risk of identity and capture for the Ripper, who withdrew. He may have been correct.

Winslow suggested that wardens from mental hospitals, more able than the police to "spot" such a person, be disguised as women and placed around the East End. Such a search might have been helped by another suggestion, that the names of all patients recently released from said hospitals as "cured" be provided so that they could be watched. Such former patients might also be recognized by the hospital wardens as they roamed the streets. Some medical men wrote in support of Winslow's suggestion. One who gave only the name "Medicus" suggested that a homicidal *maniac* would not have been organized enough to seek a secret place to perform the murder, while one suffering from epilepsy might have undergone an attack which led to murder while stimulated by the sexual act for which the prostitute had been solicited. [2]

In his *Recollections of Forty Years*, published in 1910, Winslow described his intense interest in the case and the number of days and nights he had spent in Whitechapel in his own private search for the Ripper. He claimed to have become a familiar figure in the area, not only with the police, but with the street women, who provided him with any scrap of fact or rumor they heard. Believing that the first murder occurred in 1887 ("Fairy Fay") and the last in 1889 (Alice McKenzie), Winslow attributed the crimes to one person, ". . . a homicidal monomaniac of religious views labouring under the morbid belief that he had a destiny to fulfil." [3] Prostitutes were merely his chosen targets. As the murders continued, the doctor came to believe that the Ripper might be suffering from something like epilepsy and in fact be a West End resident who lived quite civilly within a family who were totally unaware of his problem, just as he was himself unaware of any involvement in these activities. With the "double event" murder of Stride and Eddowes, and the apparent compulsive pursuit of a second victim when interrupted during the first murder, Winslow's views regarding religious monomania were further strengthened as he came to believe that the Ripper "`. . . possibly imagined that he received his commands from God.´" [4]

Colin Wilson indicates that these were advanced thoughts for the day and extraordinarily accurate based on the analyses of several more modern serial or spree murders of woman, specifically of prostitutes, derived from interviews with their murderers.

But Winslow's suggestion for a trap was ignored. He even proposed that a newspaper advertisement be run by "someone" seeking help from anyone who would like to join him in the suppression of prostitution; anyone who responded would then become a suspect. That, too, was ignored.

Gradually, Winslow added to the profile of "religious mania" what would today partly describe the psychopathic personality, one fully knowledgeable of the extent of his rage, but often unaware of events which occur during the manic moment, a person who lives a quiet, unassuming life, a person whom no one would suspect based on observable day-to-day behavior. Winslow did not identify the total lack of remorse in the psychopathic personality, the felt entitlement that the antisocial acts committed are fully justified, the self as god-center in a moral sense.

In August 1889, he thought he had identified the Ripper, even to the extent of acquiring bloodied boots from his suspect's apartment, but the police did not follow up on his detective work and the information he gave them. It seems he had met a woman who was approached by a man on Worship Street the night of Alice McKenzie's murder; she resisted but watched the man enter a nearby house and wash blood from his hands. When the house was searched by the landlord, the man was nowhere to be found. But an innkeeper told Winslow that this was the same man who had rented an apartment on Sun Street, near Finsbury Square and Liverpool Station, in April 1888, indicating that he would be there several months "on business." This character came and went late at night, quite irregularly and quite silently in his rubber boots. When the suspicious landlord searched his apartment the night of the Tabram murder on 7 August he had found a shirt whose cuffs had been washed hanging to dry, bloodstained sheets on the bed, and three pairs of boots with rubber soles, some of them stained. The tenant was known to write papers on religious themes that focused on the evils of prostitution, some of which he shared with the landlord.

Turned away by the police when he brought his material to them, Winslow went to the *New York Herald*. He was then severely criticized by the authorities for his amateur police work when his activities and theories were printed, but he took some credit and satisfaction from the fact that no more Ripper murders occurred after his story appeared. As we shall see when we pursue the case against Montague Druitt, the police did not want any murders labeled "Ripper" crimes after December 1888, as they thought they had ceased with Druitt's suicide.

Just who this person was and where he disappeared to may never be known; Colin Wilson does not provide a name or indicate whether Winslow did in his book. Winslow must have known it, at least the name used by the landlord. The suspect was apparently never questioned by the police, which, if his story was as organized as Wilson suggests, is surprising. Wilson dismisses the story pretty much on the basis that it became at the very least distorted in Winslow's own search for publicity. But there is no question the police must have been not just a little aggravated by this amateur sleuth carrying on in the press while they continued to struggle with very little success.

This "person" certainly fits Winslow's profile and the profile is deserving of consideration given its author's field of expertise. To summarize, he saw the Ripper as a quiet man, living in a community of family or friends, believing that he had been called by God to avenge sin, in this case prostitution, aware that he was in fact acting on that command, but was perhaps unaware of what he was doing or had done in the fury of the moment.

A second Victorian who was much more involved with the police and considered expert on such matters was Dr. Thomas Bond. Dr. Bond participated in the postmortem of Marie Kelly, studied the reports on the other victims, and wrote out his conclusions in a police report that still resides in the Metropolitan Police files. His first seven findings relate to the physical characteristics of the murders; the last three of his ten observations focus on his profile of a likely suspect. He judged that the Ripper had not even the anatomical knowledge of a butcher, but Rumbelow points out that Bond had seen firsthand only the murder which would give even butchers a bad name. Some other doctors involved disagreed with that assessment, arguing that some level of knowledge was evident in the deftness of organ removal, done quickly and in darkness. [5] Bond continued:

> 9. The murderer must have been a man of physical strength and of great coolness and daring. There is no evidence that he had an accomplice. He must in my opinion be a man subject to periodical attacks of homicidal and erotic mania. The character of the mutilations indicate that the man may be in a condition sexually, that may be called Satyriasis. It is of course possible that the Homicidal impulse may have developed from a revengeful or brooding condition of the mind, or that religious mania may have been the original disease but

I do not think either hypothesis is likely. The murderer in external appearance is quite likely to be a quiet inoffensive looking man probably middle aged and neatly and respectable [*sic*] dressed. I think he must be in the habit of wearing a cloak or overcoat or he could hardly have escaped notice in the streets if the blood on his hands or clothes were visible.

10. [Such a person] ... would probably be solitary and eccentric in his habits, also he is most likely to be a man without regular occupation, but with some small income or pension. He is possibly living among respectable persons who have some knowledge of his character and habits and who may have grounds for suspicion that he is not quite right in his mind at times. Such persons would probably be unwilling to communicate suspicions to the Police for fear of trouble or notoriety, whereas if there were prospect of reward it might overcome their scruples. [6]

While Bond tended toward the condition called satyriasis — sexual lust incapable of satisfaction despite repeated performances — he allows for the murderer being driven by psychological frustration or delusional religious motives. These tend to be the more modern interpretations given such crimes.

The physical appearance of Bond's suspect is similar to Winslow's — a normal man of adequate, but not overpowering strength, one for whom a normal exercise regimen would be adequate. "A man without regular occupation" did not necessarily mean "unemployed or frequently unemployed" but could also mean "one who had flexibility in managing and scheduling his occupational affairs." And he saw some possible alternative source of income in addition to or instead of a regular income. Bond's last observation that some close acquaintances or family might suspect something would eventually fit neatly into the emergence of Montague Druitt as a suspect when his family or other acquaintances reportedly voiced their suspicions to police after his corpse was hauled from the Thames. [7]

Chief Inspector Walter Dew had been the first policeman on the scene when the call came into the station following the murder of Marie Kelly. He would say in his book *I Caught Crippen* that the memories of that sight would haunt him for the rest of his life, with food and the mere sight of a butcher shop nauseating him for some time. [8]   He claimed to have slipped and fallen in the "awfulness." He rejected the notion that the Ripper was a doctor or had any anatomical knowledge, but like Dr. Bond, he had seen only the worst of the butcheries. Dew, like Sir Robert Anderson, hypothesized that someone knew who the Ripper was and what was happening, and that the Ripper was both physically and socially unobtrusive, capable of gaining the trust of the women quickly in order to lead them into the dark. Without trying to identify the specific madness suffered by the Ripper, Dew believed he was mad but disagreed with Winslow's theory that the Ripper was "taken over" by his mania, pointing out that he left from wherever he lived to go to the murder spot with the weapon in hand, consciously intent on the task before him. To Dew, the murders were willful. [9] This moves us toward the coldly calculating psychopath, totally lacking in remorse.

Edward John Goodman wrote this profile in *Sala's Journal* in November, 1892:

> . . . no vulgar ruffian, repulsive in appearance, and desti-
> tute of education, but "a most respectable" person, mild and
> suave, or cheerful and plausible, in manner, of superior culture
> and intelligence, possibly a very popular man in his own circle
> — what is commonly called "a good fellow" — in short the very
> last person whom ordinary folks would have suspected of such
> deeds as his. [10]

As we shall see, this description fits Druitt quite well. And it fits Charles Dodgson extraordinarily well.

Although Colin Wilson doubts some of the detail in inquest witness George Hutchinson's description of a man he saw with Marie Kelly late in the evening before her body was found (partly because the observations were made in the dark), this description and Goodman's three years later are quite similar. Hutchinson had seen a slim man about thirty-four or thirty-five, five feet, six inches tall, "foreign" looking, and dressed in fine clothes. He was carrying a "doctor's type" black bag. This description would play a significant role in the changing public perception that a "`toff,´ a man of education, influence and money" [11] was a more likely profile of the Ripper than had heretofore been suspected. Inspector Abberline, perhaps the most dedicated and underrated of the detectives assigned to the case for its duration, agreed with this profile, and, as we shall see later, also rejected Montague Druitt's suicide as either admissible or definitive evidence that he was the Ripper. [12]

Lieutenant Colonel Sir Henry Smith wrote his own beliefs regarding the Ripper in 1906 in his *From Constable to Commissioner*:

The series of diabolical crimes in the East End which appalled the world were committed by a homicidal maniac who led the ordinary life of a free citizen. He rode in tramcars and omnibuses. He travelled to Whitechapel by the underground railway, often late at night. Probably on several occasions he had but one fellow-passenger in the compartment with him, and that may have been a woman. Imagine what the feelings of those travellers would have been had they known that they were alone in the dark tunnels of the Underground with Jack the Ripper!

Some of us must have passed him in the street, sat with him perhaps at a cafe or a restaurant. He was a man of birth and education, and had sufficient means to keep himself without work. For a whole year at least he was a free man, exercising all the privileges of freedom. And yet he was a homicidal maniac of the most diabolical kind.

. . . But the bulk of the dangerous lunatics at large are not systematic assassins. They are only wrought to frenzy by a fancied grievance or the stress of circumstance. [13]

The medical journal *The Lancet* dated 15 September 1888, hypothesized that mania was an unlikely characteristic of the Ripper, that such a condition would not explain the extent of the detailed coordination evident in the crimes and the successful escapes. Their belief was that mania would give rise to a less premeditated attack which would not likely be repeated. [14]

The question of "sanity" and "insanity" of murderers will no doubt continue in the field of mental health and criminology. But a Dr. Henry Sutherland, an expert on insanity at the time, attributed the crimes to someone who was sane, not insane, even if the obsessive grudge had been long-standing. He argued that when murders are committed by persons who are insane, they are spontaneous, disorganized, rarely followed by mutilation, and most often followed by suicide by the perpetrator. [15]

The last of the nineteenth century experts to be discussed is Richard von Krafft-Ebing, M.D., who authored the monumental work titled *Psychopathia Sexualis, Contrary Sexual Instinct; A Medico-Legal Study* in 1893. The doctor described lust-murder, which involved the cutting, handling, and arranging of body parts, even the wish to or actual eating of them. He placed Jack the Ripper in this category based on the "constant absence of uterus, ovaries, and labia." He even allowed for cannibalism having occurred, and he hypothesized that there were ten victims. [16]

Von Krafft-Ebing defined two different abnormal sexually based conditions, one of abnormal sexual appetite as reflected in sexual acts, such as coitus, masturbation, pederasty, and bestiality (the latter two reflecting also a "defective moral sense"). [17] The second condition reflected abnormal desires, a perversion of desires, but not of act, and were based on distortions in emotions that became sexualized. Sadism, masochism, lust-murder, and the defilement of women fell into this latter category. [18] Although he linked lust and cruelty in a historical sense, he did not identify or attempt to identify the object or symbolic object represented by the "thing" upon which the sexualized cruelty was directed. We will be heading toward the former of Von Krafft-Ebing's profiles, a man who brooded over abnormal acts, some of them solitary, combined with evidence of the possession of abnormal desires. For those who wish a more technical discussion of this and other aspects of sexual perversions, *The Agony of Lewis Carroll* contains three appendices: appendix 1 discusses rage and its origins in detail; appendix 2 covers perversions as expressions of rage; appendix 3 presents historical thinking on the origins of homosexuality.

It is clear in the historical analyses that a totally new experience was involved in these crimes, that the psychopathic personality was not yet formally recognized. This is a personality founded in a combination of extraordinary self-control over the presentation of oneself to society, unbridled rage, and, if not intelligence, enormous cunning. It is the Jekyll-Hyde split without the chemicals which brought out the hidden beast in Robert Louis Stevenson's 1886 work.

While other writers have referenced theories on these murders and sexual murders in general, none has been more dedicated or thorough than Colin Wilson, whose career has been devoted to the study of murder and these murders in particular. He is most often the source of expertise regarding the psychological profile of the Ripper in other books on Jack, and he is the "dean" of "Ripperologists," a term he coined to identify the informal fraternity of amateur sleuths still hot on the trail. To attempt to develop the theoretical background for what Wilson has written would be an enormous task which I will not undertake. What follows is a summary of several notions from two of his several works, *Origins of the Sexual Impulse* (1963), and *A Casebook of Murder* (1969). My own comments are interspersed.

In his 1963 work Wilson attributes sexual perversions to boredom, a sense of worthlessness, and alienation. They represent a distortion of, a degeneration of "vitality," moving to establish a new path that will overcome the discomforting feelings about the self. Wilson quotes William Blake " When thought is closed in caves / Then love shall show its root in deepest hell." [19] as descriptive of the bored, brooding, and alienated state. In the vacuum of alienation, brooding, and fantasizing, vital forces will be turned from creation to destruction in their intent, in their ability to satisfy the creator/destroyer. From his standpoint, destruction is seen as the means to create the "new self," liberated from the alienation which consumes him.

Wilson writes that the evolution of the individual — personal growth — involves the struggle with the intellectual self and the feeling self, in ancient Greek terms, of the rule of order represented by Apollo, and the rule of chaos (unbridled sensual and sexual pleasure) of Dionysos. [20] Growth resolves the transformation from the feeling state of the child to the intellectual state in the adult. Cruelty reflects a fixation in the childlike state which is dominated by feelings. While Wilson attributes cruelty to "the outcome of surplus energy" (155) and combines this with feelings of inferiority in adults, he fails to acknowledge the role of powerlessness in the face of what the child sees as abuse of himself by parents or other caregivers in the creation of inner rage. Cruelty is an expression of power over those seen as powerless by those who feel themselves powerless, a defensive response to one's own powerlessness. Cruelty is selfish, a focus on self at the expense of others, but it usually reflects the degree to which one feels himself brutalized. It involves a depersonalization of the other person which reflects the depersonalization experienced by the self.

Wilson tends to attribute cruelty to those lacking in intelligence. While those with more intelligence do have more potentially constructive outlets for their energy, as he says, childlike emotions in one with great intelligence increase cunning and the ability to rationalize and intellectualize the cruel action as being justified "for me" even if it is not within acceptable societal norms. The cruelty may not be manifested physically, but rather emotionally and intellectually. The "civilized" arm's length economic and emotional destruction of families to satisfy one's greed is arguably no less a manifestation of cruelty; the difference is in the nature of the destruction and the physical and emotional distance from the victim. Intelligence combined with childlike feelings would tend to further intensify the fantasies, the brooding, feelings of both inferiority on the one hand and a distorted superiority on the other, all of which increase feelings of alienation as the disparity between the self, potential self, and others is emphasized. Intellectual prowess can also provide sophisticated self-delusional arguments for what Wilson calls "compensative justice," arguments which justify why the rules which apply to everyone else do not apply to "me." While Wilson does not discuss this within the religious framework, the extension of this to feelings of chosenness, not "other-worldly" voices, but feelings nevertheless, could become another in the complex list of forces that drive the compensative behavior.

Typical of the psychopath is that he is a compulsive liar (162). For his outward life, long ago made necessarily false in order to survive with dysfunctioning parents or environment, continues to be a lie. He wears the social mask of respectability to cover an interior life bent on the destruction of some aspect of that experience, people or society, either in actuality or in brooding fantasy.

Wilson references the works of Bernard Shaw, perhaps the most prolific and insightful Victorian writer on the alienation of the age. Shaw recognized that it was the hypocrisy of the day which failed to recognize the terribly destructive boredom of the upper classes and their selfish and destructive activities while it held the more obvious crimes of the lower classes in disdain. Shaw suggests that the difference between the artist and the criminal is that the former is framed in his highest moments, the latter in his lowest. But both are seeking a definition of self, a differentiation of self, within an environment filled with either boring sameness, an ingrained feeling of alienation, lack of "fit," or other alienating forces (211-12).

Finally, a most prevalent characteristic of the psychopath is that of self-pity, a brooding self-pity. This can come from a number of sources, including full awareness that the self has been destroyed by mental, physical, or sexual abuse in childhood, the felt awareness of powerlessness from an unknown source (usually experienced in the nonverbal world of infancy), or of systematic exclusion in a society's hypocritical application of its own revered standards.

In his *A Casebook of Murder*, Wilson carries the Shaw artist/criminal comparison further, indicating that *choice* is the differentiating ingredient. By *choice* Wilson means the giving in to the low and an embracing of the baser forces that come to play. What he does not say is that this giving in, especially by one with intellect and will in other aspects of his life, anticipates the application of the same forces of intellect and will to *succeed* in the destructive act contemplated.

In chronicling the evolution of murder through the twentieth century, Wilson identifies a change from the economic murders which had preceded it (either for property or to get rid of wives-as-property) to murder for "freedom," for release from boredom. From that he sees the "joy" murder, that committed for the thrilling rush of power attendant on the act. For Wilson, the Ripper murders were murders for freedom.

But it will become evident that they were more than just aimed at freedom from boredom, although it was boredom that provided the space for fantasizing. They were murders in search of freedom from a lifetime of repressed rage at forces that the Ripper felt had destroyed him. They were murders for spite, evidenced in the mutilation. For him, they represented a move from bondage toward freedom.

Wilson sees these murders as compulsive, not the result of really rational choice (a departure from his discussion regarding choice). I will differ from this in the sense that they were not so compulsive as to be done without awareness. I believe they became a willed response to feelings created by the frustration of compulsions, that all other efforts to relieve the rage had failed, that a compulsive need to seek relief in a new way pushed him to these murders. In that sense they became the choice of one who feels cornered, not by external forces, but by his own inner forces.

He depicts the Ripper wallowing naked in the bloody remains of Marie Kelly, not just killing her, but plunging into the wetness. Moving somewhat away from the notion of sexual murders in which the genitals are the target of destruction, he suggests that the Ripper was interested in bellies and wombs.

> ... Freudians will draw many inferences from this — about hatred of the mother, perhaps of younger brothers and sisters stealing the parents affection, etc. I would draw only one inference; that this destruction of the womb indicated a suicidal tendency in the Ripper; it was the place that bore him about which he felt ambivalent. [21]

We leave Colin Wilson, to return later, with one last conclusion he has in drawing a profile of the Ripper:

> It is far more likely that the Ripper was an upper or middle-class young man, with some powerful grudge against the world or his family. . . . [22]

While he clearly means "young" in chronological age, to be consistent with his comments regarding the relative dominance of childlike emotions and the adult intellect, we could also find the Ripper in someone older but extremely childlike in his emotions.

In his 1972 work Farson draws on Wilson's opinion that the Ripper experienced a "kind of self-righteous glee" in the killings, but was most likely wracked with guilt and shame later when he contemplated what he had done. [23]   He also (123) suggests that Magnus Hirschfeld's definition of sexual murder (from his *Sexual Pathology*) is relevant: "a murder in which the murderer's *sexual tension* is released through the [production] of physical injury or death [my italics]." This fits with Von Krafft-Ebing's notion regarding the degeneration of sexual acts and their meaning.

Three additional works are worthy of comment.   The first is a collection of the writings of Dr. Magnus Hirschfeld entitled *Sexual Anomalies and Perversions*, published posthumously in 1952.   In a virtual continuation of the Victorian repression of such studies (17), this work was judged obscene until it was challenged in the British courts, no doubt because of its explicitness and candor. Hirschfeld writes:

> In genuine cases of sexual murder the killing replaces the sexual act.   There is, therefore, no sexual intercourse at all, and sexual pleasure is induced by cutting and slashing the victim's body, ripping open her abdomen, plunging the hands into her intestines, cutting out and taking away her genitals, throttling her and, sucking her blood.   These horrors. . . constitute the. . . pathological equivalent of coitus. [24]

In order of frequency, the mutilation or removal of genitals is most common, followed by disemboweling, "plunging a stick or umbrella into the vagina or anus. . . then severing of breasts, and throttling." [25] Frequently abuse of the corpse will follow the murder; some examples reflect that the killer has masturbated onto the corpse.

In a hypothesis regarding the Ripper that differs from the psychopathic personality, Eric Ambler writes in 1963 in his *The Ability to Kill* that the Ripper most likely suffered from schizophrenia and committed the murders in a "fugue," after which he remembered nothing.

> . . . Perhaps, having achieved an apotheosis of horror, he had at last exorcised the evil that had haunted him.
> But what did he look like?
> We can be quite certain of two things; he looked ordinary, and he looked harmless. . . . [26]

Manfred Guttmacher and Henry Weihoffen write in their *Psychiatry and the Law* that there are essential differences from the psychopath and the occasional or hysterical murders.   Psychopaths possess fundamental character flaws, fundamentally warped skeletal personality structures, whose behavior is not organically based but whose development reflects "emotionally disorganizing early environmental influences." [27] The origins of character disorders, which offer the potential for murderous explosion, lie in the earliest years of childhood.

Lastly, Phyllis Greenacre, coincidentally the author in 1955 of the first full psychobiography of Lewis Carroll titled *Swift and Carroll: A Psychoanalytic Study of Two Lives*, writes with Loretta Bender in *Handbook of Correctional Psychology* that they find from their studies that the origins of the psychopath lie in "a stern, respected and often obsessional father who is remote, preoccupied, and fear-inspiring in his children; and an indulgent, pleasure loving, frequently pretty but frivolous mother who is often totally contemptuous of her husband's importance." [28]

I would suggest something a little further than what has been described in the discussion of "sexual murder." More fully discussed in appendix 2 of *The Agony of Lewis Carroll*, the tension created from an alienated self is released sexually in an effort to restore whole-body good-feeling to replace the bad or empty feelings. This occurs *whenever* an object, be it another person-as-object, the penis in masturbation, or other "thing," is used and abused compulsively in order to stimulate sexual pleasure as a means of restoring feelings which are overwhelmingly uncomfortable about the self, beyond just poor self-esteem. Sexual *murder* becomes the most obscene distortion of the same fundamental underlying dynamics.

Furthermore, if we assume (safely) that these women were unknown to the Ripper, then they were representatives of something and someone. They were symbols for "woman" in the broad sense and for "mother" in the narrow. While the mutilations were acts of spite and the results of fantasized retribution, the handling of body parts and possibly wallowing in them had three psychological components. First, there was the wish to merge with the mother-symbol who was loved as well as loathed, to bathe in her essence (a woman's blood, evidenced in menses, was believed to be the nutrient of life in early Victorian times and going all the way back to the ancient Greece). Second, there was the wish to annihilate the merged mother/self as an act of symbolic murder/suicide. And third, there was the wish to remove in some cases the sexual organs and possibly consume them as an effort to *possess* that which the Ripper wished for but did not have, in this case the wish of a homosexual for the organs that would bring him into harmony with his feeling state. Of course, this is an ambivalent wish, one also filled with loathing for organs that represent the hated birth mother.

There is one more area which is so much more obvious today than in even the just recent past. It is the extent to which sexual murder (sexual crimes in general) is an expression of rage which seeks tit-for-tat retribution for sexual abuse in the childhood life of the murderer, an act of retribution for the betrayal inflicted by, or perceived as tolerated, by parents as primary caregivers.

The search for deeply ingrained symbolism in the actions taken brings us not just to the apparent presence of ritual in some of the murders but to the whole question of the role that religious beliefs may have played. If we accept the notion that there may have been an equally distorted view of religious matters on the part of the Ripper, and incorporate religious symbolism into the act of these sexual murders, we could have, in the consumption of blood or human flesh, a reenactment of the symbolism of Christian communion. In this case the most beloved is "consumed" in order to produce a merger with the loved one. In other cultures, consumption of the hated one incorporates his powers into the self. In the Ripper case, the mother figure was both loved and loathed.

Or, in a very different way, the entire "ritual" of eating the victim could have been performed and intended as an obscene parody of revered church ritual. If the Ripper were one who was battling either external organized religion or his own inner love/hate relationship with God, or, who at this stage was taking on a devil/incarnate position against God, strong forces could have been at work to attack revered religious ritual.

Another psychological dynamic which could have been at work has been mentioned historically, but not really attributed to suspects. That is the wish to lead, not just participate, in social reform. While the late 1880s had seen the rise of socialism in London, the Christian "message" has always had in its teaching, if not its practice, the "Good Samaritan" ethic, the active participation in the relief of the oppressed. Even the Reverend Samuel Barnett would see a good side to these murders from his mission at St. Jude's in the East End when he observed that they were bringing attention to the plight and blight of the area and were causing the diversion of public resources to bring improvements. [29] So, within a Ripper profile, we might seek a frustrated social reformer, one who was unable to identify a role for himself which would have impact, who had always wanted to make a contribution to social and moral reform but did not have the inner resources to do so, perhaps could not focus on a single area, or had visions of grandeur over what might be done which produced only feelings of inadequacy as he saw himself day by day, year by year, doing nothing.

If we now combine emotional immaturity, really infantile immaturity, with a fervor to *do* something significant based on motives founded in religion or social reform, or with the search for existential freedom, we can begin to contemplate that the Ripper was an older man. He no longer needs to be the more typical sexual murderer in his twenties or thirties but could be in his forties, fifties, or even sixties if he were physically strong enough. The dynamic that "time is running out" becomes a weighty and relevant emotional factor as the intellect recognizes the inevitable passing of years and the fear or fact that opportunities to accomplish the driven tasks are disappearing.

Finally, we could find in the Ripper profile signs of cowardice. George Bernard Shaw states it well in the words of Andrew Undershaft in *Major Barbara*: "Hatred is the coward's revenge for being intimidated." [30] Hate for self is turned to others as a way of restoring self-esteem; outwardly focused destructive feelings are substituted for inner feelings of self-loathing due to one's fear of being destroyed by what should be felt as only normal assertiveness in conflict. If we combine the frustrated social reformer (who should have recognized the hypocrisy of West End prostitution as a better target than those "in the business" due to their poverty), or the moral avenger ("down on whores") with cowardice, we locate the attacks on prostitutes in the East End rather than the West End. It was purely and simply a safer place to vent hate assertively and indiscreetly.

I would suggest that in summarizing a profile of the Ripper, we need to marry (at least) two schools of psychological thought. Were these murders committed for freedom, for restoration of "self" consistent with the theories of Alfred Adler, perhaps Heinz Kohut (self-psychology) and an existential philosophy, or were they murders committed by relentless drives subverted in the unconscious mind? There are aspects of both in them for they reflect the eruption of the most archaic (originating in feelings of infantile omnipotence) destructive feelings combined with a search for escape from the consequences of those destructive feelings, the total alienation of self from self and from the world.

Second, while any one "force" working with enough strength could be enough to tip the balance from "sanity" to "insanity," the more forces we can find at work in a suspect, the more deeply alienated and therefore pathological we would find him. And the more likely we would be able to draw a conclusion regarding motive.

What we are seeking, then, is a person (or persons), most likely male, who manifests some or all of the following characteristics:

1. arrested emotional development
2. anger at mother, women in general, and family
3. possibly homosexual, although not necessarily so
4. filled with rage and spitefulness
5. one who uses people, especially women, as objects
6. presents differently in society than his inner life reflects, the hallmark of a psychopathic personality
7. self-destructive, compulsive modes of sexual expression
8. alienation from self and society
9. an underachiever *based on his own measurement*
10. independence in allocation of time and resources, all of which contribute to opportunity
11. victim of psychic, physical, or sexual abuse as a child
12. evidence of some combination of intellectual abilities and boredom, the inability to organize talents productively
13. a long period of violent fantasizing
14. adequate physical strength and ability
15. filled with childish self-pity
16. adequate knowledge of the female anatomy
17. child of a stern and remote father, with an over-involved mother who devalued the father in the family
18. evidence of strong emotional religious feelings, of chosenness or of religious alienation, or both
19. evidence of wishes to participate in social reform in a meaningful way but feeling inadequate to the task

Ideally, if we can satisfy this profile in a suspect, we can then search for evidence that this specific person moved from brooding fantasy to action. We will have an even stronger case if we can identify the content of the fantasy.

Chapter 3

A Life of Motive

It is when we turn to the question of motive for the Ripper murders that we are confronted with the inner life of any suspect; for it is inside the person that the seeds of destructive behavior lie. Lacking unchallengeable physical evidence, the presence of motive becomes a crucial piece of a circumstantial case against a Ripper suspect. Colin Wilson has criticized Ripper studies that attempt to force motive onto a particular suspect without adequate evidence. He encourages the alternative solution, i.e., to find a suspect who fits the motive profile and then work to integrate the known facts with the suspect to see if a fit occurs. If there is a strength to this book, it is the identification of a suspect with motive who divulged his fantasy world for all to see, albeit in the guise of children's literature.

On the other hand, if there is anyone in Victorian England (perhaps even today) who would have been considered the least likely suspect in these murders, it is Lewis Carroll. Even the thirteen or more serious biographies, including the first by his family that began in the year of his death, 1898, give no hint beyond eccentricity, sexual constraint, or "religious struggles" of the extent to which Charles Dodgson's inner life was filled with rage. By every societal measure, Dodgson lived a life of fame and some fortune through his pseudonym even as he maintained the privacy and anonymity of an Oxford don when he so chose. So far from anything remotely like these murders was his visible life that if he had indeed been found bending over a victim with blood on his hands, he could no doubt have escaped suspicion by proving his identity and claiming he was secretly helping a "fallen woman" as part of the Oxford University mission in the East End — Toynbee Hall.

In many ways, just as *The Agony of Lewis Carroll* could have been titled "The Making of a Serial Killer," this chapter should be titled a "Summary of the Inner Life of Charles Dodgson"; it carries its chosen title because Dodgson's inner life, for nearly his entire life, *constituted* motive. Before proceeding on to biography, the sources for that material need explanation. The facts of Dodgson's most visible life are taken from the biographical studies of others and from his own diaries, both published and unpublished, as well as those letters that have been published as part of biographies or in the two-volume *The Letters of Lewis Carroll*, edited by Morton Cohen. It would be too much to say that this "public" life constituted a total facade, but very much a facade it was. For behind the "looking-glass" lay quite another interior life, which, while it sometimes poked through in the letters and diaries, existed mostly in coded material that he incorporated into his children's stories and poems.

The means for Dodgson's encoding of that self-disclosure about a quite different life was a word game in which he is known to have excelled — anagrams. This game, a delight for children as they begin to gain competence in spelling and vocabulary, consists of forming new words and phrases simply by the rearrangement of the letters in given words or phrases. In his *Sylvie and Bruno*, for example, Dodgson toys with his readers when he has the fairy Bruno make the word *evil* out of *live* just by "twiddling" his eyes. Of course, another word, *vile*, can also be derived, as can *veil*, a continuation of the game Dodgson leaves to readers. In anticipation of things to come in this unreal world of games, note that the word *viler* is an anagram for *liver*, the abdominal organ which became a target for destruction and most importantly, ritualistic display, in the Kelly murder.

The game becomes considerably more complex, however, as the length of the word increases, or as entire phrases, sentences, even paragraphs become rearranged to form entirely new sentences and paragraphs or just image-laden phrases. Anagrams are at their best when the theme of the formed anagram answers to the theme of the original. Their validity as "evidence" (as opposed to pure coincidence) in drawing inferences and conclusions regarding Dodgson's inner life lies primarily in the thematic consistency and the fact that he left clues in his works regarding their presence. Occasionally, he even provided illustrations whose relevance existed only in the anagram, not in the story. Invariably in his writing, he surrounded words and phrases which should be examined more closely with quotation marks or underlined them, which when printed, became italicized words and phrases. Within the text of his emerging nonsense, such phrases or sentences tend to create inappropriate or surprised responses from the characters to whom they are directed, a suggestion that the reaction may not be to the words as spoken, but to the inner meaning hidden in the anagram to be formed.

Some examples should suffice. Then, as biographical content warrants, those that are applicable may be presented without detailed examination.

There were only two occasions when he pointed out the presence of strange material specifically, and they constitute two of the most important disclosures in his works. Both occurred in the Preface to *Sylvie and Bruno* in which he points to two specific sentences in the work that he described as "dreamlike suggestions." The first of these was the statement by his character Lady Muriel: "It often runs in families, just as a love for pastry does." [1] That statement was made in response to one by a character with the nonsense title, "His Adiposity, the Baron Doppelgeist," who told Lady Muriel that "My ancestors were all famous for military genius." If we take all three statements in turn, treat them as three distinct anagrams, and rearrange the letters, we derive three quite different statements. "His Adiposity. . ." becomes "O, I pity Dodgson, his path a rebel spite." The "pastry" sentence, which on the next page in his story he suggests would be more appropriate if it had been said by the libertine character Eric Lindon than Lady Muriel, becomes "I stir for pederast unions as often as family love." And in the third, "My ancestors...", Dodgson appears to place the blame for his psychic state on his parents' relationship as first cousins, "I was a terror from all my incestuous family genes." [2]

The second sentence that he points out in his Preface appears on page 332 of *Sylvie and Bruno*, as Eric Lindon's *badinage* about his past. He is responding to Bruno's inquiry as to whether he had ever been a servant.

> "Lower than that, your Royal Highness! Years ago, I offered myself as a *slave* — a `Confidential* Slave,´ I think it's called?" [Dodgson's emphasis] [3]

When we rearrange this sentence, we have an anagram similar in theme which identifies more fully the totality of degradation, the lower-than-slave nature of the fagging experience from public school, a position that often required much more than running errands and polishing boots for the upperclassmen:

> Lewis Carroll suffered so as loyal, fag, love-slave, as an honest gay search, I think. Oh, say I intended it a family threat! [4]

Studies in the origins of male homosexuality (for which "gay" as used here is a very early word which, at the time, pointed more to the prostitute-like behavior of women than that of men or of an inner same-sex orientation), identify unsound relationships between boys and their mothers (too close, female dominating in the marriage) and their fathers (remote with the child, appearing weak in the marriage and family). They also point to preadolescent and adolescent homosexual experiences, especially if traumatic, and to homosexuality as an act of rebellion against society. So, this anagram fits into theory and suggests that Dodgson may very well have "joined in" with what began as aggressive assault against him (at age twelve), what we would call rape today, as a way to survive and relieve the trauma of the attacks. This is a common psychic and behavioral defense mechanism. We see an example of it today in the inner cities where boys will join gangs to survive, but revert to more acceptable behavior if they are removed from the threatening environment.

In later works, anagrams emerge with much angrier and more sexually explicit themes, such as the "Marchioness of Mock Turtles" which becomes "O fuck mother's incest morals." (*Fuck* is a valid Victorian word.) And, in what I believe to be thematically the crowning piece of his works as they reflect his struggles and possibly predictions of these murders, we have the opening verse to "Jabberwocky" from his *Through the Looking-Glass and What Alice Found There*. This verse is considered by many to be the greatest piece of nonsense literature in the English language as he created words with sounds which sometimes seem to have meaning, although they do not, at least on the surface. The full poem is presented below with Dodgson's chosen illustration on the facing page:

Jabberwocky

Twas brillig, and the slithy toves
 Did gyre and gimble in the wabe:
All mimsy were the borogoves,
 And the mome raths outgrabe.

"Beware the Jabberwock, my son!
 The jaws that bite, the claws that catch!
Beware the Jubjub bird, and shun
 The frumious Bandersnatch!"

He took his vorpal sword in hand:
 Long time the manxome foe he sought —
So rested he by the Tumtum tree,
 And stood awhile in thought.

And, as in uffish thought he stood,
 The Jabberwock, with eyes of flame,
Came whiffling through the tulgey wood,
 And burbled as it came!

The Jabberwock

Source: *Through the Looking-Glass and What Alice Found There*, Chapter I.

> One, two! One, two! And through and through
> The vorpal blade went snicker-snack!
> He left it dead, and with its head
> He went galumphing back.
>
> "And hast though slain the Jabberwock?
> Come to my arms, my beamish boy!
> O frabjous day! Callooh! Callay!"
> He chortled in his joy.
>
> Twas brillig, and the slithy toves
> Did gyre and gimble in the wabe:
> All mimsy were the borogoves,
> And the mome raths outgrabe.

The story continues:

> "It seems very pretty," she [Alice] said when she had
> finished it, "but it's *rather* hard to understand!" (You see she
> didn't like to confess, even to herself, that she couldn't make it
> out at all.) "Somehow it seems to fill my head with ideas
> — only I don't exactly know what they are! However,
> *somebody* killed *something*: that's clear, at any rate —"

Here we have what is most likely the clearest disclosure of
Dodgson's rage, its target, the nature of his efforts to both soothe
himself and separate himself from the grip which possessed him. It is
also the clearest foretelling of the Ripper murders as appears in the
works published prior to 1888. In fact the opening verse was written as
part of a family game, then published in 1871.

Many analysts have interpreted the poem as masturbatory in
theme. If we treat the opening verse as three anagrams, the first two
lines together as the unit they are based on punctuation and the last
two separately, we have a totally different poem, clearly masturbatory in
theme, which also identifies what and who was killed symbolically. We
also see an introduction which sets the theme for the body of the poem
that follows. The anagrammatic solution is:

> Bet I beat my glands til,
> With hand-sword I slay the evil gender.

A slimey theme; borrow gloves,
And masturbate the hog more! [5]

Within Dodgson's world of words and anagrams, and, until they were not enough, I believe he "slayed the evil gender" with *words*, the anagrammatic reworking of *sword*. Sidney Halpern points out that the dragon/monster, as displayed in the illustration which accompanies the poem, is a symbolic representation of the mother-figure across civilizations and cultures. [6] Psychoanalyst Masud Kahn and others identify the penis as a symbol of mother in masturbation. All of this ties together as an act of self-mutilation as a substitute for abusing a mother figure, with individual freedom from the controlling mother-image and the self-abusive act the goal, but dependent on a resolution of the psychic rage directed at that mother figure. [7]

Now, when we examine the body of the poem in this light, each verse in sequence, we see first an exhortation to beware the grasping, controlling nature of the mother figure, followed by an allusion to the length of time during which the assault was plotted, then a clear masturbatory fantasy founded in the penis-as-mother, with no attempt to hide either the sound/sense of *burbling* or the Victorian pornographic meaning of *came*. This is followed by a striking out with the sword at the head of the mother figure, then a withdrawal from the assault followed by praise received from someone, what appears to be a male adult figure. The imagery is of removing the head of the "dragon" in retribution for the head-removing metaphorical castration inflicted on him. But then, as if the slaying of the figure is not adequate for relief, the poem closes with a repetition of the opening theme, which, in its anagrammatic reconstruction, reflects the recognized failure of masturbation as an effort to self-soothe, as an effort which will be repeated but is doomed to failure: "And masturbate the hog more!"

Was this entire poem a foretelling of violence to come, a part of the brooding and plotting that began twenty years or more before the Ripper murders? Or were the murders plotted later and designed to bring to life this fantasy that a tormented Dodgson never dreamed he would have the courage to execute? Was he foretelling that even the killings would not satisfy, would not provide relief, that when brought to life, they, too, would be repeated, without a relief that satisfies?

A very similar theme was introduced earlier in *Alice's Adventures in Wonderland* when the Queen of Hearts, herself a mother of the errant Jack of Hearts and a Dodgson mother-figure, threatened everyone with the famous refrain "Off with her (his, their) head (s)!"

Metaphorically, this means of retribution for wrongs committed became mother-taught.

There is one other pivotal series of anagrams which should be identified before we continue. These involve the mysterious number "42" which appeared throughout Dodgson's works. There was "Rule Forty-two" in *Alice's Adventures in Wonderland*: "All persons more than a mile high to leave the court." Rules 1 through 41 were never defined. In *The Hunting of the Snark: An Agony in Eight Fits*, we find "Rule 42 of the Code" which directs: "No one shall speak to the man at the helm, and the man at the helm shall speak to no one." A character in the *Snark*, the Butcher, left forty-two boxes carefully packed and marked on the beach.

The first rule reads, in anagrammatic reconstruction: "Let not holier thoughts reveal cheap animal mores," a manifesto that a Jekyll-Hyde existence is very much the plan for his life. The second reads: "No one shall spanketh the hot male meat, and the hot male meat shall spanketh no one," an obvious continuation of masturbatory imagery. The latter is totally consistent with Dodgson's line from the *Snark*, highlighted in his Preface as being the one most likely to warrant the charge of being nonsensical, "Then the bowsprit got mixed with the rudder sometimes." This line has been seen as reflecting gender confusion, but it also reflects a theme of sodomy as the bowsprit was the most projecting part of the ship, therefore, a penis allusion. However, more explicitly, the line transforms to: "To mother: Disturbed, I themed the worst pig sex with men." [8]

The origin for "Rule 42 of the Code" lies, I believe in a wood block found among other children's things beneath the floorboards of the Dodgson home at Croft during reconstruction in 1954. Found there was a piece of wood that contains words written in what is believed by biographers to be Dodgson's (childhood) hand:

> And we'll wander through
> the wide world and
> chase the buffalo. [9]

If we remove eight letters, bringing the fifty letters down to forty-two (I find no anagram which uses all fifty) we have a manifesto to the world that the life lived will be a facade, a charade of respectability hidden behind a "looking-glass," with the hope that it will last beyond the grave.

"Bluff a rough, sordid, heathen world, and cheat death." [10]

What we find in a detailed study of his works written as an adolescent and up until the time of his death are repetitions on the same themes and same imagery. He used this means of incorporating his anger into his entire body of literature as his means of venting an insatiable rage. It was a sense of the inadequacy of that means of venting that led me to wonder whether he had in fact taken a more active, demonstrative, and compelling way to bring angry yet sterile words to life in physical acts of violence.

This work would become quite a different one if the literary pursuit of these anagrams became the focus. Several more will be mentioned as they fit into the story of his life. What their presence demands, however, in understanding his life and his possible involvement in these murders, is that they became his way of telling his story and of expressing himself in a hateful, spiteful, time-consuming, obsessive task *for a lifetime*.

And it is here that those who come to believe that the evidence for Dodgson being Jack the Ripper is overwhelming must take on a sympathetic view of him as also a victim. For he was in many ways no less a victim than those so destroyed by the Ripper. The remainder of this chapter reviews that destruction as it summarizes my more technical work *The Agony of Lewis Carroll*, which provides what heretofore has been interpretive evidence provided by others of inner ugliness with concrete evidence of the nature and origins of that ugliness.

What we find is a boy who was destroyed in childhood, first by seductive and coercive parenting practices that attempted to mold him into a replication of his father — rather, into an extension of his father's wishes for himself. This loyal and conforming perfect child, who gave his all to meet parental expectations, even learning Greek and Latin at age five, was then sent, stammering, effeminate, innocent, unathletic, and precocious into the violent English public school system where it appears he was homosexually raped from the earliest weeks throughout his six years there. It was at Rugby where the worst of the attacks occurred, the school he entered exactly forty-two years before these murders occurred.

It was during this period that I am increasingly convinced he suffered what we would recognize today as a psychotic break from which he never recovered. His experience at age fourteen could only have been akin to that described in the *New York Times* in which a nineteen-year-old boy was imprisoned with eleven other inmates in a four-bed cell. When he was to be psychologically tested, he wrote nothing but "Help me! Help me!" on the test form. It was later learned that he had been raped every hour on the hour for forty-eight hours by cell-mates.

[11] One could easily imagine that "11" or "48" could bring back terrible memories of trauma during his life.

Going now beyond my original thinking, whatever Dodgson endured there, he became a psychopath who focused first on secretive antisocial acts and eventually on multiple homicides and mutilations. His emotional life stopped growing; the seeds of rage already laid blossomed forth, and he set himself on a path of childlike revenge against his family and society. Life became obsessed with getting even, filled with spite, a constant search for retribution. The primary target of his rage was his mother, whose favorite he had been and whose task in the family it was to guide and protect him. After her death when he was nineteen, his targets became the symbols-of-mother. His overriding and controlling feelings were of profound betrayal and abandonment by her; later that rage extended to his father, who, fully knowledgeable of the school environment, appears never to have warned him about it. Just as he had been used by his parents as their thing-object, as their parenting practices demanded that he become an adult early and reflected their denial of him as a child, he, in turn, treated the women in his life, even the children with whom he had what appeared such close and affectionate relationships, as thing-objects. They met his emotional needs and provided a testing-ground for the incorporation of smut in the nonsense he wrote for their enjoyment and consumption. The Ripper victims also became thing-objects whose sole purpose was to meet the emotional needs of the killer.

On an intellectual level, Dodgson engaged in a lifetime struggle with good and evil. A faith that God would deliver him was replaced by a sense of Christlike chosenness to suffer, then followed by or combined with a belief in his behavior as not only justified, but ordained. And at all times these feelings were laced with strong negative feelings that even God had abandoned him both at school and in his early adult life of prayer for relief from his turmoil (as evidenced in his diary manuscripts). At times he may have seen himself as the devil-incarnate.

Colin Wilson describes these crimes as existential in nature, as an effort by the Ripper to define himself as separate from what he felt were the forces controlling his existence, personal as well as societal. This was explored more fully when we discussed the psychological profile of the Ripper in the last chapter. This lifelong battle that Dodgson waged was very much existential in nature, but with emotional tools that had long since been destroyed. When such a condition exists, emancipation can lead, not to successful individual release, which demands that emotions "keep up," but release *based on* the annihilation of the controlling force or its symbolic representation. It is the infant kicking back at his parent, but with the strength and potency of the adult.

But I get ahead of the story.

While nearly all of this material appears in *The Agony of Lewis Carroll*, I am particularly indebted to biographers Stuart Collingwood, Ann Clark, and psychobiographer Phyllis Greenacre for nearly all of the factual details. Again I have provided citations for material which seemed unique to a source.

Charles Lutwidge Dodgson was born on 27 January 1832, the third of what would be eleven children born in quick succession. He was the first boy, named Charles after his father, grandfather, and great-grand-father. As his parents were first cousins, a sure indication of family emotional fusion, he was also named after his great-uncle Charles Lutwidge. In a similar fashion, his older sister and their first child Frances was named after her mother and even carried the same nickname of Fanny.

Charles' father was a stern, remote, strongly opinionated Anglican cleric in the remote village of Daresbury in the county of Cheshire. He had chosen the simple parish life despite his extraordinary performance at Oxford University during which he had taken a rare double first in both the classics and mathematics. Life was lived on the edge of poverty as the stipend from the Church was only marginally adequate for the family of ten children born there. This was true despite the fact that their income was supplemented by the glebe farm on which they lived and derived income from the sale of produce and rental of the land. To further augment his income, the elder Dodgson translated ancient texts from the Latin for his benefactor, Dr. Pusey, who became leader of the Oxford Movement within the church, and he accepted students in what was originally the "family" school. When Charles was eleven, his father was appointed Rector of the parish at Croft, and the family moved to the new town and rectory and a new life in the upper middle-class.

Charles' mother is somewhat of an enigma in biographies; little is known about her. She came from an upper middle class family, her father was a civil servant. But there are also claims that her early roots lay in the titled class. A silhouette profile done at a fair the family attended in 1840 depicts a woman with a somewhat regal look but who was not attractive. She had a pronounced Roman nose, more Roman even than her husband's. [12] I have long suspected that the mutilation of the noses of two of the Ripper victims may have its origins in this hated face and facial feature.

None of the other children seem to have passed on anything of significance about their mother. Given the opportunity to do so in the family approved biography written in 1898 by Charles' nephew (by his sister Mary), Stuart Collingwood, they failed to do so. What they did present was a description of her which was attributed to Charles and confirmed as originating with Dodgson by a later biographer with close family ties, Langford Reed, in his 1932 work *The Life of Lewis Carroll.* [13] She was

> one of the sweetest and gentlest women that ever lived, whom to know was to love. The earnestness of her simple faith and love shone forth in all she did and said; she seemed to live always in the conscious presence of God. It has been said by her children that they never in all their lives remember to have heard an impatient or harsh word from her lips. [14]

There is no question from the only published sample of her writing style that the children (Charles at that time as the letter's recipient) were at the center of her life as she sent Charles one million kisses to share with his siblings. But the description is quite different from the mother-figures he parodied in his children's' books — the Marchioness of Mock Turtles, the Duchess, Queen of Hearts, or Red Queen, although later ones in *Sylvie and Bruno* were softer.

Returning to the world of anagrams, I came to believe as others had that this description of his mother was not "real." It certainly would describe a "perfect" mother, too perfect, one with whom it would be impossible to disagree or rebel against in even the slightest way without feelings of enormous guilt. She would have characteristics of the castrating mother who, through seductive sweetness and love, yet overpowering goodness, would prevent the individual from emerging, of forming himself by being at times in opposition to her. Rebellion would risk the loss of the love and protection which poured forth, along with all the feelings of specialness and acceptance which can accompany such outpourings of love, not for the child as he is, but for what he is as the mother's "created thing." Suspecting that the description might be, if not dripping in sarcasm, at least a distortion of his feelings about her, indeed, perhaps a looking-glass reversal of those feelings, I treated it as an anagram, rearranged the letters, and believe I found the truth. She was

> one of those sweet and gentle women that hobble blest, healthy, tempted children. As tenacious as a dog she never let them live their own lives. As her thin, misshapen, favorite

charmed her, I came to resent every word from her lips. So, a horrid freak — a timid phony — sneered, revolted, wasted a talent, and showed how vile filth vanishes in foolish nonsense. [15]

These feelings, whenever they emerged, were hidden behind a childhood filled with what many would perceive as an idyllic environment. But the conforming Charles was perfect in every way as he excelled in his studies at home, in the way he entertained his younger sisters with plays he wrote, puppets he made, clever magic shows, and later the publication of his poems in family-prepared books. He built a "love" train from a wheelbarrow and other farm implements, but in the rules he wrote for its operation, he told how if one is injured he must be run over by the love train two or three times before aid would be provided. Love's curative attributes could already be seen as overwhelming and annihilative of self-development.

He, along with his sisters, stammered throughout his life, just enough to inhibit spontaneous speech except in structured situations. Significantly, the stammer disappeared in the presence of the children with whom he socialized as an adult.

Shortly after moving from Daresbury to Croft, Charles was sent off to Richmond Grammar School, about ten miles away. It was his first experience living away from home and his first exposure to public school, even to boys other than his brother and Sunday-friend Thomas Vere Bayne from Daresbury. Within a week he wrote a letter to his sisters Fanny and Memy in which he described his first days. This letter is pivotal in understanding what happened to him, for in it he describes an innocent enough game called "Peter, the red lion" which involved boys with their eyes closed poking fingers into mouths. But in his closing, he sent a strange message to his eight-year-old brother Skeffington:

> MY DEAR SKEFF:
> Roar not lest thou be abolished.
>   Yours, etc. [16]

At the age of twelve, Charles sent his brother his first message in anagrammatic form. For in rearranging the greeting and message, we derive: "Ask mother about the red lion; safer boys fled." [17] We learn from Victorian slang dictionaries that *peter* was a word for *penis*. We learn from the remainder of Dodgson's life, as reflected in his writings, that *lion* would have a dual meaning to him, as would *Peter*. In later life, although he secretly adored the attention he received as Lewis

Carroll, especially from the children, he avowed a wish never to be lionized. It was at this time that he was introduced to the Greek love of which he had most likely read in his childhood studies.

After a successful stay at Richmond, successful by every academic measure, although his headmaster warned his parents in a letter that there was some risk of him deviating from sound character if he came to recognize his cleverness over others, [18] he went on to Rugby, the next level of schooling in preparation for his destiny at Oxford University.

Rugby was quite typical of the public school at the time, housing boys from age eight to twenty-two in the same buildings with what amounted to a total absence of adult supervision during the night hours. Writers increasingly disclose the extent to which vice was rife in the schools, so devoted during the day to the study of Greek (in the case of Rugby seventeen of twenty-one hours per week), sports, and religion, and at night to fighting, fagging, and unspeakable sexual practices involving one or more boys. *Fagging* involved the practice of older boys using the younger and more vulnerable boys to perform services for them. While on the surface, these "services" involved running errands and shining boots, for many they involved what could only be considered homosexual rape given the age and size differences and the isolation that peer pressure produced for those who complained.

While in his adult years Dodgson made only two references to his experiences during those four years, and only then referred to them as nighttime annoyances, it would seem that they were far more than that. Nighttime became a terror for him throughout his life, leaving him an insomniac much of the time. It was during the night that much of his rage and anger vented itself, both (most likely) in the masturbatory practices about which he wrote in his coded manner and in the work of hate-driven anagram creation that consumed much of his loneliness. He would write in a serious poem titled "The Valley of the Shadow of Death":

> ... "O bitter is it to abide
> In weariness alway:
> At dawn to sigh for eventide,
> At eventide for day."

... [As morning approaches, following a night of visions of a woman-figure]

> The morning-mists grow thin and clear,
> and Death brings in the Day. [19]

Written when he was thirty-six and referencing "half a life behind," which would be the school period, the theme seems to be in the title and the anagram formed from an italicized phrase in the first line (the only one in the poem): "Gay men lived as things. . . and died." [20] His days and nights were filled with horror and loathing, but also brooding and fantasizing, the slow death of continued alienation.

It was while he was at home during the Rugby years that Dodgson began to incorporate anagrams into the stories and poems he wrote and published under his parents' auspices. While they were really family affairs, he was the prime contributor.

And it was during this period that he began honing his skills in the creation of anagrams, but it would not be until he began focusing on children's stories that the vehicle for and direction of his rage expression became clear.

In the meantime, he completed the Rugby years during which he gained as many academic awards as a student could obtain under the rules and prepared for several months for entry to Oxford. Two days after his arrival there and one day before his nineteenth birthday, his mother died quite unexpectedly at the age of forty-seven. He was not present at the end, and the only recorded family reaction was a description of him as seeming melancholy for several months. I strongly believe that given the strong love-hate feelings he had toward her that this melancholy reflected a normal mourning but also a mourning that she would not be present to "receive" the venom he was already including in his writings. For he was up until this point publishing with her approval and assistance, while she was quite unaware that he was hiding material in his coded anagrammatic form.

The details of Dodgson's life at Oxford are not well known. He did well, nearly replicating his father's performance when he received first class honors in mathematics and second class in the classics in 1854. He did so well that he was offered a studentship to continue on, and remained there as a tutoring don until his death in 1898. It was during this period that he began to keep a diary, but the early volumes disappeared, probably just from neglect, in the interim between the time Collingwood used them in 1898 for his biography and their discovery in the basement of a family home when their publication became a goal to celebrate the hundredth anniversary of his birth in 1932.

At the request of biographer Derek Hudson, a handwriting analyst, Dr. M. J. Mannheim, examined two letters from Dodgson, the "Dear Skeff" letter and one written during the Oxford days. The change in personality is striking. In the first, Mannheim sees a boy experiencing some immediate anxiety, but in general one, who at age twelve, appears inappropriately set in his personality, so adultlike as to have bypassed adolescence, with an outward focus totally devoted to pleasing others. This is the picture of the "perfect" child, who has totally denied himself and lived up to the expectations and wishes of others. At the completion of Dodgson's education, Mannheim sees a young man, still mature beyond his years, extremely set in his personality, but with a totally inward focus and "a very rebellious mind." [21] This is the profile of one whose inner world is at least partially destroyed, one who is now focusing on psychic survival of the self, with the way to do that moving toward unconventional means. It appears that psychic energy was now focused on managing a catastrophic split.

Oxford at the time was a place where homosexual activities could and did take place with relative freedom from criticism or the criminal repercussions which were more subject to risk outside of the school environment. The extent to which Dodgson was involved in them is not known, in fact was never raised as possible in all the early biographies.

It was from this safe haven that he began his struggle to teach mathematics. The teaching experience was not a good one. He was constantly disappointed at the lack of interest shown by students, always uncomfortable with the teaching process, most likely over the lack of control he had over unmotivated boys and his stammer in their presence. The diaries during this period indicate that a profound boredom was setting in, a lack of enjoyment and fulfillment from his assigned tasks, and nothing challenging to fill his private time. It was now that he began his ventures into children's' nonsense, an effort that would continue until *Sylvie and Bruno Concluded* was completed in 1893. He appears to have been assisted in these efforts by two friends, Thomas Vere Bayne, who had become by this time a fellow don, and Henry Parry Liddon, like Bayne three years his senior, and a don he had met while a student at Oxford.

Returning to the world of anagrams, we can perhaps sum up Dodgson's school experience by drawing from a poem titled "Clara" which is published (rarely reproduced) in *Useful and Instructive Poetry*. This work ostensibly includes poems from his childhood, but I believe this one was written later and included there in the notebook, which was not published until 1954. Its theme is sexual in tone as Clara awaits the arrival of her husband to join her in bed, fearful of letting him "in." The fear may be related to the final line which reads: "He's only been drinking too much gin, / And got dead drunk." [22]

If "Rule 42 of the Code" is invoked, and two letters are removed from the 44 before solving anagrams, we can derive at least six different statements:

Rugby turned a keen Dodgson child into a demon king.

But kin and Richmond led keen Dodgson to gay urning. (*Urning* was one of the Victorian words for *homosexual*, a word which did not exist until later in the century.)

Stingy mother bore kind, nodding [in obeisance], angled [Dodgson stood with a backward tilt], eunuch don.

Oh, Liddon, Bayne, Dodgson trick the game, nude urning.

In drunk den night agony, mired don suckled hog bone. (*Bone* was slang for *penis*, with *hog* better supported as a "dirty fellow" although it appears in the former context on several occasions.)

Bared urning don king mounted holy chaste don king. [23]

All of these, although somewhat awkward in structure, reflect the kind of life lived by many students in the unsupervised dormitories of the public schools, where violence was rife and sexual activities were homosexual, brutal, experimentally deviant, and orgiastic in nature.

There came a time in Dodgson's studentship that he was required to continue on with the vows of priesthood in the Anglican Church. He requested a dispensation from the requirement both because of his continued interest in attending theatrical productions, an activity specifically prohibited for Oxford priests by his superior Bishop Wilberforce, and presumably because of his stammer and its effect on his ability to preach. After Liddon interceded on his behalf, he was allowed to remain as a don without proceeding to full priesthood.

The remainder of Dodgson's life was lived in what can only be described as proper respectability, even if there was eccentricity evident. It is this record of his life that fills the biographies, suggesting disturbances, some sexual, some religious in nature, but all indicating that he was able to keep whatever they were in check. It is only the discovery of the hidden material that allows us to examine that life for more sinister motives, some conscious, some unconscious.

There are five aspects of his adult life deserving of focus in this work. The first is his relationship with family, men, women, and the bevy of prepubertal girls with whom he spent so much of his time. The second is the role that photography, an all-consuming hobby for a number of years, played, especially with the young girls. The third is the character and personality he presented to the world and what his two ongoing afflictions — stammering and migraine — suggest lay at the foundations of that character. A brief review of his writing activities will give us a sense of the way he aged and the kinds of things included in his themes. Finally, we need to examine his religious struggles and what seem to have evolved as his beliefs regarding salvation and eternal punishment.

Relationships

Dodgson's relationship with his father was a distant one throughout his adult life until the latter's death in 1868. The few letters published reflect only routine business matters, one of them being advice from his father regarding insurance. Diary entries indicate that father and son walked together when he visited the family at Croft, and they attended Masonic *fetes* together in the 1850s and 1860s. How tickets were obtained is not known. My efforts to determine if his father were ever a member of the organization were unsuccessful, but this subject is pursued further in chapter 5.

His relations with his sisters can only be described as extremely supportive, evidenced especially at their father's death when he took over management of affairs and helped them settle in a new house in Guildford, called "The Chestnuts," where they lived until after Charles's death. With all but sister Mary unmarried, Charles was apparently looked on with awe and admiration, due no doubt to his success with the books, his generosity in providing for them from his royalties, and for the way he helped manage their affairs with the outside world.

It is only when we know what was happening secretly that we find that the love so evident was matched with a seething hate beneath the surface. Fully aware of his attitude toward his mother, we can easily see the biting sarcasm in his letter to Mary on the birth of her first son (Stuart, who would become his biographer) as he told her in a two-sentence letter punctuated with exclamation marks that he hoped she would do for her son what his own mother had done for him and that he could think of no better wish to make to the infant at that time.

Anger in anagrammatic form would emerge, this time with sister Lizzie, when he wrote her on the subject of eternal punishment. She wrote back, objecting to receiving an "argument" from him, and he apologized, saying he was only trying to clarify things for her. His argument on the surface was that there were at least three meanings to the phrase "I believe in the doctrine of Eternal Punishment." He went on to break down three possible meanings and the implications of taking any one of the positions. By anagrammatic construction, however, the phrase can take on two additional meanings: "I'd be proven insane if I let the lion meet her cunt" and "I believe the Fathers condemn penile nutrition." [24]

There is no question, however, that by every visible measure he was a perfect brother to his sisters but even more so with his brothers. Here, he seemed to be sincere, although one cannot dismiss the notion that he was placing the entire family's name at risk should his writings ever be exposed. Quite importantly he guided them to schools that were considerably more gentle in their educational approach than he had experienced at Rugby, seemingly very sensitive to their never having to go through what he did. It would only be in his diary that he criticized his brother Edwin for going to Zanzibar as a missionary when he felt there was so much work to be done in England, perhaps an ominous foretelling of his own contribution to the missionary effort. Coincidentally, it was during the Ripper murders that he was guiding his nephew Stuart through Oxford University, recording in his diary that they were meeting quite regularly.

Except for a very small circle of friends in the Oxford community and the contacts necessary to meet with his publisher, Macmillan, Inc., Dodgson is believed to have avoided pretty much all contact with men. His aversion was such that he would even explicitly exclude husbands when he invited their wives to dine. There is no question that he was more comfortable with women, usually the mothers of the children whom he entertained. There is no indication that he attempted any serious relationship with any of the adult women in his life.

It was the children who were his focus; and again it was the young girls, since with few exceptions he would avoid or exclude boys from his life. While he was already beginning to be known as a storyteller among the children he would meet at the beach, it would not be until the Liddell family moved into the deanery at Christ Church, Oxford, that he befriended their children so openly. And it was Alice Liddell, who would later be celebrated as the heroine of the *Alice* books, who unquestionably caught his eye, although as one reads the diary manuscripts, the even younger Fredericka was very much a favorite.

After telling the story of Alice while on a boat ride on the river near Godstow in June 1861, he was badgered by Alice and her siblings to write the story down. He proceeded to do so and presented her with a handwritten *Alice's Adventures Under Ground* in February of the following year. Further encouraged to publish the work by adult friends, he nearly doubled the original work, engaged John Tenniel, political cartoonist for *Punch* to do the illustrations, and published *Alice's Adventures in Wonderland* in 1865. The book met with immediate commercial success even though some of the reviews were more guarded. It was not the typical or approved Victorian children's story.

As one examines the original work and its longer published version, one finds that the inclusion of hidden material began early and only grew more sophisticated. Perhaps the most famous of the riddles from *Alice* is the question asked at the Mad Tea Party, a riddle which has remained a mystery for well over a hundred years: "Why is a raven like a writing desk?" In the Preface to the sixth edition written in 1896, Dodgson provided an answer, although he denied that it had an answer when originally written:

> Because it can produce a few notes, though they are *very* flat: and it is never put with the wrong end in front! [25]

The first part of his answer responds to both notes as sung by the raven and as written, but the second part does not appear to respond to the riddle. What it does respond to is the anagram formed from the riddle and its suggestion of "gay" anal behavior: "His kind Lewis a gay knave writer" or "Lewis his kind, a gay knave writer." [26] As we can see, at age thirty-one, he provided a question with no answer, suggesting that we examine the question more closely. And, two years before his death, he was still toying with his audience, moving just a little closer to the true meaning of the line. The book is filled with anagrams and clues to examine things very closely.

John Tenniel worked under Dodgson's close supervision in all of the illustrations, although his apparent inclusion of likenesses that resembled current political figures has caused many to believe that Carroll's work was primarily political parody. In the work he handed to Alice Liddell, however, all of the illustrations were his own. Of particular relevance is one picture of the grounds of the Queen's courtyard, in one corner of which is a scene that has baffled Freudian analysts since it was first noticed. For two courtiers are kissing, while one appears to be holding the other's penis, his tights having been turned down to expose himself. This might be dismissed as an interpretation of an unclear picture (much less ambiguous in the first edition copy) if we did not find a confirmation for it in the second of the *Alice* works, *Through the Looking-Glass and What Alice Found There*, published in 1870. Early in the story Dodgson has the Red King, a chess piece, writing a memorandum of his feelings while Alice "assists" at the end of the pencil. He writes: *"The White Knight is sliding down the poker. He balances very badly."* The italics are Dodgson's and represent the clue to examine the sentence, which rereads: "Ah, ye! When I slid down the lonely knave's tights I grabbed the prick." [27]

These kinds of constructs, some more explicit, some less, fill the works, including his book of serious and nonsense poems for adults published in 1869 *Phantasmagoria and Other Poems*, which title itself is an anagram: "Ah, pants and orgasm hero poet am I!"

What is of interest here in this work is just what role the children were playing in his emotional life. There is no question that he was entertaining them with his stories. They flocked to him as a Pied Piper, a rare adult who met them on their own level and patiently taught them, told stories, read the bible, made puzzles and played games. The thousands of letters he wrote to them are filled with just delightful material.

Yet something much more sinister was going on. For, whether attacking them as possessing the sexuality he wished for himself, a sexuality he both hated and loved, the sexuality that would have allowed him to avoid the trauma of public school, or of attacking their parents as surrogates for his own parents, he was penetrating them repeatedly *outside their awareness* with his clever smut-laden anagrammatic nonsense. He was using them as objects for his own enjoyment even as he was delighting them with his company and entertainment.

Since publishing *The Agony of Lewis Carroll* some have disagreed with my conclusion that he never abused the children physically, that he never touched them carnally. I persist in this belief. He had too much to lose if he ever did touch them beyond the kissing and hugging that he did do with them, for he would have lost access to the only emotional world in which he was comfortable. For him to have even masturbated in their presence beneath his clothing I find totally inconsistent with my understanding of him. Again, he would have risked detection by parents and governesses when they called for their children. Of the nearly two hundred children he befriended, only two or three parents limited his access to them without accompaniment, especially in his rooms. One of them was Mrs. Liddell.

So hungry was he for the adoration he received from them, an adoration perhaps akin to his memories of that provided by his mother, he carried a black doctor's type bag on all his trips, a bag filled with toys and games, pins and bows — things to allow him to engage with young girls he met on the train, at the station, on the beach, or in and around the theater district. There is no question that these children provided both the calm of innocence in his turbulent world and also the calm which came from his ability to exercise a control over them that violated that innocence.

Several biographers have hypothesized that he had wished he could have married one of the children, with Alice Liddell often named, along with Ellen Terry, a child-actress who as an adult maintained his friendship as she became a renowned actress on the London stage. Given what was lying underneath the surface, I reject this notion totally. Marriage was not in his plans.

What we do find in his letters to these children who drew away from him as they reached puberty was the same use of anagrams in their letters as he used in his works, often sexually explicit. The psychological pattern is interesting, for they, as themselves mother-surrogates, were abandoning him at the same age at which he experienced feelings of abandonment by his mother. This replication of the betrayal brought out the same rage, this time directed to adolescent girls.

Photography

Dodgson acquired his first camera in 1856 and was an avid and talented hobbyist until he suddenly abandoned it in 1880 after twenty-four years. While he took many photographs of adult friends and Victorian notables that he met from his fame as "Lewis Carroll," his favorite subjects were the little girls. Having built a studio atop his quarters at Oxford so as to have proper lighting, he spent many hours both posing the girls in costumes he would acquire from his theater acquaintances and many more hours with them in the dark room developing the pictures by the "wet" process then required. The mysteries of that process are well documented in stories by the children who stood wide-eyed in the dim light watching the picture emerge.

This hobby became such a compulsion to him, partly due to the involvement with the children, partly due to his propensity to compulsive processes, that he often complained of having too little time for his work, even as he would fit in hours for this hobby. The reasons for his abandoning something so enjoyable are not known. There had been introduced about 1880 a more modern "dry" process, much easier to use, but which tended to produce somewhat inferior prints. He may have given it up rather than compete with something inferior.

But he had also, for several years now, been photographing children in the nude, always extremely sensitive to any objection by parents or child to do so; he took only those who were willing and not the least bit uncomfortable. There was an incident with one of the children about this time; he kissed her, only to find that she was already past puberty. Both he and her mother were not happy. An incident such as this, one that would risk his reputation, may very well have brought about a discontinuance of the hobby and possible loss of his friends. I suspect, however, that it was primarily the work load that lay before him, as the two *Sylvie* books were already under way, filled with anagrams he had been collecting for years. (He had called the material "litterature" in the Preface to the work, an intentional mis-spelling.) He had also been curator of the Common Room for several years, itself a time-consuming activity.

My sense is that the photography with the children provided not only another way to attract and control the children through the posing process, but a search for his own wished-for feminine image in the innocent age at which his own emotional growth stopped. A frustrated artist, never happy with his own renderings, photography allowed him to capture "perfect images" of the wished-for self. He was never attracted to the girls who were "too cute," preferring instead the plainer ones with some asymmetry in their faces. Was he seeking to capture the same plainness and asymmetry which made up his own appearance, only in an idealized form? In the preparation for the illustrations of Sylvie in the *Sylvie* books, he went so far as to suggest to his artist, Harry Furniss, that he travel here to see a perfect nose, there for perfect eyes, somewhere else for perfect legs, providing Furniss with the addresses of the girls to be used as models. With photography by this time long abandoned and his own years advancing, this became the means for capturing the wished-for image.

Character and Personality

There is no question but that Dodgson was recognized as eccentric, even by Victorian standards. He ate sparsely, [28] consistent with his five feet, 9 inch very slim frame, walked with a jerky gate, although there was no known deformity, and tended to tilt backward when he stood. Except for wearing a white straw hat when boating, he dressed conservatively in black, occasionally adding a festive touch with gray rather than black gloves. He wore gloves always, claiming to the children that they carried "love" inside them. Psychoanalysts have attributed a masturbatory connotation to the practice, [29] an interpretation consistent with his own explanation.

He was a perfectionist in everything, a personality feature often interpreted as a technique for hiding internal chaos. He kept things meticulously clean and in order, created elaborate methods for managing his many letters, kept records of his dinner guests, including what they ate and the seating arrangement. He fussed about the drafts in his apartment and devised a way to control the temperature in each room.

He intruded constantly in the work being done by his artists. John Tenniel, after he told Dodgson that he could do no more illustrations for him, told Harry Furniss that he doubted he would be able to work with him at all. Furniss threatened to quit on several occasions, once when Dodgson demanded to see work in process. Furniss barred the door and Dodgson withdrew; Furniss in fact had done nothing, claiming that what Dodgson believed would take seven years of effort would take him less than a week. When pressed to seek out child models, Furniss used his daughter to create Sylvie. Dodgson was not unaware of or untouched by Furniss's attitude for he hid an anagram in the last work, *Sylvie and Bruno Concluded*, playing on a phrase from Shakespeare's *Hamlet*: "The funeral baked-meats did coldly furnish forth the marriage tables," [30] which he used in a context which is the reverse of the original. (The re-marriage followed the funeral in *Hamlet*; the funeral followed the marriage in *Sylvie and Bruno*, but Dodgson used the phrase anyway.) Reconstructed, it reads: "Harry Furniss called me a harsh, demented tart, but I faked the glib fool." [31] There is no question but that Furniss was unaware of the material hidden in the works.

Dodgson was very much a loner at Oxford, although he did manage the Common Room where the residents ate and socialized. His fame and fortune which came from certainly nonacademic endeavors, was tolerated, as were the lion-seekers in search of "Lewis Carroll." He came into conflict on several occasions with Dean Liddell over University matters, drawing on his facility with the pen by writing papers and pamphlets on subjects of interest. Even on those occasions one sees evidence of anagrams in every title he chose for those papers.

For a very long period he did not preach at all, although that was attributed to his stammer. In his later years, about 1886 and onward, he returned to preaching, either at the University (often for the servants service) or at Guildford when he visited his sisters.

He published a number of books in mathematics during the years that he was publishing the nonsense, but, never having learned calculus, they are really just clever presentations of material rather than contributions to the subject. These books served two purposes, although we must recognize that his mind was elsewhere. They presented the image of making an academic contribution, and most likely satisfied his father, himself a mathematician-hobbyist, while he was alive. "Papa" never quite understood his son's success with the nonsense, but recognized himself in it as he was also an excellent raconteur and creator of nonsense for his children as they were growing. And mathematics did give him a diversion from the rage-filled obsession with the other material. His last serious work was in symbolic logic and is considered by many to be a contribution to the field, although it is rarely used.

While most writers comment heavily on Dodgson's insomnia, his character is perhaps most evident in two additional afflictions which troubled him throughout his adult life — stammering and migraine. In the modern literature on the latter, he is considered to have suffered all of the classic symptoms. [32] The etiology and dynamics of both reveal a deeply disturbed personality, a more modern interpretation which has moved away from more physically oriented explanations.

Stammering reflects the early presence of overinvolved perfectionism, of controlling parents who intrude on the learning process of speech as well as other childhood self-coordinating efforts. As adults, stutterers tend to overmanage their affairs, especially everything to do with speech. They constantly search for manageable words, place themselves in ritual positions in relation to the crowd in the room, focus on words as if they had lives of their own, and resort to magical rituals like covering the mouth. (Dodgson drew a caricature of himself teaching with his hand over his mouth.) They tend to focus on women for friendship and for assistance in speaking, often letting the mother-surrogate speak for them in a group. Their inner world is filled with self-loathing, poor self esteem, yet a sense of specialness. There is a constant fear that they will be exposed as frauds. Alienation from self and others is at the core of the personality.

Migraine manifested itself in Dodgson's life in distortions of vision which are believed to be properly reflected in the *Alice* stories by the body expansions and distortions that took place and the dream-like states of *déjà* and *jamais vu*. The personality behind this recurring affliction reflects enormous stress, feelings of hate directed toward people avowed as loved, a repressed hostility, and the presence of "superficial interpersonal relationships, sexual maladjustment, and obsessive preoccupation with moral and ethical issues." [33] The personality is usually constricted, perfectionist, rigid, emotionally constipated, and excessively ambitious.

In Victorian times the causes were believed to lie in a hereditary taint and in masturbation, either of which could lead to madness. These beliefs may very well have fed right into Dodgson's need to blame such things as his parent's consanguineous marriage and his own private practices as the latter represented the state of contemporary knowledge and therefore perhaps supported fears about his own well-being.

Religious Struggles

Any discussion of the religious struggles so evident in Dodgson's private and public writings is faced with the question of whether they represented a part of the facade, part of the "bluff" so evident in other aspects of his life. But there is neither need for a judgmental conclusion nor for any conclusion at all, for it seems that all roads lead to the same place, that is, that he moved toward a position of specialness or one of total trust in the saving power of Christ to overcome life's weaknesses, either of which allowed him to define the moral environment in which he lived. If we conclude that he totally abandoned the faith in God in which he was raised to the point of becoming his own god-center, we only further identify the extent of the psychic damage already done. If we conclude that there was a struggle to the end of his life, then we further identify the totality of torment with which he lived a lifetime.

It appears that somewhere in adolescence, as a means of psychic survival, Charles virtually took on a persona that combined aspects of the Greek culture in which he was so educated as well as the Christian. This persona was that of Orestes, a mythical youth and hero exalted in plays by Euripides and Aeschylus. The story is one of family betrayal, abandonment, and violence, highlighted by Orestes' murder of his mother and her lover, after coming to the belief that he was commanded by the god Apollo to do so in retribution for her murder of his father. In the story, however, Orestes had also been abandoned to what he described as the shame of the homosexuality in the Greek schools. Hounded for a lifetime by the Furies, symbols of guilt, whose task it was to avenge the acts of children against parents, Orestes fled from land to land until finally he sought a trial as his only possibility of exoneration and relief. Pleading that he had only acted in conformity with divine will, he was judged "not guilty," but only after the tied vote of the jury was broken by the goddess of wisdom, Pallas Athena. These themes appear in Dodgson's *Alice's Adventures in Wonderland*.

In his 1953 work *Man's Search for Himself*, Rollo May describes the Orestes story as a powerfully symbolic search for survival by a child against parents who have overwhelmed him. [34] Just as Dodgson did when he attacked his father by the inclusion of prayers and biblical material from which the same anagrammatic themes can be derived, May sees the rebellion as not just against mother, but against both powerful parents and the effect their troubled relationship has on the child. The Orestes story is in contradistinction to that of Oedipus, the Greek hero that Freud used in his Oedipus complex, where the boy attacks the father over the love of mother, fearful of being castrated as retribution for stealing his mother's affection.

Dodgson took on this task of attacking his mother, then his father, with "words" as a means of psychic survival, but incorporated it as a command to do so as retribution for her abandonment of him to the "Greek love" in the public schools, the very same circumstances experienced by Orestes, who told his mother before he killed her (with the sword) that she would be ashamed to hear what he had endured at the school to which she had sent him.

As we examine Dodgson's diary manuscripts during his thirties (the first volumes were lost), we find the most heart-wrenching prayers to God for relief from unnamed activities and "hardness of heart." This is the period during which the two *Alice* books were being written. These were dismissed by biographers as "normal bachelor temptations," but I believe they were much more than that. The prayerful theme can be paraphrased as "You know I want to change. You have the power to change me. I entreat you to do so."

These entries slowly disappear, giving the sense that a feeling of either abandonment by God has taken over or that the activities he is engaged in are a test by God and therefore must be continued, a continuation of the suffering, a parallel of the Christ experience. This latter notion emerges in his later writing on religious matters and eternal punishment, especially his letters to those who are suffering.

These writings contain a movement from the traditional Anglican beliefs, such that he began to see eternity as "a long time" during which repentance could always occur, that the opportunity for repentance did not end with death, that one could not even deny the devil the possibility of repenting at some point, and finally, that the saving power of Christ was *enhanced* and by implication the more to be celebrated by the most heinously evil acts committed by someone who might at some point repent and prove the marvelous efficacy of Christ's redemptive act.

In her seminal work *The Field of Nonsense* published in 1952, Elizabeth Sewell views Dodgson as having assumed godship in his world of nonsense, where he was total master of words and their meaning and of the actions of his characters as well. [35] It would seem that he extended this allusion into his theology and life.

In the Preface to *Sylvie and Bruno Concluded*, published in 1893, just five years before his death, he referenced two biblical quotations. The first was "Hallowed be Thy name" from the Lord's Prayer, a phrase which forms a number of thematically explicit anagrams. The second was "From hardness of heart, and contempt of Thy Word and

Commandment, Good Lord, deliver us!" This very theme that appeared in his diary can be reworked into the Orestes theme, with the prayer answered: "I hated pederast thorn, a worst fury! Don't condemn! A command from God saved don from Hell!" [36]

On the other hand, his diary tells us that he was in virtually daily attendance at chapel, was even one of the last to attend until services were suspended for lack of interest on the part of students and faculty at Oxford. On the surface, there is every indication that there was a struggle going on.

But, when we examine his writings closely, we find evidence of game-playing, anagrams, and sexually explicit themes, just as we have seen in his letter to his sister. One prayer which may have originated with him, "Teach us this and every day to live more nearly as we pray," perhaps coincidentally, perhaps not, forms an anagram whose masturbatory theme and imagery are exactly the same as "Jabberwocky": "Today I slay ye, mother! Sway viper! Hurl a venereal spend." *Spend* was Victorian slang for semen. [37]

So, we are left with no answer to the question of Dodgson's true religious experience. Even on his death bed we find no answer. He asked his sister to read him his favorite hymn which he said ended "Thy will be done." The hymn is a prayer for a total trust and acceptance of God's will, which feeds right into both a sincere fear of the unknown as well as a perverted sense of chosenness. And, surely he was perfectly aware that at least three anagrams can be formed from the refrain: "Ill done, why bet?" "Ill done, bet why." "Beeth wild only." [38]

As we close out this chapter we certainly are left with the question of whether the material presented is a fair review of a complex life. If there is anyone about whom more has been written in the last hundred years than Jack the Ripper, it is Lewis Carroll. Biographers unquestionably focus on the events in his life, which by any measure was filled with interesting contacts and activities. I have totally ignored the hundreds of plays that he attended, his diary-filled critiques of them, and his contacts with a variety of Victorian notables. But I have concluded that these activities were not self-satisfying, were undertaken to ward off underlying boredom and support facade maintenance.

But biographers have avoided interpreting a darker side that is mentioned but not pursued, due without doubt to what has been a lack of hard information. Although Morton Cohen acknowledges some dark sexual drives in Dodgson's penchant for socializing with little girls, he concludes in his 1995 work *Lewis Carroll: A Biography* that Dodgson was able to contain in typical Victorian fashion all behaviors which might be considered deviant (he also ignores the coincidence of so many anagrams in Dodgson's titles and works). Psychoanalysts write with more assurance of that darker side, of the ugliness beneath the fun and nonsense, the violent themes in what are considered children's works. They write with total conviction that their interpretations are sound. The confirming evidence of that ugliness lies in the extensive use of anagrams within his entire body of literature as a means of self-disclosure and rage expression.

What that disclosure tells us is how an innocent child was destroyed by (well-intentioned) parental abuse and institutionalized hypocrisy, nearly all of which he blamed on his mother. His life became virtually consumed with surpassing that hypocrisy in every private way, a nearly total facade. It is such a facade that one can look, it seems, reliably at the opposite of his professed belief or statement as the cynical position he is propounding beneath the surface, often verifiable within the anagrammatic material to be found there. On the other hand, he provided enormous enjoyment to untold numbers of people while hiding darker motives, including an effort to "bluff the world and cheat death" by carrying into the history books the image he chose to present to the world and spent a lifetime creating.

The Jekyll-Hyde theme is a recurring one in this work. In her article "Must We Ban Sade?" Simone de Beauvoir described the Marquis de Sade in similar terms and generalized her comments in ways which very much apply to Charles Dodgson.

> There are certain "sexual perverts" to whom the myth of Dr. Jekyll and Mr. Hyde is perfectly applicable. They hope, at first, to be able to gratify their "vices" without compromising their public characters. If they are imaginative enough to see themselves, little by little, in a dizziness of pride and shame, they give themselves away. ... Surprise is like that of a child who keeps striking at a vase until it finally breaks. He [Sade] was playing with fire and still thought himself master, but society was lying in wait. [39]

> ... Sade tells us that his ultimate attitude [of social defiance, described later (183) as intended 'to outrage the laws of both Nature and Religion'] has its root in resentment. [40]

De Sade expressed his outrage over twenty-seven years of imprisonment in Vincennes, the Bastille, and Charendon. Dodgson expressed his rage over a lifetime of imprisonment within his own mind.

Unlike de Sade, society was not "lying in wait" for Dodgson; indeed he fooled the society of his day to such an extent that it is difficult even today to comprehend and accept the reality and depth of his charade.

Additional biographical data appears in later chapters to support material specific to them. Readers should leave this chapter fully aware and convinced (short of my duplicating *The Agony of Lewis Carroll* here) that communication about himself and his expression of rage in anagrammatic form are a virtual fingerprint in the Dodgson personality and character. He told the dark side of his life within coded material in his works. And we can see that the themes of these anagrams were no different at age sixty-one than they were at forty-one, thirty-one, or twenty-one, that they constitute evidence of a lifetime of motive. We will also find as we move along what I believe are other self-disclosures very pertinent to the story of Jack the Ripper.

Chapter 4

The Ripper Letters and Poems

Any effort to analyze the communications received by the police and media which claimed authorship by Jack the Ripper is faced with a number of problems, nearly all of which have been well-covered by other writers. Over the short period between the August and December murders, there were literally thousands of letters and cards received each week by the police authorities and newspapers that claimed either that they were from Jack the Ripper or offered suggestions for his capture. [1]   Their points of origin eventually extended around the globe. Excited by the audacity of the crimes, the thrill of the chase, an antiestablishment sentiment, and the increasingly critical press editorials on the ineffectiveness of the police efforts, a portion of the population sought vicarious thrills by contributing their small part to the confusion that reigned.

These letters ranged from claims of having committed the most recent killing to predictions of when and where the next would occur to identifying where and when "I" (or someone else) could be found. Through a painstaking sorting out process that began very early and was continued over the years by researchers and writers, no more than four of the letters and poems are currently considered authentic, or, more appropriately, given the highest likelihood of being authentic. Some have held from the beginning that none are, with Sir Robert Anderson, a main (although by all accounts inept) player in the police investigation claiming in his *The Lighter Side of My Official Life* that the most accepted letter was concocted by a newspaperman whom he suggested he could identify. On the other hand Rumbelow, [2] who opts personally for no more than two being authentic, notes that a Dr. Thomas Dutton, a specialist in microphotography and member of the Chichester and West Sussex Microscopic Society at the time confirmed that of one hundred twenty-eight letters he examined "at least thirty-four were in the same handwriting." He found the writing greatly disguised and the composition intentionally inconsistent as spelling and punctuation would at times be incorrect, then correct elsewhere in the letter. Rumbelow goes on, although, to question the veracity of the doctor who claimed to have a print of the "Juwes" message washed off of the wall at the order of Sir Charles Warren, although he never produced it.

This investigation focuses on two aspects of the letters and poems not heretofore considered and benefits from having a suspect who was a master of words, their alternative meanings, their origins, and who left a proliferation of both letters and poems as well as the incorporation of coded self-disclosure and other communication within his famous writings. From this we can draw an inference as to whether Charles Dodgson's literary "fingerprints" are incorporated in the writings of Jack the Ripper that were already believed or suspected of being authentic. The patterns to be pursued are the use and meaning of language and the extent to which we find the presence of anagrams with structure and content consistent with those found in Dodgson's writings. We are searching for relevant meaning in the anagram, but even more importantly for a consistent relationship between the original material and the anagram.

Most likely due to its poetic cadence and diabolical play on the nature of the crimes and psychological condition of the murderer, the most memorable communication is the poem used in the Epilogue to this work:

> I'm not a butcher,
> I'm not a Yid,
> Nor yet a foreign skipper,
> But I'm your own light-hearted friend,
> Yours truly, Jack the Ripper. [3]

This jingle was received by Scotland Yard and was considered to be authentic by Sir Melville Macnaghten, as he reported in his *Days of My Years*. [4]   The original did not appear in the microfilm files, so no handwriting analysis could be done.

One of the patterns of Dodgson's communications regarding self-disclosure in which he used anagrammatic structures was that the statements made in the open and those hidden in the anagrammatic reworking were both "true" if they were statements of fact.   In his purest anagrams, the theme of the material, both source and anagram, were identical. We see the first pattern here. The message in the clear is self-evident; he denies being a butcher, Jew, or sailor, all of which classes were either generically suspect or the source of specific suspects throughout the investigation. He then tells us who he is, in a statement that could not be clearer even though it seems and has been historically taken as a terrible, taunting play on the emotions. He then closed in letter-writing fashion with the by then recognized trade name.

In a line by line rearrangement of the letters we have a new "poem" subject to analysis:

> But mother, I *can*!
> O, I'm dainty!
> Rip no gay peter foreskin.
> I hated mother; fury built in don grew.
> Jury, our tricks will trap ye!

The implications of these anagrams are very important to the further analysis of this crime and the implication of Dodgson in them. First, in the critical fourth line in which he identifies himself as "light-hearted friend," it identifies the mother as the object of the rage lying behind the crimes, a rage and target already presented in much of the literature on Jack the Ripper and in the analysis of Dodgson. Furthermore, in a most cynical and spiteful way, she is addressed here personally. Second, he states that he "can" commit the crimes. This implies a possession of knowledge and both a physical and psychological ability to perform, and, given the nature of the acts, to endure both the murders and mutilations. By the time this was received he had already proven his ability in all three areas in addition to an ability to avoid capture. This notion of enduring is an important one for the murders had increased in audacity and ferocity to a point where the inability to endure any more after the Kelly murder became a nearly universal explanation for why they ceased. It was believed that the killer's mind had given out and that he most likely committed suicide. In this analysis, however, endurance is believed to be part of a cunning conscious plot to increase ferocity to its most obscene limit. It would be fainting, the loss of consciously willed control, not "lunatic insanity" that would become the preplanned limit which would cause him to stop. This will become a recurring theme as we move forward.

For purposes of thoroughness, a second anagram on this line should be identified: "Moan, true bitch!" It would appear that Emma Smith and Martha Tabram were made to suffer, especially the former, who was left to stagger home and then to the hospital where she died. Of the murders with the more patented modus operandi, except in the case of Kelly, who was clearly heard by two people to cry out "Oh, murder!" and Chapman, who possibly shouted "No!" it does not appear that "moaning victims" were in the plan. This is consistent with the hypotheses that the victims were first strangled as part of a way to eliminate the potential for detection by their crying out. [5] With the victim seen as a mother surrogate, however, there is the likelihood that during the mutilation stages the murderer was driven by the image of a living and moaning victim, a frenzy of rage directed to an "as if living" person rather than the very different psychology involved in the mutilation of a long-dead corpse. For with the quickness between the death and mutilation of these women, there can be no question that vital organs were "as if" alive as victims were found to be still warm, with little or no signs of *rigor mortis* having set in.

The second line "I'm not a Yid," for poetic structure, the lack of rhyme, and class identification purposes could have very easily ended with "Jew." But with the chosen word the line reworks to "O, I'm dainty!" With Dodgson both statements are true. He was seen as very effeminate in both speech and manner, at one point parodied by his students as "Louisa Caroline" in a play on his pseudonym Lewis Carroll. As with many of Dodgson's anagrams, word selection was based on the anagrammatic fit. Long held theories as to the murderer's background and apparent knowledge of anatomy, along with the hypothesized strangling, gave rise to the notion that a Jewish slaughterman may have done the killings in the ritual manner of the *sochet*. [6]

The third line "Nor yet a foreign skipper" provides two suggestions. First, he is not a sailor. In addition he may be implying that emigration would be his means of escape should he feel that the police were closing in on him. Dodgson was not a foreign traveler, having left the country only once in 1867 to visit Russia in the company of his friend Henry Parry Liddon. His closest friend, Thomas Vere Bayne, whom I suspect to have been a participant in some ways, was, however a frequent vacationer to the continent (usually with Liddon) during the summer break at Oxford. Bayne's diaries reflect that he was in fact in Dover with Liddon the evening of 31 August when Nichols was murdered. They were awaiting to cross to France the following morning. Bayne reports that he returned on 5 October. He was in England on 7 August when Martha Tabram was murdered, and on 9 November, when Kelly was murdered. Was the writer implying that while one of the pair was at the moment a "foreign skipper," he himself was not yet one?

The anagram formed from the fourth line is typical of many found in Dodgson's works; "Rip no gay peter foreskin." Here we have suggestions of sodomy, a "gay" service within the Victorian heterosexual use of the word and the homosexual sense in which Dodgson seems to have been an early writer. [7] Sodomy is considered by Rumbelow to have been the service that Jack the Ripper sought from his victims (though perhaps never carried out) in order to place himself behind his victims and allow for either strangulation or left-to-right throat cutting that would both prevent his detection in advance by the victim and being covered with blood afterward. [8]   Sugden, on the other hand suggests throughout his work that victims were strangled from the front, laid down and the throats cut starting on the left side while the killer knelt on the right of the victim, thus avoiding the spurting of blood on himself; this explains also the extent to which blood was absorbed in the clothing toward the back of the victim.   Based on the speed with which the victim was killed, however, it would appear that either scenario was possible.   As we have seen, *Peter* was Victorian slang for *penis* and was associated with Dodgson's pivotal and traumatic experience at Richmond Grammar School where he was introduced to the mysterious game "Peter, the red lion" during which he was most likely experienced his first homosexual assault at age twelve. [9]

I believe the fourth line is confessional: "But I'm your own light-hearted friend."   It represents a brazen admission that he knew his many now adult child friends would never associate with him.   The anagram formed from the line is also confessional: "I hated mother; fury built in don grew."   This is, of course, the theme of *The Agony of Lewis Carroll*, and the word *built* has significant meaning.   Dodgson disclosed clearly in his hidden material a notion (well supported by theories of human development) that rage is built from the earliest moments and throughout childhood by assaults against the emerging self by significant caregivers.   Here he could be saying that it only grew increasingly intense as life went on, was never relieved, and finally reached an explosive level.

The anagram from the mocking last line "Yours truly, Jack the Ripper" identifies the cunning plotting that took place to avoid, not only capture, but most likely conviction should he be caught: "Jury, our tricks will trap ye."   The implications of this statement are pursued further when we explore Dodgson's diaries but can include the use of disguises which would allow him to move around in the East End in something other than the rigidly formal black suit he wore as a don.   I believe an additional trick involved the sophisticated use of distortions of Masonic ritual, politics, and secrecy, which created a diversion as it brought about self-conscious and inappropriate action by members of the police force who belonged to the organization.   As chapter 5 describes, Dodgson had the wherewithal to know many of the Masonic secrets, most likely had issues with the organization, and may have begun his attack on them many years earlier in parody in his works.

The second and third Ripper letters to be examined are the ones almost universally considered authentic.   The first was received 29 September 1888, the morning of the "double event" murder of Stride and Eddowes.   It had been post-stamped on the 27th at London East

Central and was addressed to "The Boss, Central News Office, London City." Several writers suggest that it was really posted on the 28th, the date on the postal stamp not having been changed properly at the post office. Police records indicate that the news office forwarded it to the police with a note indicating they thought it was a joke. [10] It was written in a perfect school-boy type handwriting.

25. Sept. 1888.

Dear Boss
    I keep on hearing the police
have caught me, but they wont fix
me just yet. I have laughed when
they look so clever and talk about
being on the right track. That joke
about Leather Apron gave me real
fits. I am down on whores and
I shant quit ripping them till I
do get buckled. Grand work the last
job was. I gave the lady no time to
squeal. How can they catch me now.
I love my work and want to start
again. You will soon hear of me
with my funny little games. I
saved some of the proper <u>red</u> stuff in
a ginger beer bottle over the last job
to write with but it went thick
like glue and I cant use it. Red
ink is fit enough I hope <u>ha. ha.</u>
The next job I do I shall clip
the ladys ears off and send to the
police officers just for jolly wouldnt
you. Keep this letter back till I
do a bit more work, then give
it out straight My knife's so nice
and sharp I want to get to work
right away if I get a chance.
Good luck.
        Yours truly
        Jack the Ripper
Dont mind me giving the trade name.

A note was written at right angles to the letter in a hand that appears a little less precise and stylistic than the main letter:

Wasnt good enough
to post this before
I got all the red
ink off my hands
curse it.
 No luck yet. They
say I'm a doctor
now ha ha. [11]

This communication was followed by a postal card received on 1 October which further referenced the crimes and the letter, but this time written in a handwriting considerably less precise than the first.

I was not codding
dear old Boss when
I gave you the tip,
You ll hear about
Saucy Jack s work
tomorrow double
event this time
number one squealed
a bit couldnt
finish straight
off. had not time
to get ears for
police thanks for
keeping last letter
back till I got
to work again.
 Jack the Ripper [12]

The writing is in the same style but less precise even than the note accompanying the letter. The finger smear from "the red stuff" is clear in the microfilm. Whether or not the ridges of fingerprints are still visible in the original is a good question and might provide an interesting police analysis with a Dodgson letter in the Lewis Carroll Collection at Bryn Mawr College in Pennsylvania, which is said to have a pretty clear finger print of the author.

As Rumbelow points out, [13] if the posting date had been 30 September instead of 1 October the knowledge reflected in the letters could only have been possessed by the murderer. But since the posting was on 1 October, there had been newspapers containing enough detail to support the content, for in both the murder of Stride and Eddowes the knife marks appear to have been efforts to remove the ears. While the Ripper had failed to do so in the Stride murder, which all agree was interrupted, there was more than enough time to do so during the mutilation of Eddowes.

In any event, three days later, copies of the letter and card appeared in the newspapers, presumably as an effort to bring forth someone who might recognize the handwriting. Comments from the police records indicate, however, that they were leaked to the press and that the investigation would have gone much better without their publication. For it was the publication of these letters, in which the self-styled trade name "Jack the Ripper" first appeared, that the public fancy was teased, and the volume of what are believed mostly false letters from the Ripper grew. Now as then, it is difficult to sort out valid letters as many contain words and images similar to those published.

The letter presents a number of interesting questions and coincidences. First, there is the handwriting itself which reflects the rigorous discipline of the schoolmaster. Analysts often despair in attempting to draw meaning from Victorian handwriting because it was so uniform and lacking in individual style due to the physical discipline often meted out when deviations occurred during the schooling process. This writing has that quality. Needless to say, after reading Dodgson's diaries, which reflect remnants of this type of writing but in fact show a much more individual style, I was surprised to find Bayne's diaries written in this perfect hand, even at his then age fifty-nine.

Even more surprising, after reading that the word *Boss*, an American word at the time, had given rise to suspicions that the Ripper might be an American, the word *Bosses*, used in normal context (with a somewhat different "B" than the suspicious letter) was discovered in a single place in Bayne's four volumes of diaries — an entry for 1 August 1888. On the 7th, Martha Tabram was killed. On the 16th, Bayne's diary reflects a deterioration in handwriting as he reports he can barely move from gout. What caused theh increased stree? On the 23rd he reports he and Liddon have decided to leave for France on 1 September; and on the 31st he writes that someone by the name of Smith "says there is no reason I should not go abroad with a tranquil mind." [14] This kind of comment appeared on several occasions, each of them reflecting likely sarcasm when one is aware of Bayne's participation in

Dodgson's anagram development. Is it possible that this letter was written by another Dodgson friend as part of a grand trick being played on the police by Oxford friends? Could Dodgson or yet another person have added the postscript, the only part of the letter which appears to be in a slightly deteriorated hand? The envelope which contained this letter is in schoolboy hand, but somewhat different, with the "B" appearing more like that in Bayne's diary but with the s's less precise.

As we look at the greeting "Dear Boss," we find the Dodgson pattern of being able to derive multiple anagrams from the words used. For by letter rearrangement we have "Dare, Boss," possibly a statement of the relationship between the writer and Ripper and possibly a play on the original pseudonym Dodgson chose before selecting "Lewis Carroll." He had chosen "Dares," which was rejected by his publisher, after which he provided several alternatives, including "Lewis Carroll." "Dares" has long been believed to be a reference to his birthplace, Daresbury, but it much more likely had meaning in the hateful word games he began to play in his children's works. We also can derive "Sob, dears," a play on the emotions of the public. "Sores bad" might refer to the sores of gout experienced during the month of August and recurring throughout stressful parts of Bayne's life, including later in 1888. Another very meaningful anagram will be more understandable when we examine *The Nursery "Alice"*.

Thirdly, and of even greater significance, is the use of certain specific words. The first is *fit*, which appears twice. In its first use, it means convulsions, perhaps of laughter as he responded to the joke about "Leather Apron" (John Pizer). The second use — red ink being fit — uses the meaning "suitable." The word *fit* was a favorite of Dodgson's, and proved to be a pivotal one in the development of my earlier work. For he used it in *Alice's Adventures in Wonderland* when he had the King of Hearts inquire of the Queen whether she ever suffered from fits, which could have meant "convulsions" or even "uncertainty as to gender" in Victorian usage. When she responded that she never did, the King said that the statement in question did not fit her. Then the King waited for a response from the jury on the pun he had just made. In other words, it was not suitable. Here in two short pieces of Ripper communication, we have the very same word meanings appear and in the same sequence. Dodgson would later use the word in his mock epic poem *The Hunting of the Snark; An Agony in Eight Fits*, a poem which appears directed in secret to the annihilating experience of sodomy (harking back to his public school experience) while on the surface it depicts the hunt for an unknown monster. In this case, *fit* takes on another valid meaning, that of a "stanza" in poetry.

The second significant word which appears in the letter is *buckled*: "I shant quit ripping them till I do get buckled." While never explicitly stated by writers, implicitly the statement has been interpreted as an arrogant challenge that he will continue until he is captured and placed in irons. But a second meaning returns us to the notion of continuing until he faints for *buckled* also means "collapsed." I believe there is sound evidence, which will be shown later, that it is fainting which in fact ended the spree — interrupting it with Marie Kelly, but more definitely ending it with the murder of Frances Coles in 1891.

Why does he underline the word *right* before *track*? Is it because he is pointing to the latter word's two meanings, the wrong track being the sequence of theories police were entertaining, the right track being that he was using the rail system? Chapter 14 explores the geography of these crimes in detail, including their proximity to the surface and underground rail stations.

Another and in some ways more obscure hint is the presence of seven words inappropriately punctuated by someone otherwise skilled in schoolboy writing practices. [15] Neither *wont, shant, ladys, cant, dont, wouldnt,* nor *wasnt* (in the postscript) contain the apostrophe that should be present. Only the word *knife's* is correct.

Dodgson had a peculiar way of using this piece of punctuation, one which he defended on several occasions quite vehemently. For in addition to the single apostrophe to replace the "o" in "not," he insisted that a second apostrophe should be used to replace letters in a contraction if in fact both words were shortened. In this letter he would have shortened *shall not* and *can not* to *sha'n't and ca'n't*, as can be found in his children's books. Did the writer of this letter leave this clue by using only one apostrophe correctly in the entire document, as if to demonstrate that the proper rules were known? Is it coincidence that the apostrophes are also absent in the words requiring them in the card received the following day, while in some cases a space is left as if to show that it belongs there and was intentionally omitted? The facsimile's of both letter and card would certainly have reproduced the punctuation if it had been there, given the clarity of both film images.

In a strange coincidence of timing, just weeks before this letter was sent, on 1 September 1888, Dodgson focused on these words in a letter to his friend Nellie Knight and referenced them and this earlier letter to her again on the 18th in a letter to her sister. The words emphasized were *wo'n't, sha'n't,* and *hasn't.* Unfortunately for these purposes, Morton Cohen, editor of *The Letters of Lewis Carroll*, modernized the spellings to eliminate the idiosyncrasies; but I am quite sure the peculiar punctuation was present in the original since it did constitute the discussion in the letter. [16]

Finally, and perhaps most obscurely, is the effect created by the postscript on the letter written with the paper turned on edge. Dodgson had a peculiar practice in letter writing. He kept papers of various sizes in his stock and always chose one that would accommodate exactly the length of the letter he planned to write, ostensibly so that no paper would be wasted or excessive postage required. This postscript written as it was, causes the page to be filled vertically, at least. As already mentioned, however, it also appears written in a somewhat different style and may have been placed differently to accentuate the fact.

"Jack the Ripper"

The first "Dear Boss" letter which included the apology for using the "trade name" introduced two notions regarding the murderer. First, he wanted to be known by a chilling pseudonym. Second, by implication, this would not be a single event. Where did the name "Jack" come from, and is it possible to associate it with Dodgson? Again, we turn to the multiple meanings of words, as this one, too, appears to have been carefully chosen.

The first and most obvious derivation of the name is from Victorian slang which identified "John" or "Jack" as a customer of a prostitute, much as is used in the language today. In Dodgson's case, he also viewed himself as "gay" in a very early use of the term with its connotation of "prostitute," as the word was associated with promiscuous behavior to include sodomy, mutual masturbation, and other prostitute-like behavior.

Dodgson has been identified with numerous characters within the body of his children's books, although mostly with those either benign or at most somewhat eccentric. These include the White Rabbit from *Alice's Adventures in Wonderland*, the bumbling White Knight from *Through the Looking-Glass*, the young boy Bruno from *Sylvie and Bruno*, and several others. In *The Agony of Lewis Carroll* I suggested that the Knave of Hearts was very much a Dodgson character as he was tried by his mother, the Queen of Hearts, for a crime which remained ambiguous throughout but which many interpret as a search for identity. Dodgson searched for a lifetime to determine why he seemingly was so punished for never having committed a crime. (We will return later to where the Queen's interminable cry "Off with their heads" fits with these murders.) The Knave of Hearts within the playing card deck which was the basis for the story's characters is also the "Jack of Hearts."

Appropriate for letters to arrive later "from Hell," this one is signed by someone who also knew that "Jack" is a nickname for the devil.

Perhaps even more intriguing, however, is a real "Jack" who appears in the diary manuscripts, but who never appeared in the published version. As we explore the very early interest in this person, we are confronted with the question of just how early in his life Dodgson may have planned some sort of caper that might parallel the legendary (for many years) criminal exploits of John (a.k.a. "Jack") Sheppard. On 17 November 1857, Dodgson noted that Bayne had found a copy of the *North Hampton Mercury* dated 23 November 1724, no doubt as part of his activities as archivist at Christ Church. In it was an article about the death of the notorious criminal and escape artist which had occurred on the exact day 133 years before. The diary entry itself is filled with mathematical formulae that calculate the chances of the coincidence of the anniversary being notable, with Dodgson finally settling on odds of 2500:1. One could wonder what else Dodgson might have had on his mind that would create such interest in the odds of the anniversary of *this* event occurring on *this* date, as a review of any newspaper from the past could create "coincidences" of the current day being an anniversary of many past newsworthy events.

Who was this Jack Sheppard? John Sheppard was born in 1702 in "Spittle-fields," the location of the Jack the Ripper murders. He built an early adolescent career of petty burglary into a legend of house breaking and jail escapes by his early twenties, crimes for which he was executed. In addition to his brother, he had a partner in crime called "Hell and Fury."

> ... we hope the Publick will contribute the utmost to defend themselves against [him]; especially such, upon whom he has vowed a bloody Revenge. . . . [He swore] that there should not one remain an Evidence to swear against him; that he would increase the Number, as well as heighten the Quality of his Crimes. . . . [17]

At one of his trials at the Old Bailey, there were so many admirers and spectators that it took fifteen minutes to clear the courtroom when his trial was complete. He challenged the police that there was no lock or key that could hold him. When asked on one occasion if anyone had helped him escape, he identified God as his assistant. Sheppard was sentenced twice to death, but escaped both times from Newgate Prison until he was captured and chained to a staple in the floor with a three-hundred-pound weight attached. There, as usual, he "held court" with an adoring public, and, against all odds, escaped again. Although uneducated, he wrote two taunting letters to his captors with a fifteen line poem to one, delivering the latter himself while in a disguise. Both were signed "John Sheppard." Captured again and for the last time in late October, remaining unrepentant despite frequent attendance at religious services, he was hanged on 23 November at the age of twenty-three. He struggled to the end, despite being in shackles, and was found with a pen knife, most likely passed to him by an admirer. Fearful that his body would be taken for use in medical experiments, the crowd stayed with it until he was safely buried. A poem in his honor appeared in the *British Journal* five days later. A play entitled "Harlequin Sheppard: A Night Scene in Grotesque Characters" played for a while in a Drury Lane theater, and a three-act farce comparing his exploits with those of Julius Caesar was written, but never performed. He had become in a few short years a folk hero and legend to his generation based on his arrogant challenge to authority and despite what was considered the heinousness of his crimes. [18]

It is easy to see here many similarities in the modus operandi used by both Jacks. Both were tricksters, extremely capable of stealth and escape. Both communicated with their captors and challenged them to try to catch them.

Whether Dodgson ever pursued any further inquiry into the case of Jack Sheppard beyond that mentioned in the diary entry, or in fact modeled an escapade of crime after that committed by Sheppard, can only be surmised. However, that Dodgson would pursue more background on something that he calculated would occur in only 1 out of 2500 chances is totally consistent with his obsessive character. And the resources for research certainly existed at Oxford.

It would not be until 16 days after the murder of Stride and Eddowes that the letter believed most authentic would be received by George Lusk, chairman of the Vigilance Committee that had been formed by Whitechapel residents to increase public awareness and provide a vehicle for placing public pressure on police and political officials. For that letter accompanied a small package which contained what medical authorities determined with some certainty was the missing portion of Mrs. Eddowes left kidney. This letter certainly suggested that there would be an effort to outrage the public and authorities with the utmost in depravity, the consumption of human parts.

From Hell

Mr Lusk
     Sir
          I send you half the
Kidne I took from one women
prasarved it for you tother piece I
fried and ate it was very nise. I
may send you the bloody knif that
took it out if you only wate a whil
longer
         signed Catch me when
you can
         Mishter Lusk. [19]

On the 18th Mr. Lusk turned the package and note over to authorities. Dr. Openshaw immediately judged the kidney as human in origin, obviously placed into a preservative shortly after its removal. Later pathological analysis determined that it was a good match for the portion and connective tissue left in the mutilated body of Catherine Eddowes. No communications provided clues as to the removal or disposition of the uterus which had also been taken away in this murder as well as that of Chapman earlier.

The brazen flaunting of the atrocity committed, only to be raised another notch in the forthcoming murder of Marie Kelly, raised community and police concerns to new levels. There was no question now that they were dealing with a madman who had descended to the depths of depravity. The address "From hell" only added to that belief.

What was the hell that provided the domicile from which these events were conceived and executed? The answers to this are complex and take us into the areas of psychology and religion. While considerably more discussion has already taken place regarding Colin Wilson's works *A Casebook of Murder* (1969) and *Origins of the Sexual Impulse* (1963), it is appropriate to note that he identified a key ingredient to such seemingly motiveless murders as intellectual boredom. Referencing the famous Leopold-Loeb murders in America, he indicates the young men had no economic pressures on them, no externally defined challenge to which to devote their energies. Wilson suggests that in many ways these Ripper murders were the first "20th Century... crimes of boredom" committed "as a protest against the meaningless of life." [20] An examination of Dodgson's diary manuscripts, more than the published diaries, reveals numerous expressions of boredom, particularly during the early years. Teaching was a problem for him, provided a justification for his remaining at Oxford, but brought precious little satisfaction. "`[It is clear that] ... Dodgson had an abundance of leisure: he had few duties involving peremptory claims upon his time. I do not suppose he was ever idle....´" [21]   Oxford had no objective criteria with which it measured the performance of its dons; once there, they remained, barring some sort of disgrace. Dodgson worked essentially unsupervised. Gradually, he incorporated numerous and varied activities to fill the void, not the least of which was the writing of children's "nonsense" but also included his photography, the hours spent with his little girl friends, long walks at times over twenty miles, and numerous recorded rail trips to London and its environs. This lack of external pressure, of demands to test his energies, was characteristic of Dodgson's entire life.

While Rumbelow identifies brooding over unfilled sexual desires by high-dominance men as the time-filling activity which leads to sexual murders (minimizing an acknowledged presence of mother-hate), [22] Wilson identifies excessive sexual fantasizing as the cause. [23] Chapter 2 explored the sexual nature of these crimes and the extent to which perverse sexual activity becomes the means for restoring an alienated self from feelings of rage rather than as being primarily driven by sexual appetites.

Photography became a consuming hobby until he suddenly stopped in 1880. Untold hours were spent in the company of his child friends, entertaining them, and, in turn, being entertained by them. At times he experienced great loneliness when he was at the beach with no children to turn to. Hours were spent on the train between Oxford and London as he visited his publisher, his many social friends, or attended the theater. He carried the black doctor's type bag filled with games and puzzles which he used to gain the attention and friendship of any young girls he met on the journey. Whether it was solving mathematical problems for his own enjoyment or for publication, or creating puzzles and games for the amazement of the children, keeping his mind active and attention focused was an obsession. In a mathematical work titled *Pillow Problems*, he stated that solving mathematical puzzles without notes, while lying awake, was done to ward off unholy or skeptical thoughts which appear to have intruded constantly if they were in fact not entertained and nourished, a part of the brooding dynamic. In 1882 he made himself available and was elected to be the curator of the Common Room at Christ Church, Oxford, in part to become more active as he judged himself becoming more and more a recluse. While pursued by biographers as evidence of his enriching if somewhat peculiar life, in many ways, knowing the underlying rage was all-consuming, these activities served as distractions from an inner life of boredom and brooding *for him*. His was a life of endless activity, much of it self-indulgent efforts to keep busy in the face of nothing meaningful to do and no inner resources to really enter the world arena to change things.

From Hell

Dodgson completed *The Nursery "Alice"* in December 1888 and published it in June 1889. It is a pivotal work in our analysis of Dodgson's involvement in these crimes and has a chapter devoted to it. At the end of this work, however, he included a page titled "Cautions to Readers," the first paragraph of which reads:

> On August 1st, 1881, a story appeared in *Aunt Judy's Magazine* No. 184, entitled "The Land of Idleness, by LEWIS CARROLL." This story was really written by a lady, FRAÜLEIN IDA LACKOWITZ. Acting on her behalf, Mr. CARROLL forwarded it to the Editor: and this led to the mistake of naming him as its author. . . . [24]

In his 1987 work *Lewis Carroll and the House of Macmillan*, Morton Cohen [25] traces the history of this "Caution" noting that the name of the "author" changed from that above, a resident of Berlin, to "Miss Cato Schaap," a resident of Rotterdam, then back to the German woman in a series of corrections to his "List of Works" until he finally told Macmillan & Co. to withdraw the notice from further publications. Cohen questions whether the names are anagrams and wonders just what games Dodgson was playing, but offers no alternatives. Was this an intentional effort on Dodgson's part to create confusion regarding the authorship of something written in a very different style than that which he normally followed?

I suggest that the two names are in fact anagrams, but make a more complete thought when combined. For we can derive a statement which answers directly Dodgson's denial that he wrote "The Land of Idleness" and identified the boredom that consumed his life. By combining the two, we derive: "O, if wit lacks, I, a miscast chap, laze around." If we take the names individually, we derive "If wit lacks, I laze around" from the first, and "O, a miscast chap" from the second.

The story itself is interesting and follows the same thematic pattern found in his other works. It is written in a single long paragraph which runs for nine pages, tells of a girl named Lizzie, another seven year old, just like Alice, who is so lazy that she can't even muster the energy to accomplish the only two tasks required by her mother — to do her lessons and complete two rows of knitting each day. In fact, she cannot even knit two stitches before becoming tired.   Typical of Carroll's stories, she begins to dream of being taken to another land where her wish to be where she will have to do nothing at all will be satisfied by her being served by others. She is carried away by the birds nearby — to THE LAND OF IDLENESS (Carroll's capitals) — where she finds kings, queens, and other inhabitants unwilling to do the simplest tasks for themselves, least of all to do anything for her. Thoroughly bored and frustrated, now wishing to be where she can do something, anything, she awakens and resumes happily the simple tasks her mother had assigned her.

   Who is the author? I believe it is Dodgson himself for the tell-tale clues are there. We find characters with the names from his other stories: the king (from the *Alice* works) the baker (from the *Snark*), and the gardener, a character from the Sylvie books, not yet written, but one who will take on great meaning in the search for the Ripper. Like Alice, Lizzie is seven years old, the very age Alice said life most likely should end in *Alice's Adventures in Wonderland*. Whether Dodgson is disparaging his younger sister Lizzie is not known. The presence of his unique use of quotes (although inconsistent) in *ca'n't* and *wo'n't* and the use of capitalization of THE LAND OF IDLENESS to suggest we focus on the phrase, also the title, as an anagram, is present. In solving the title as an anagram, we find, not only a repetition of its theme, but the same theme brought out by Colin Wilson.   That is, that for some, boredom *is* — constitutes — hell: SON SAT, DEFINED HELL. For in truth, nothing provided a really satisfactory relief for Dodgson, a relief that would prove to be truly self-restoring activities and draw him away from the brooding which produced so much hate-filled verbal assaults on his mother and women in general within the violent imagery hidden in his works.

   But, typical of many of Dodgson's titles, more than one anagram can be derived, and, as usual, they all seem to have themes consistent with his overt or covert life.

> Defend the loin, lass!
> Then d'file noses, lad!
> Sin, thee! fondle lads!
> Then defile lads, son!
> Fondle less in death.

Son defiles the land.
Deafness: the don ill.
I'll send on the deaf!
No, I'll send the deaf.
The "self denial" don.
I sensed the fall, don.

Regarding the issue of "self denial," virtually all biographers acknowledge that Dodgson indulged himself on the one hand in whatever amused him — children, theater, and hobbies — while on the other hand he presented himself as the totally controlled, albeit eccentric, Victorian gentleman. Whether or not this anagram points intentionally to the notion that self-indulgence is a likely outgrowth of boredom, lack of outward focus, and intense brooding which can take place in that environment can only be guessed. In any event Dodgson's tell-tale presence is evident in a number of clues associated with this material in which hell-on-earth is defined for the bright, educated, directionless, alienated self.

Dodgson was deaf in his left ear. Much of the imagery regarding "lads" is consistent with themes of pederasty which appeared in the most explicit of the anagrams already seen. The last one is an interesting allusion to my work and to his own prediction in *Sylvie and Bruno* that the artist's "art" would one day crumble. In any event, the creation of multiple anagrams, filled with brooding and fantasizing, represents a task created to fill idle hours (except for those studying such things, of course, although I am not unaware of what might have been Dodgson's amusement regarding research into his life!).

It would be in November 1894, that he wrote his own sister Lizzie his letters on "Eternal Punishment," in which we have already seen "at least three" anagrams.

Another aspect of Wilson's hell is that "hell" is relative to each individual's situation. Dodgson really tells us the same thing but in a way which few parents or children would pick up. Lizzie was bored with lessons and knitting; the Victorian girl's lessons were quite purposeless because the opportunities for women beyond marriage (and childrearing) and working as governesses were quite limited so lessons would be boring for a girl. They also became a significant issue in his own childhood as there was little relief from them in the family-operated school. Lizzie's knitting requirement was also boring because it consisted of "two rows per day" with no mention of a purpose other than the repetitious stitching. When she fell asleep and found herself in a place even more boring, she returned happily to the state of boredom provided by her mother. Dodgson in many ways was parodying Victorian culture's dictum "Mother knows best" just as he had parodied a number of "morals" in *Alice's Adventures in Wonderland*.

A second area where we find hell defined is in the works of the Reverend Frederic Farrar, who preached and wrote on the subject of eternal hope. His work *Eternal Hope*, published in 1878, is considered a seminal one on the subject and one which greatly influenced the Anglican church of the day. [26]   Dodgson's association with it is reflected in the copy he kept in his library (as listed on the auction sheets) and in his writing on the subject of Eternal Punishment, a concept he increasingly came to reject in favor of one of hope.   It is clear from Dodgson's writings, although he takes the concept considerably further than Farrar, that he came to believe that one had all of eternity, a "very long time" to repent his sins if he indeed died in the state of sin and that even the devil should not be assumed incapable of final redemption.

If we conclude analytically but not judgmentally that Dodgson was in essence totally destroyed psychologically by his experience as a child, we can see that in everything he did he extended morality beyond all societal proscriptions, a fundamentally necessary ingredient to perversions if they are to have any hope of giving a sense of self-restoration to the destroyed self.   One can see that Dodgson may very well have carried his inner religious beliefs on this subject to the same extremes, virtually identifying himself as the Devil incarnate. His library contained many volumes on devil worship and black magic to provide him with knowledge of that area.   But by further examining Farrar's work, we can see that he defined what a hell-on-earth would be, a description that seems very much like Dodgson's inner world.

In his chapter "Consequences of Sin," Farrar describes Gehenna (a word we'll see later) as

> not a burning prison, but a polluted heart.   Alienation from God: hatred of truth; hatred of purity; a hard, bitter, railing, loveless spirit; mean, base, selfish, sensual desires; these are the elements of hell. . . .

> Which way I fly is hell, myself am hell,
> And in the lowest deep a lower deep,
> Still gaping to devour me, opens wide,
> To which the hell I suffer seems a heaven.

> Hell is a temper, not a place. So long as we are evil, and impure, and unloving, so long where we are is hell, and where hell is there we must be. [27]

> ... Have any of you said, "Because we may never cease to hope, therefore we may go on in sin"? Ah, if you have said that, you must indeed be in a gall of bitterness and a bond of iniquity from which it is clear that no horrible dread of an endless hell has saved you! Dare any one, who professes and calls himself a Christian, say in his heart, "Let us continue in sin, that grace may abound"? [Rom. vi.I.]
> ... My brethren, there are two kinds of sin — wilful sin and willing sin. Wilful sin is that into which, because of the frailty of our nature, because of the strength of passion and temptation, — not loving, but loathing it — not seeking, but resisting it. . . . [This is the kind of sin from which we seek redemption.] But there is another kind of sin, — far deadlier, far more heinous, far more incurable, — it is *willing* sin [Farrar's italics]. It is when we are content with sin; when we have sold ourselves to sin; when we no longer fight against sin; when we mean to continue in sin. . . . [28]

The first of these notions, that the redemptive miracle of Christ is further enhanced, made further miraculous by the fact that greater and greater sin is still subject to final redemption, seems to be one that Dodgson came to embrace. The second fits very much with what is a recurring theme regarding these murders and a Dodgson connection — that they were performed as acts of will and not of uncontrolled passion or emotion.

Farrar continues, [29] drawing on themes totally consistent with those of Orestes, the persona Dodgson assumed when he emerged from the trauma at school. Orestes, believing he had received a command from the god Apollo, murdered his mother to avenge her murder of his father, with images of serpent progeny, of those suffering from insomnia ". . . for whom the `furies have taken their seats upon the midnight pillow. . .´" (145). Other themes also appear, including the effects of guilt, and of tainted hereditary blood, a preoccupation with Dodgson, whose parents were first cousins. But the primary issue pertinent here is the sense of "chosenness" that Orestes felt and that Dodgson seems to have also felt, that this good, perfect, child was chosen to suffer for a reason. This feeling can and it appears did become so distorted that all acts, even murder as an act of retribution against the evil one, became justified. Farrar writes:

> . . . and so the boy and the youth, healthy, and bright, and gay, and even, in his folly, the grown man, believes that it shall not be so with *him*; that he will repent in time; that he is the darling of Providence, *he* is the favourite of Heaven, *he* the one who may sin and shall not suffer. . . that God will indulge *him*. . . . [30]

Within the vocabulary and preoccupation of the day, much of Farrar's imagery regarding "sins of habit" (151) points to masturbation, considered perhaps the worst of sins. It was an obsession with Dodgson in the imagery hidden in his works. Of course, *gay* had a very different meaning for him than it did for Farrar. What we also see is the notion of "being sent," one which appears in the literature on Jack the Ripper and one which will appear later in hidden material and in the diaries.

It is interesting to note that Dodgson's friend Henry Parry Liddon was preaching at St. Paul's Cathedral, London, in the mid 1870s on the immortality of the soul. A loyal disciple of Dr. Pusey, he supported the notion that the soul of the sinner was not destroyed at the moment of death (the then official position of his church) and implied that salvation could occur at some point after death by a corrective process possible between death and the last judgement. [31] It would only be after this final judgement that restorative processes would no longer be possible, but that the annihilation of the soul would not occur at either time. We can see that a redefinition of hell was occurring at this level of the church also. At first, Pusey opposed Farrar's views, but he later softened his position.

This extensive excursion into the religious theme of Hell supports the material in the anagram "Son sat, defined hell," not only in the sense that "hell *is* boredom" but that in the bored and brooding state in which Dodgson lived, he in fact defined hell as being for him here on earth as he rejected the notion of Eternal Punishment. In any event it would appear that he is telling us most seriously the origins of the motivations behind these murders.

There is another letter that appeared in the Metropolitan Police Files which I believe may be authentic, although it does not appear in any of the literature as so. The handwriting is quite different, with a very obvious vertical motion that might be a disguise. I have chosen it for the words used and its contents. Unfortunately, I did not obtain a copy for handwriting analysis.

Hell

26/11/88

Dear Boss
Was not that jolly a scare about that woman
who thought that Jack the Ripper. they
think they have got hold of my description.
I laughed myself into fits over that
I have got a jolly lot of false
whiskers and moustachios in my
"black bag". The last job was nice
& clean. I carried away a
part of her. (Conundrum Try to
find what part). I am going
to do another on Friday. &
I shall give the police a
enough running about on
Christmas. Jack the Ripper [32]

This letter is dated after the Kelly murder. Again we have the
appearance of Hell as the return address. The word *fits* appears also,
but by this time, *fits* could represent an imitation of the letter that
appeared in the newspapers. The "black bag" had appeared in the
newspapers as the press hypothesized that a doctor might be involved
and observed the number of people with such a bag among witness
observations. The focus on disguises is interesting as I feel that
disguises play a large role in the ability of Jack the Ripper to move about
the area undetected. The theater was Dodgson's hobby by this time,
photography already abandoned. He acknowledged on several occasions
the extent to which he had access to the backstage and how he had
drawn on his acquaintances among the actors, actresses, and children to
acquire a supply of costumes in which to pose the children. In his *The
Investigation of Murder* Francis Camps writes that the

"description of a well-dressed man, 5 ft. 6 ins. in height, with
dark complexion, dark eyes, bushy eyebrows and a thick
moustache, [is] in fact almost the stage villain. [33]

Although he never acted on the stage, Dodgson had all the knowledge of acting and directing that could have made this his finest stage
production. It is clear that he played a Jekyll-Hyde role in public

throughout his adult life as he presented a person quite different from that which appears hidden in his works.

The use of *conundrum* is pure Carroll, as he was always creating them either within his mathematical or word puzzles. The postmortem on Marie Kelly had been completed by the date of this letter. Four doctors had worked six and a half hours reassembling her mutilated body in order to determine if any parts had, in fact, been removed from the room. They satisfied themselves that Kelly's heart had been removed and perhaps some other portions of parts which were never found, even after a careful examination of the ashes in the fireplace. [34] The public had been assured that no parts had been taken away in the *Daily News* of 10 November, their claim made on indisputable authority by the Central News. The ultimate cynical game would have been to perpetuate doubts about whether anything had been missed, since by this time the burial had taken place. In the public domain only the killer would know for sure the answer to the conundrum.

The following letter, undated both in writing and in receipt is another which alludes to Boxing Day in the use of "Christmas box." This day after Christmas is when the British give their gifts to merchants and other service providers, public as well as private.

> Dear Boss
>   You have not caught
> me yet and you are not
> likely to. I shall keep on at
> my work for I love it, and
> I will send you something
> for a Christmas box.
>   Yours Jack the Ripper [35]

What relationship does Boxing Day 1888 have with Dodgson? What would make it a day on which to plan a murder? For over six months Dodgson had been working with Savile Clarke, the producer of children's theater, including *Alice in Wonderland* which Dodgson had approved but not written, to revive the production by opening on 26 December, Boxing Day, 1888. It was to star Isa Bowman, one of his favorite child friends with whom he spent many weeks during that summer both at Oxford and his summer retreat at Eastbourne. Part of that negotiation included engaging Richard Mansfield, the American actor/producer to produce this play. Mansfield had been the producer and lead in the stage adaptation of Robert Louis Stevenson's *Dr. Jekyll and Mr. Hyde*. Mansfield himself had been a Ripper suspect, based partly on a letter to the police or newspapers in which the writer suggested that no person could undergo such a realistic transformation to Hyde and create such a stage frenzy as just a *tour de force* in acting. He wrote that Mansfield could not be acting and most likely left the theater and committed the murders after transforming into Hyde. [36] Out of his own concerns that it was inappropriate to continue the play while such real life murders were taking place and unwilling to exploit the situation, Mansfield gave a final performance at the Lyceum in early October as a benefit for the homeless in the East End and closed the play after a very successful run of just ten weeks. For a man living a Jekyll-Hyde existence, certainly aware of the work's publication just two years earlier, fascinated by his mysterious "Rule of Three" (to which we shall return in the discussion of Masonic ritual), a murder on the 26th, combined with the stage Jekyll-Hyde producer himself opening a revival of the stage adaptation of his most famous children's story, could have provided Dodgson with a thrilling "triple event." But, of course, we know of no murder on that date; Rose Mylett was killed on the 20th.

"Eight Little Whores"

Another of the communications believed to be authentic is the following poem, one of the very few that has survived among the several received:

> Eight little whores, with no hope of heaven,
> Gladstone may save one, then there'll be seven.
> Seven little whores begging for a shilling,
> One stays in Henage Court, then there's a killing.
> Six little whores, glad to be alive,
> One sidles up to Jack, then there are five.
> Four and whore rhyme aright,
> So do three and me,
> I'll set the town alight
> Ere there are two.
> Two little whores, shivering with fright,
> Seek a cosy door way in the middle of the night.
> Jack's knife flashes, then there's but one,
> And the last one's the ripest for Jack's idea of fun. [37]

This poem is interesting for three reasons. The focus on eight women, perhaps accidentally, perhaps not, tallies exactly with the number of women in the Dodgson family for he had seven sisters and his

mother (although she had died when he was nineteen). We know that
Dodgson had a great deal of hate directed to his sisters, even Mary,
believed by all to have been his favorite. This number eight and the
other symbolic use of numbers in the body of Dodgson's literature
(three, forty-two, thirteen, forty-six) suggests strongly to me that
Dodgson's original plan may have included "at least" eight killings, a
symbolic one for each of the women in his family.

Second, notice the similarities in meter and rhyme with a poem he
wrote in 1883 and published in *Rhyme? and Reason?* titled "A Game of
Fives." Notice also that in the Ripper poem the number of whores
decreases as age (undefined except as the point of time when death
occurs) ceases to progress, is terminated, while in this poem the ages of
the girls increase while their number remains the same. There is a
virtual "looking-glass" reversal. In both poems, the fate of the named
group is described as a change occurs.

A Game of Fives

Five little girls of Five, Four, Three, Two, One:
Rolling on the hearthrug, full of tricks and fun.

Five rosy girls, in years from Ten to Six:
Sitting down to lessons — no more time for tricks.

Five growing girls, from Fifteen to Eleven:
Music, Drawing, Languages, and food enough for seven!

Five winsome girls, from Twenty to Sixteen:
Each young man that calls, I say "Now tell me which you
   mean!"... [38]

The third reason for focus on the "Eight Little Whores" poem,
which is included in Dutton's handwriting as likely authentic, [39] is the
content of the anagrams that can be formed from each line, which have
been numbered below for ease of reference.

1. Hero poet hit! He leaves night with new fool.
2. Thomas Vere Bayne led on seventh; all get seen.
3. We never shoot frig till, all in, she's begging.
4. O, I, the lone, thin, gay, heel king enter cunts, arses.
5. Beg, dole whores! I tax all evil tits!
6. He kept the jar of uteri enclosed in vase.

7. A raw hymen felt rough, horrid.
8. Seed a mother, don!
9. Low at night, I test Hell.
10. O, here we retreat.
11. Who views her left to right slit with grin?
12. Oh, they dieth for a zany, meek, wit: i. e., C. L. Dodgson.
13. There! Just as sent! Knife flesh! Hack bone!
14. Hep! I donated for the nastiest of Jack's funerals!

These represent the best of several anagrams which contain similar themes for those few lines that seemed to have more than one solution. Alternative themes and solutions were sought for all lines and for the entire poem and none were found. All of the words have been validated as appropriate Victorian usage in regular and slang dictionaries.

Line 2 would refer to the murder of Martha Tabram, reported by some writers to have occurred on 7 August but which most now believe took place on the 6th. It was committed during the time when Bayne's diary reflects that he was in England. Tabram was killed with thirty-nine stab wounds, unlike the later victims, with what experts believe were two different knives. There was considerable discussion as to whether the killer was ambidextrous, and some as to whether there was more than one killer. Authorities were amazed that the killer could escape detection with so many police in the area. This anagram suggests awareness that they were viewed, and that there were perhaps more than two involved, even if some were diversions or lookouts.

Line 4 suggests anal as well as vaginal penetration, both of which occurred with the knife in several of the murders. Although it is unclear in some of the mutilations, accounts which describe the trunks as having been opened from the anus to the chest area, it is possible that the knife was thrust into either the vagina or the anus before moving upward. Of course, in a broader sense the line could be just describing "gay" behavior according to its most accepted Victorian meaning, that of prostitutes.

Perhaps it is worth here a brief excursion into Victorian pornography, specifically a book titled *Cythera's Hymnal*, published in 1852, ostensibly by Oxford University Press, no doubt a phony attribution. In his *The Worm in the Bud*, Ronald Pearsall suggests that some of the poems and "nursery rhymes" are of such quality that they could have been written by Carroll, although he provides no strong suggestion that they were. [40] If we examine the imagery in some of them, we see a reenactment of Ripper violence. On several occasions in his diary, Dodgson decried some of the printed material that was coming out of

Oxford. Is it possible that he brought these obscene and violent scenes to life in another escalation of atrocity?

From "The Gallant Gentleman," we have:

> ... But while she thought, and schemed, and reckoned,
>   I caught her by her velvet bum,
> Produced my prick, and in a second
>   Poked it up to kingdom come.
>
> So long, so stiff, that in that grind
>   It pierced its inward way so far,
> I feared 'twould issue out behind,
>   Like Love's intestinal cigar.
>
> I poked her till she could not lift
>   The fringéd lash of either eye,
> I poked her till the dripping shift
>   Seemed never destined to be dry.
>
> And still as sombre death we lay
>   Till Cupid's bow again was strung,
> Then, like a tigress on her prey,
>   Upon the emboweling shaft she sprung. [41]

Or another, from "The Poisoned Wound":

> ... The Queen that night neither sighed nor groaned,
>   But with new delights did quiver,
> For the dildo for past neglects atoned,
>   And almost lifted her liver.... [42]

As we have seen in the Ripper murders, livers were cut, one removed. Eyelids were nicked with the wounding "instrument," all rage based — "for past neglects atoned." In an obscene distortion of the characters from "Alice," with Kelly's heart removed, had she become the Queen of Hearts or a mother-substitute, the Queen of H-A-T-E-R-S.

Line 5 suggests the ultimate tax and the authority to tax, consistent with a claimed "divine right."

Line 6 reflects a purpose and disposal of at least two uteri which were removed and disappeared during two mutilations. Authorities speculated at one point that they were being sold to satisfy an American who was said to have advertised for uteri, or that they were for use in medical experiments, although the doctors involved in the autopsies denied that the removed organs could be used for any legitimate medical purpose. Wilson interprets the removal as indicative of a wish to destroy the very origins of the self — a suicidal metaphor. Some sexual murders with cannibalistic overtones suggest that uteri are removed to be eaten, a metaphorical devouring and annihilation of self-origins. This anagram would suggest that they were saved, most likely in a preservative, just as the kidney had been before it was sent to Mr. Lusk, and "displayed" virtually as trophies on a mantelpiece in a way similar to what a sportsman would do. A small amount of preservative chemical had been poured or spilled onto Marie Kelly's body. [43]   At one point suspicious men were seen in deer-stalker hats, which became a suspect trademark, and perhaps a very appropriate disguise for Dodgson, who publicly criticized "sport" as well as vivisection even though he appears to have used the latter as a mask for hiding a defense for bestiality. [44] This conflicts with the letter that indicated that the kidney had been eaten, but possibly supports the notion that it, too, may have been in the same jar with the uteri.

Line 9 returns us to Dodgson's insomnia and his lifelong problems with the nighttime, believed to have its origins in the sexual assaults he endured at night while at public school. In his own, although understated description, he indicated that school would have been much more enjoyable except for the "annoyances" at night. Throughout his life, the nighttime appears to have been the time when much of the brooding, plotting, and violent anagrammatic construction took place.

Line 10 suggests that there was a lodging close by to which Jack the Ripper could disappear. Those who thought the killer was an out-of-towner were suspicious that he may have had quarters in London. Dodgson mentioned in his diaries [45] that he might advertise in *The Hunting of the Snark* for a rental house in London to be used as a studio by artists when he was not there, but he never seems to have run the advertisement. This theme will reemerge later in more explicit form. Again, we see the suggestion of more than one participant.

Line 13 suggests a divine mission to kill the prostitutes, another theme that will recur and one that was popular when the theory was that Jack the Ripper might be a religious fanatic "commissioned" to avenge the evils of prostitution or to create through the murders public awareness of the terrible class inequities that existed and put public pressure on authorities to improve conditions in the East End. The word *there* could be *three*, and suggest that three people were involved in the actual mutilations, a notion not supported by any of the experts on the postmortems but another that will emerge in later chapters.

Line 14 is the eeriest of all. This poem was received just days prior to the nastiest of Jack's murders — that of Marie Kelly. Her funeral was in fact paid for by the elderly clerk in the local parish, who invited public contributions to construct a headstone (although not enough money was received to do so). Donations had also been invited for the burial of Stride and Eddowes as the community began to come together in its common concern for these women as poor victims. *Hep*! is slang for *Attention*! or *Now hear this*! but did not imply a knowledge of social graces, a more modern American meaning. Is it possible that this was an arrogant prediction of the murder about to take place?

There are two letters that appear in Wilson and Odell's *Jack the Ripper* which deserve a brief mention. The first was cited briefly in chapter 2 regarding the profile of the Ripper. It was believed to have come from a medical person who used the name "Medicus." [46] The writer suggested that most likely the murders were not those of a maniac who would not have sought a secret place for the crime, but that he might have had an epileptic attack with homicidal impulses while engaged in a sexual act with the prostitute in a dark place. Unless the writer was a very narrow thinker, this is patently absurd, as the scenario would require that this otherwise well-intentioned epileptic just happened to have a six-to-eight-inch knife in his possession, ready to use it in a time and circumstance that prevented a cry from being given or heard. Is it coincidence that this letter comes from someone whose pseudonym is an anagram? "Die, scum!" *Scum* is a correct Victorian allusion.

The second letter was written by a P.S.R. Lunigi to Dr. L. Forbes Winslow, most likely in response to his proposed "solutions" and recommendations which appeared in the press. [47] This letter arrived just prior to the murder of Marie Kelly and forecast a murder on 8 or 9 November, perhaps in Clapham, perhaps in the West End. Was this a letter from the Ripper giving serious consideration to raising the ante by moving against the home of upper-class "discreet" prostitution? Or was it an effort to bring about a transfer of police forces away from the East End? Is it coincidence that "P.S.R. Lunigi" forms "at least" (recalling Dodgson's reference) three anagrams, one of which would forecast the mutilation that would accompany the removal of Marie Kelly's heart, and severe damage to a lung, one of which describes perfectly a Dodgson skill with words as puns, and the third of which further reflects his facility with anagrams and reinforces a sense of meaning in the removal of rings from the hands of Annie Chapman? "I rip lungs." "I pun, girls."

"Plus, I grin!" Were two *rings* stolen from Chapman or did two perpetrators with Cheshire cat *grins* steal away in the night? *Cat* was Victorian slang for *prostitute*, having much the same meaning as *gay*. Dodgson and Bayne were from County Cheshire.

This concludes the discussion of the letters and poems available in the Scotland Yard files and the literature. The taunting nature of these communications, possibly authentic (even if some cannot be confirmed by handwriting analysis), is further enhanced and made more authentic by the presence of hidden, often explicit, often self-incriminating statements which are historically consistent with the known facts of the Ripper murders. Others reflect the attention to minute detail which carefully prepared communications, intended to confuse yet at the same time leave clues as part of an overall effort to titillate the self is totally consistent with Dodgson's pattern of communication in the main body of his literature.

Chapter 5

The Masonic Connection

It would not be until the BBC television broadcast of a fictionalized dramatization of the Ripper murders in 1973 that a public connection was made between those killings and Freemasonry. Even then the notion was not fully developed. The much maligned Stephen Knight would pursue the subject even more fully and with more conviction in his 1976 work *Jack the Ripper: The Final Solution*, which was then followed by a powerful and controversial exposure of Freemasonry in his 1983 work *The Brotherhood*. In fact, the Masonic connection, first brought up by Walter Sickert's son as he narrated the supposedly true story told him by his father, was weighted heavily by Knight in the total credibility given the son's incredible story.

The link to the Masons was supported by the message that was found written in chalk on a hallway wall on Goulston Street where there was also found the remains of blood in the sink and nearby a piece of the apron that had been cut off from that worn by Catherine Eddowes. This message was:

> The Juwes are not
> The men that
> Will be
> Blamed for nothing. [1]

First found as part of a hasty search of the area when the police sensed that the Ripper was on the run after the Eddowes murder, the message was protected until Sir Charles Warren was fetched and, hopefully with the help of dawn's light, until it could be photographed. Despite protestations to the contrary from detective David Halse, including suggestions that just the word *Juwes* be either covered or erased, Warren is said to have erased it himself after it had been copied onto a scrap of paper by Constable Long. Warren claimed then and in a letter later sent to the home secretary that he feared a neighborhood uprising against the Jews. [2]

There was confusion between the two officers involved, for while one version was as above, the other read:

The Jews are
The men That
Will not
be Blamed
for nothing [3]

The discrepancy, caused by the fact that one was drawn from memory and the other from notes taken at the scene, could not be resolved during the inquest, but it did little to change the meaning of the phrase, if, indeed it had one.

Knight's hypotheses regarding Masonic involvement supported two of his arguments. The first was that Sir William Gull, Physician in Ordinary to the Crown and a high ranking member of the secret organization, had indeed committed the murders in order to protect the monarchy against the blackmailing efforts of the small group of prostitutes, headed by Mary Ann Kelly, who knew the details of the Prince of Wales's son Eddy's secret marriage to a Roman Catholic and the fathering of her daughter. Second, he suggested that the erasure of the hand-written message ordered by Sir Charles Warren, himself a high level Mason, was also part of the cover-up. In this scenario, Warren most likely recognized the ritual nature of the murders, and most certainly recognized *Juwes* as a Masonic word; he then ordered the erasure, not for his stated reason that it might incite an anti-Semitic riot, but to destroy evidence that Masons were involved, even if he did not know fully the details of the plan.

In his 1989 work *Jack the Ripper: the Uncensored Facts* Paul Begg contradicts Stephen Knight's claim that *Juwes* was a word with Masonic origins or usage. [4] According to the *Oxford English Dictionary* the word was already an obsolete form of the word *Jews* in Dodgson's time. I did not find it in the Masonic literature which Dodgson kept in his library.

Howells and Skinner reject entirely any Masonic connection primarily on the basis that the murders were not true enough to the ritual described in Masonic documents to identify them as evidence that they were committed by a Mason or were intended to be identified as Masonic in origin. [5] What I reject is the notion that the killings were done as part of a plan to intentionally have the organization blamed as a means of intimidation — the Knight thesis — for it would be only a small group of Masons that would be able to put two and two together. As it is, it took nearly a hundred years for the association to be made in the print media. For a loyal Mason to reveal such a secret as a way to intimidate prostitutes ignorant of its symbolism is a ludicrous notion.

What I do suggest as possible is that in the rush of the moment, given that all but one of the murders was committed, not so much in haste as with due deliberation in a short period of time, an effort was made to give them a ritual appearance somewhat true to the Masonic tradition in order to at least create confusion, at most disparage the organization and high ranking members in the government having the responsibility to stop the slaughter. In short, this, too, was part of the cunning plot which took place, planned by someone who was not himself a Mason but who had at his disposal detailed knowledge of the organization's secret inner workings and symbolism, and who had an axe to grind with the organization.

Charles Dodgson not only had that knowledge but had obtained it from a source intent on exposing the powerful organization as fundamentally steeped in the bankruptcy of hypocrisy. The Masons, representing the power of the establishment, were a perfect target for one who perceived himself as the alienated, lifelong victim of ruthless hypocrisy and who, in numerous other ways, had for a lifetime attacked every hypocrisy by doing it one better as his means of attacking society.

Innocuously listed on page 53 of Jeffrey Stearn's *Lewis Carroll's Library*, a publication which identifies the contents of Dodgson's library at the time of its disposal at auction shortly after his death, is "Freemasonry, A Ritual and Illustrations of, and the Orange and Odd Fellows Societies. . . ." The full title of the work, found in the Burns Collection at Boston College, adds where the ellipsis points are: "also an Account of the Kidnapping and Murder of William Morgan, who divulged the ridiculous and profane usages of the Freemasons; Abridged from American Authors." This book was published in England in 1851 and, except for time appropriate modifications, contains as complete a description of Masonic ritual and history, along with assessments of those very much opposed to it, as any of the many other exposés reviewed (see Bibliography), including Knight's. In addition, it details the murder of the high ranking American Mason, Captain William Morgan, believed perpetrated by fellow Masons motivated by his disillusioned disclosure of Masonic secrets in his work *Morgan's Freemasonry Exposed*, published posthumously.

A lengthy introduction to the work in Dodgson's library provides numerous quotes from British and American churchmen and from articles in religious newspapers, all of them condemning the organization as fundamentally corrupt, and, in its claims of divine origin (and allegedly evidenced by greater Masonic loyalty to regular meeting attendance than church attendance) a quasi religion. These include such passages as:

... Masonry is to the modern world what the whore of Babylon was to the ancient ... degrading the command of the Most High, which says, "Thou shalt not kill." [6]

... We had no idea that "Freemasonry" was such a compound of folly and profaneness. The perversion of the Holy Scriptures: the insults offered to heaven, in their profligate mocking of prayer; and the horrifying abuse of oaths, with which they are chargeable, render them a reproach to human kind, and prove that purity of character is no qualification for membership in a society into which they are omitted. (ix, quoting *Christian Advocate*)

... In some ceremonies, Holy Scripture is so used and perverted as to render it shocking and impious. (ix, quoting *Methodist New Connexion Magazine.*)

... [describing Morgan's murder as] a moral dementation — a diabolism for which neither reason, nor humanity, nor civilisation, nor law, nor religion, can afford the most specious apology. (xii)

... the *princes* among the people [not the poor or ruffians] [italics and brackets in the original] appear to have matured the plot and directed its execution.
[The crime was believed executed and covered up in the legal system by high ranking American Masons.]

... We are compelled to notice a species of exultation that the acts have been committed, visible in those who seem to triumph in the belief that no responsibility for them, attaches to themselves or others, who can be reached by the laws. We have been still more surprised and disgusted by hearing numerous individuals, of decent manners and deportments in other respects, treat with levity, and as wholly unimportant to the community at large, these scandalous violations of private rights, and gross insults upon offended justice. (xxiv)

... found the whole system to be, what the world now knows it to be, a sink of moral corruption, where every species of intrigue and hypocrisy is carried on under the veil of ANTIQUITY, MORALITY, AND CHARITY. (xxxiv)

In addition to a detailed description and condemnation of the use of murder and treason (in the case of Morgan's murder the subverting of the legal system) to protect the *organization*, the work contains the following material relevant to the Ripper murders:

Twenty-four pages of illustrations which depict ritual handshakes, body positions, ceremonial seating arrangements, and costume. These include the approximate body positions of the murder victims described in eye-witness reports — legs spread apart and drawn up (no question also in the position for copulation, which would have placed the male in what is known as the "Missionary" position and totally consistent with Victorian pornography's "worshipping at the shrine"), arms outstretched in one pose, one hand at the waist (Kelly's hand was stuffed into her abdominal cavity at the waist), another on the breast.

A detailed elaboration of the induction ceremonies at the various degree levels and the oaths required. This includes the description of the punishment to be inflicted to the initiate member who divulges Masonic secrets — a slitting of the throat from left to right (not the fate of Captain Morgan, who was beaten and drowned).

Identification of the oath taken at the highest degree, that of Royal Arch, and the one most controversial in labeling the organization as sinister, in that the candidate pledges:

> ... I furthermore promise and swear, that I will assist a companion royal arch Mason when I see him engaged in any difficulty, and will espouse his cause so far as to extricate him from the same, whether he is right or wrong. ... I furthermore promise and swear, that I will keep all the secrets of a companion royal arch Mason (when communicated to me as such, or I knowing them to be such,) without exception. * [The author of the *Rituals* footnotes] I have seen this point in the oath given in three different ways, that is, the phraseology of the sentence varied, but it always covers or comprehends murder and treason; sometimes it is expressed, — murder and treason not excepted.
>
> ... To all which I do most solemnly and severely promise and swear, with a firm and steadfast resolution to keep and perform the same, without any equivocation, mental reservation, or self-evasion of mind in me whatever; binding myself

under no less penalty than to have my skull smote off, and my brains exposed to the scorching rays of a meridian sun, should I knowingly or willfully violate or transgress any part of this my solemn oath or obligation of a royal arch Mason. . . [after which he kisses the book seven times]. [7]

The full denunciation quoted above derives heavily from the disclosure that the initiate at each level of the organization is not made privy to the nature or contents of the oaths to be taken until, in full regalia standing before the membership or leadership, he, in fact, takes the oath. At each level except the last, the use of "murder and treason" is usually specifically *excluded* as a valid means of action. In that way, it was concluded that members believed in the upright nature of things and participated in good faith in the many good works that were and continue to be done. The inclusion of murder and treason as acceptable at the highest level, and the believed use of them in a specific case against a fellow Mason was a shocking surprise; the ritual words were suddenly not just symbolic, but carried the weight of "moral suasion."

The origins of Freemasonry are detailed in the work. The lore identifies that the organization was founded by Hiram Abiff, who participated as a Master Mason in the building of Solomon's Temple. He was later murdered by three member betrayers — Jubela, Jubelo, and Jubelum (who arguably became known collectively as the "Jews") with *Jubela* becoming a word to mean "the epitome of betrayers." When tried, each was required to define his own execution:

JUBELA: O that my throat had been cut across, my tongue torn out, and my body buried in the rough sands of the sea, at low water mark, where the tide ebbs. . . .

JUBELO: O that my left breast had been torn open and my heart and vitals taken from thence and thrown over my left shoulder. . . .

JUBELUM: O that my body had been severed in two in the midst. . . [and] my bowels burnt to ashes in the centre and the ashes scattered by the four winds of heaven. . . . [8]

Again, while the Ripper murders were not perfect matches for any of these forms of "executions of betrayers," the throat slitting is clear in all victims; the removal of breasts, heart, and vitals was clear in the murders of Eddowes and Kelly; Chapman's small intestines and flap of abdomen had been placed on or by her right shoulder, according to testimony of Dr. Brown, the doctor involved in several of the inquests.

And, they had been attached with a cord [9] to hold them in place. There were also flaps of skin over the left shoulder, while Eddowes's kidney had been removed. It is possible that some body parts, although not Kelly's, were burned in the fireplace of her apartment. The similarities are undeniable with consequences for all three evident in the Kelly murder and mutilation.

As an obsolete form of *Jews* with or without Masonic significance Commissioner Warren could very well have recognized *Juwes*; and it could have led to confusion regarding the meaning of the phrase, already a conundrum with the double negative present in either recorded version.

In what has all the earmarks of a staged event, although perhaps made part of the record due to the word confusion, just prior to the murder of Stride, Inspector Abberline reported that a man accompanied by a woman shouted "Lipski," an anti-Jewish epithet, in the direction of an observing Jew named Schwartz, who fled, fearful the cry was aimed at him. Another man was seen observing the couple also ran off in the same direction. [10]   If a double-event murder had been planned for that night, both Mitre Square as the preselected locale for the second murder and the piece later proven to have been cut from Eddowes apron and found with what were most likely human bloodstains near the scene of the "Juwes" message, could not have more of a symbolic connotation. For Mitre and apron are deeply symbolic items in the Masonic craft and organization's ritual themes; both of them were fully described in the book in Dodgson's library. [11]   Here in the double event, we are surrounded by Masonic and Jewish allusions at the same time that the message appeared.

Because Masonic themes and symbols draw on many ethnic and religious cultures and practices from East and West, it is difficult to conclude that what could be interpreted as Masonic parody in Dodgson's work is not drawn from other material. Throughout his works we have the mysterious "Rule of Three." "Three" is a significant number in Masonic lore, but also appears in many other cultures. The numerous nonsensical hierarchical titles which appear in *Sylvie and Bruno* and *Sylvie and Bruno Concluded*, both published after the murders, could be Oxford, church, or government parody, but they could also be Masonic parody, as the Masonic organization itself appears in many way to have provided (in its origins especially, as royalty eventually was included in its ranks) an opportunity for the working man to participate in a hierarchical organization with much pomp and ceremony which paralleled those from which he was excluded by birth or decree. *Sylvie and Bruno* ends with the inspirational cry "Look Eastward! Aye, look

Eastward!" —— perhaps a reference to the revered Masonic "direction," perhaps also a play in its anagrammatic restructuring, "Take low roads! Aye, take low roads!" on the perceived hypocrisy of the organization. This anagram is totally consistent with other hidden material in the work.

As we move into Dodgson's world of anagrams we find another Masonic symbol used correctly. Shortly after he gave Boston Latin School permission to use *Jabberwock* as the title to its literary publication, he was very offended by an "irreverent" article they wrote and told them so in no uncertain terms. [12] This criticism was followed by a conciliatory letter in which he offered a "lump of sugar" (he surrounded the phrase in quotes, one method of signaling that the phrase should be examined) as a sign of reconciliation for the "Black Draught" which had preceded it. While "Black Draught" meant "strong medicine" in Victorian times, it also referred to ale. But he was offering something more than "a lump of sugar to make the medicine go down." The reconciliation was, I believe, a false one, for the "lump of sugar" was really, in reconstruction, "foul rump gas" emanating from the "Black Draught" he had previously offered them. In Masonic ritual, a lump of sugar is used to represent "Hidden Manna" [13] from heaven, the traditional Judao-Christian symbol of reconciliation.

Another Masonic secret appears to be the basis for a system of writing in the dark that he "invented." In 1890, Dodgson published such a system which he called a "Typhlograph," but which he later renamed (on a friend's suggestion) to "Nyctograph." When he introduced it, he claimed he had used it quite successfully for some time when he awoke at night with an idea he wished to make note of and recommended it be adopted by the blind. By using a template filled with rows of small squares, the writer could form letters by tracing a pencil in the dark from corner to corner and along the edges, making "characters" of lines and dots, moving from square to square without being able to see any of the paper or writing. [14] As one examines the "characters" themselves, they bear a noticeable resemblance to the secret cipher code used by Masons to encrypt messages, even if Dodgson made several useful improvements. Two alternatives of this cipher were published in *Rituals* [15] in their complete form. Depicted on the following page is my rendition of Dodgson's instructions for the Nyctograph (n.) and one version of the Masonic cipher code (m.).

Of course, all of the above is hypothesis. There is a presumption that Dodgson owned the *Rituals* in the relevant time frame, that he read them, and that he had strong feelings toward them. It is indisputable, however, that he had a relationship with the Masons, although

Nyctograph
and
Masonic Cipher

	A	B	C	D	E	F	G
n.	⠡	⌐:	⊏	⊐	⌐	⌐.	⌐⸳
m.	⌟	⸱⌟	⊔	⊡	⌞	⌞⸱	⊐

	H	I	J	K	L	M	N
n.	⌐⌐	⸱⸏	⸱⌟	⌐⸱	⌞	⊓	⊔
m.	⊐⸱	□	⊡	⊏	⊏⸱	⌐	⌐⸱

	O	P	Q	R	S	T	U
n.	◻	⌐⸳	⸱⌐	⌐⸱	⌐	⌐	⸳⸳
m.	⊓	⊓⸱	⊏	⊏⸱	∨	∨⸱	>

	V	W	X	Y	Z
n.	⸳⸳	⸳⸳	⌐⸱	⌐⸱	⎓
m.	⸫>	<	<⸱	∧	∧⸱

it is uncertain just what that relationship was. The diary manuscripts at the British Library reflect that he often attended the annual Masonic *Fete* held on Commemoration Day. He went in the company of his father prior to the latter's death in 1868, but makes no mention of how the required tickets were obtained. Inquiries at the Library and Museum of the United Grand Lodge of England in London determined that the younger Dodgson was not a member, a study having already been done in response to a prior inquiry. My request for an investigation as to whether the father had been a member evoked, after some effort over a period of weeks, an indeterminate response pending more information on what specific lodge (among the thousands that existed) he might have belonged to and his title. [16] This is an area where more investigation could be fruitful in determining whether any hate the son may have had for the Masons had evolved from hate for his father based in no small part on what he perceived as his hypocritical abandonment to the sexually violent public school experiences.

The *Fete* itself appears to have been an opportunity for the father and son to socialize together, but on one occasion Dodgson recorded surprise in his diary at the humor his father found and expressed with such animation to some off-color songs included in the entertainment. This reaction was not the image of his father that he had or behavior that had been encouraged for him within the family. After the elder Dodgson's death, the son continued to attend the festivities, often acquiring tickets for men and women friends, but from sources that he did not reveal.

Perhaps the strongest implication of Dodgson's presence in these murders and their Masonic connection lies in the mysterious statement on the wall that opened this chapter, a statement perhaps written in the haste of the flight to Mitre Square after the murder of Stride (which experts believe was interrupted by the threat of detection), after the murder of Eddowes, or perhaps hours before since the hallway with its convenient basin had been preselected as a place for retreat. Or, perhaps it was written by someone else, with his knowledge or direction.

For the Dodgson "fingerprint" is there in its full presence. Like he had done in his literature with such things as the inimitable riddle "Why is a raven like a writing desk?" in *Through the Looking Glass*," an impenetrable message is the sign of the presence of an anagram. Is it possible that "The Juwes are the men that will not be blamed for nothing" is an anagram for *"Jubela mother! This rotten game'll end when we both faint!"*? For here we have not only the mother-image identified as the target of the murders, but a repetition of the Masonic theme, the identification of "mother" as "betrayer," classification of the murders as a cunning game, possible suggestion of a second participant, and finally, another appearance of the recurring theme that the murders were an act, not of "lunatic" passion, but of will, murders which would, by design, increase in horror and end when the control mechanism of consciousness was finally lost.

In what became a surprise coincidence in the research for this work, the presence of another anagram from this statement may very well suggest conclusively the meaning of the "Rule of Three." In my earlier work, I encountered on several occasions "at least" three relevant anagrams from the same statement. It was in Dodgson's letter to sister Mary on the subject of Eternal Punishment that even he used the phrase "at least three" when he suggested there were at least three meanings to the statement "I believe in the doctrine of Eternal Punishment." We have already seen the two anagrams that can be formed, both of which reflect the use of the penis.

Here, also, we have several additional anagrams that very much fit into the history of the investigation, even if the theme was not what was recognized or published at the time of the murders: "Widen the thin net! Blame the rat, Mason, W. Gull, for the job!," or "Need the thin women haters blame, taint W. Gull for the job?" or "Hint: net, detain, blame the women hater W. Gull for the jobs!" etc. This suggestion that Dodgson implicated Gull through his anagrams begs for the existence of some letters or other open communication which he might have sent to newspapers or even government officials, most likely under a pseudonym. I have found none in any sources, nor would I expect that they would have been saved. They would have been destroyed as coming from a crank.

Dr. William Gull, physician to the Queen, a hater of women? Charles Dodgson emotionally involved, with an axe to grind, with William Gull? The biographies of both men make no mention of the other. Yet they met on opposite sides of two very charged public issues, albeit through a third person. And those subjects were vivisection and "sport."

One of the theories on the Ripper murders was that they were the work of a demented vivisectionist. A "trademark" seen among suspected men in the area was the "deer-stalker" hat. Did Dodgson combine his own hate for women with two practices which Gull publicly embraced and which were judged by opponents as reflective of at least a callous disrespect for life, at most horribly cruel and grossly hypocritical. Did he incorporate them into his own attack on women and society? Was this

yet another instance of one-upping an accepted societal practice he
viewed as hypocritical?

Chapter 6

The Vivisection Connection

If there was a pattern found in my exploration of Dodgson's life as having Jekyll-Hyde qualities, it was that he embraced the highest ethical and moral principles publicly while in secret he hid what appears an intellectual and emotional embrace of their most degraded opposites. This became not only ingrained in his personality but an obscenely designed parody of the Victorian hypocrisy that had destroyed him as a boy. He appears to have done this in every area, virtually as a goal, with religion and its threat of eternal punishment the only area where there may have been evidence of a struggle remaining. This duality appears also in the area of "sport," a Victorian euphemism for "game" hunting, and vivisection, the use of "lower animals" for medical experimentation.

The Victorian Age was typified by the rise of science, the turning away from "unproven" principles, beliefs, and theories. The work of Charles Darwin changed the entire thinking regarding the origins of man. Investigation needed to be done on specie members to identify and classify. Nowhere was this more true than in the study of human physiology and medicine. The practice of doing this research on cadavers was being displaced by increased work on living animals and charity cases — particularly and mostly women — in hospitals. As reports filtered out of the universities, early "research laboratories," and hospitals regarding the increased presence of investigatory or surgical procedures being undertaken with minimal, if any, anaesthesia, the cry for regulation emerged. In 1875 the Society for the Protection of Animals Liable to Vivisection was formed. Spearheading the effort was Frances Power Cobbe, an early suffragist and ardent antivivisectionist. Out of that effort came the Cruelty to Animals Act, passed in 1876, and challenged unsuccessfully by the medical community in 1883. The Act limited the amount of experimentation that could be done using domes-ticated animals and very much codified the principles already informally guiding the British Association (physicians) in 1871:

(1) No experiment which can be performed under the influ-ence of an anaesthetic ought to be done without it.
(2) No painful experiment is justifiable for the mere purpose of illustrating a law or fact already demonstrated.

(3) Whenever, for the purpose of new truth, it is necessary to
    make a painful experiment, every effort should be made
    to ensure success, in order that the sufferings inflicted
    may not be wasted. [1]

As can be clearly seen, these principles are so broad that they are
for all intents not enforceable. They depended totally on the ethics,
skill, and good will of the practitioner or on the integrity and courage of
whoever present among his peers might report abuse. Needless to say,
this did not satisfy the antivivisectionists, and Cobbe would later introduce an effort to totally abolish the practice of vivisection.

Dodgson's involvement in this issue began with a letter titled
"Vivisection as a sign of the times" which was published in the *Pall Mall
Gazette* on 12 February 1875. An unpublished diary entry on the 24th
notes that the letter was written on the 8th. What is of interest in this
entry is that he also notes having received a very flattering letter from
Miss F. P. Cobbe regarding the letter and his participation in her
cause. [2] He signed the letter with his pseudonym, for some reason not
wishing to be identified by his given name. Essentially the letter
attacked Reason and Science as destroying the feeling person, with
vivisection a "sign of the times" and trend toward heartlessness.

Quoting excerpts from Dodgson's article which touch on Cobbe's
themes:

> ... How far may vivisection be regarded as a sign of the times,
> and a fair specimen of that higher civilisation which a purely
> secular State education is to give us? In that much-vaunted
> panacea for all human ills we are promised not only increase in
> knowledge, but also a higher moral character... [i.e.], a scien-
> tific education tends to improve moral conduct. ... "Can the
> man who has once realised by minute study what nerves are,
> what the brain is, and what waves of agony the one can convey
> to the other, go forth and wantonly inflict pain on any sentient
> being?" ... When I hear of one of these ardent searchers after
> truth giving, not a helpless dumb animal, to whom he says in
> effect, "*You* shall suffer that *I* may know", but his own person
> to the probe and to the scalpel, I will believe in him as recog-
> nising a principle of justice, and I will honour him as acting up
> to his principles. "The thing cannot be! cries some amiable
> reader, fresh from an interview with that most charming of
> men, a London physician. "What! Is it possible that one so
> gentle in manner, so full of noble sentiments, can be

hardhearted?   The very idea is an outrage to common sense!" [3]

The use of "a London physician" is interesting, but the reference could very well be a generic one (as others in the letter seem to be), as Gull could present both charm and imperiousness, the latter often as a "devil's advocate." Being made Baronet in 1871 and gaining the position of physician-in-ordinary to Queen Victoria no doubt represented a reward for a number of skills, not just his successful treatment of the Prince of Wales from near death. Gull was known for often quoting noble sentiments, biblical in nature, although he considered himself a "Christian agnostic." [4]

Continuing the letter, Dodgson decries the absence of religious and moral training in secular education.

> . . . The world has seen and tired of the worship of Nature, of Reason, of Humanity; for this nineteenth century has been reserved the development of the most refined religion of all — the worship of Self. For that, indeed, is the upshot of it all. The enslavement of his weaker brethren. . . the degradation of woman — the torture of the animal world — *these are the steps of the ladder by which man is ascending to his higher civilisation.* Selfishness is the key-note of all purely secular education; and I take vivisection to be a glaring, a wholly unmistakable case in point. . . and when the man of science, looking forth over a world which will then own no other sway than his, shall exult in the thought that he has made of this fair green earth, if not a heaven for man, at least a hell for animals. (Italics mine.) [5]

There is no question that Dodgson's position was overwhelmingly in support of Cobbe's cause for her work was directed not only to the treatment of animals, but to the abuse of children and women.

> Frances Cobbe located the source of sadism in English life in the systematic flogging of children. Boys, and occasionally girls, were routinely birched, and Cobbe shrewdly felt that a great deal more than discipline was involved [i.e., sadism]. [6]

Cobbe attributed later beatings of women as learned behavior from early childhood experiences. Flogging was the primary means of discipline in the public school system, where Dodgson was schooled. To what extent he was flogged in the family school he attended until nearly twelve years old has not been recorded, may have been a family secret. Indications are, however, that he was punished more by the writing of impositions than by the birch in the formal schools he attended.

Again referencing an unpublished diary entry, on 2 March Dodgson noted that he had heard from the secretary of the Society for the Prevention of Cruelty to Animals (Northern Branch) who had sought permission to use the letter on a flyleaf to be circulated. He granted the request.

His next and what appears to be last foray into the arena occurred in May when he submitted an article titled "Some popular fallacies about vivisection" to the *Pall Mall*. Another unpublished diary entry notes that they declined to publish it, claiming that the fallacies were unheard of. Even in the diary (for future biographers?) he wrote the defense that while five of his points were original, he had seen eight others in the *Pall Mall*. Dodgson's response to that rebuff was to send the manuscript to Miss Cobbe, who, in turn, had forwarded it to the *Fortnightly Review*. The diary entry for 19 May 1875, notes that he had heard from the editor, a Mr. Morley, who indicated they had accepted it for publication. It was published on 1 June 1875.

The article presents eleven statements used to defend and justify vivisection and follows with his "logical" attack on each. Dodgson's primary argument throughout the article is that regardless of the pain endured by victims of vivisection, the damage done psychically to the vivisector is far greater. For regardless of good motives, the heart (of surgeons) will eventually become hardened to the existence of pain in the other. Within this context he writes:

> It is humiliating but an undeniable truth, that man has something of the wild beast in him, that a thirst for blood can be aroused in him by witnessing a scene of carnage, and that the infliction of torture, when the first instincts of horror have been deadened by familiarity may become, first, a matter of indifference, then a subject of morbid interest, then a positive pleasure, and then a ghastly and ferocious delight. [7]

He concludes the article with:

> And when that day shall come, O my brother-man, you who claim for yourself and for me so proud an ancestry — tracing our pedigree through the anthropomorphoid ape up to the primeval zoöphyte — what potent charm have *you* in store

to win exemption from the common doom? Will you represent to that grim spectre, as he gloats over you, scalpel in hand, the inalienable rights of man? He will tell you that this is merely a question of relative expediency — that, with so feeble a physique as yours, you have only to be thankful that natural selection has spared you so long. Will you reproach him with the needless torture he proposes to inflict upon you? He will smilingly assure you that the *hyperaesthesia*, which he hopes to induce, is in itself a most interesting phenomenon, deserving much patient study. Will you then, gathering up all your strength for one last desperate appeal, plead with him as with a fellow-man, and with an agonized cry for "Mercy!" seek to rouse some dormant spark of pity in that icy breast? Ask it rather to the nether mill-stone. [8]

When the issue of vivisection again came to the fore in the early 1880s as part of a movement to ban it altogether, both Cobbe and Gull were in the middle of the fray. A sample of Cobbe's writing reflects an effort to feminize the arguments. Drawing from a letter to Prime Minister Gladstone reproduced in a pamphlet we have:

> ... Like the witness stretched upon the rack, Nature, put to the question by Torture, answers with a lie. ... [9]
> ... And she [Nature] is very woman, whose real law is sympathy, whatever to shallow and loveless observation it may appear to be. For she reflects to each one who approaches her, precisely the image he presents to her. ... [10]
> ... Reduced to butchery, and this as of the most revolting description, science now obtains from its science, not the finest intellects, but the hardest hearts. ... [In the ways of man versus woman] The head is all, the heart is nothing; sense is all, conscience is nothing; intellect is all, character or disposition nothing; consequences are all, means are nothing; having or seeming is all; being or doing is nothing; body is all; soul is nothing; temporary is all, the eternal nothing; inhumanity is humanity and not love but self. ... [11]

In her article "The Janus of Science" published in the *Contemporary Review* of April 1882, Cobbe attacked Gull directly, including one observation dripping in sarcasm regarding a presentation he made in which he quoted statistics on the number of dogs that had died in medical experiments, making a simple error in addition:

If Sir William Gull finds that $3 + 11 + 2$ amounts to 6, I should venture to offer him a copy of Colenso's Arithmetic, out of consideration for his patients, to whom his peculiar view of the First Rule might prove of importance in a prescription for psychic. [12]

Sir William Gull's "The Ethics of Vivisection" was published in the *Nineteenth Century* in March 1881. We see in his comments the kinds of presumptive upper-class godlike arrogance that would make Dodgson-as-Jekyll bristle, but Dodgson-as-Hyde salivate in self-justification.

> ... Our obligations to the lower creatures arise out of ourselves. It is due to ourselves that we should treat them with tenderness and kind regard. Dominion over them has been put into our hands, and that dominion, from the demands of our intellectual and moral nature, must be intelligent. In killing and eating an animal, we are on the same level as the carnivora; in using them for our sports, we are on the ordinary level of man; but in using them intelligently for the advancement of beneficent knowledge, provided that this be with a due sense of proportion between the benefit and the pain, we are justifying the highest purposes of our intelligence. [13]

Acland, the son-in-law of Sir William Gull, would conclude in the biographical summary that opens his *Collected Letters*:

> Few men of eminence have during their lifetime been more freely criticised. This arose partly from the novelty of some of his opinions, and partly from a certain prejudice against his somewhat imperious manner, and his seeming dogmatism in regard to his scientific inquiries and his therapeutical conclusions. [14]

Gull was very much a self-made man. (Drawing on Knight's work) he was the son of a barge-owner who worked the Lea River and was raised by his widowed mother (along with four surviving older siblings) from age eleven. He became dedicated to following a career in medicine early. By means of some strong mentor support, sheer dedication and hard work, he was recognized for his achievements with the highest award when he obtained his M.D. degree from the University of London. Eventually a Fellow of the Royal College of Physicians, he served much of his life as resident physician of Guy's Hospital. Riding on the crest of his Masonic connections, the credit given him by Queen Victoria in saving her son, who would become Edward VII, from typhoid, Gull rose to be perhaps the best known doctor of his time. By some unknown means, he left an estate of £ 344,000, an enormous sum for that time or its inflation-ravaged equivalent today. [15]   It is difficult to draw dependable references from Stephen Knight. For example, when he quotes Gull's "The Ethics of Vivisection" (Knight's page 192), he describes Gull as "Arguing that `the good we may obtain to ourselves by physiological experiment should outweigh the immorality of the process´ and that `our moral susceptibilities ought to be bribed and silenced by our selfish gains´" he omits Gull's opening of the sentence: "It is no doubt a weak and unworthy argument, that. . ." followed by his insistence that the moral position is and must be clear. [16]

While Knight suggests, indeed, bases his case on the notion, that Gull acted the vivisectionist among poor women in the asylum at Guy's Hospital, including the "wife" of Albert, duke of Clarence, I could find no verification of the assertion. Based on historical sources, Gull himself was a physician and practitioner, not a vivisector. But he avidly supported the practice, without regulation, arguing for self-discipline among ethical practitioners and for the enormous benefits to be gained in relieving pain and misery in the long run.

Before tying all of the preceding together, when quoting from Dodgson's first letter "Vivisection as a sign of the times," I italicized the phrase *"these are the steps of the ladder by which man is ascending to his higher civilisation."* This allusion appears to be a reference to the themes depicted in four drawings by William Hogarth, eighteenth-century English artist. There can be no question that Dodgson either had copies or knew of them, for an unpublished diary entry on 24 March 1882 reflects that he had acquired a Hogarth collection of 117 pieces, but that he did not plan to keep all of them.

These four engravings carry the title "The "Four Stages of Cruelty." In them are depicted increasingly progressive acts of cruelty, beginning with the abuse of dogs, cats, and chickens by children, then the adult abuse of beasts of burden, then of women in the street, and finally, what appears to be a woman on the operating table. She is being disemboweled; as her intestines are gathered into a barrel, her head is lifted up by a hoist connected to a screw driven into her head, and a dog picks at her heart, which is lying on the floor. Officiating over the event is an academician with a pointer apparently explaining the procedure to the assembled crowd, some of whom appear to be there for their entertainment.

Dodgson's suggestion that the doctor-as-vivisectionist is at the height of this evolutionary ladder reflects accurately his whole public position on the issue.

What we have seen thus far is the benevolent Jekyll image Dodgson presented to the world on the issues of both vivisection and sport, his connection to Frances Cobbe, and indirectly to William Gull as her antagonist and a visible leader of the vivisectionist movement. But, as in all things, lurking behind the facade, driven to "*Bluff a rough, sordid heathen world, and cheat death*" lay the Hyde persona. For it is in the disturbed emotional world that we begin to identify the reality between these connections and the possibility that Dodgson was the perpetrator of the Ripper crimes.

I believe strongly that Dodgson's involvement in the controversies of vivisection in 1874 was in anticipation to his forthcoming "epic" poem *The Hunting of the Snark: An Agony in Eight Fits*, which was published two years later. By taking a public position on the subject of "sport" and vivisection using his "Lewis Carroll" pseudonym, he accomplished the goal of using his fame to help the righteous causes, but more importantly, to position himself to avoid criticism regarding the "hunting" theme of his poem. For that poem, with all the various interpretations that are possible and have been made, is filled with masturbatory and anal erotic undercurrents. The proof of this lies in the title, then in other word games used extensively by Dodgson to create his own "dictionary." As with all of his titles, this one, too, is an anagram for hiding disclosure or sexual imagery. These anagrams include: *"None hunt the King of Hearts in the gay night fits"* (with *hearts* amenable to being re-worked to *haters*); *"They, the Uranian kings, often hit on night fags"*; and *"The king of urnings hateth any Onanite fights."* *Uranian*, *Onanite*, and *urning* were early whispered words for *homosexual* before the latter word was invented later in the century. The annihilation of one of the Snark hunters when he finally confronts the Snark alone relates to Dodgson's annihilation experienced at Public School where he was (as I believe he discloses it) subjected to repeated anal assault. [17]

His "Some popular fallacies about vivisection" appears to have been written very quickly in response to Frances Cobbe's praise for the earlier letter. If we accept Dodgson as a woman hater and one who abused women *in secret* while he embraced them in public, this appears to have been an opportunist's delight, particularly after the *Pall Mall* sensed something wrong in the absence of "fallacies." Now he could use Frances Cobbe, carrying a first name he detested — his mother's — to help him publish his hidden defense of bestiality. The anagram from the title of his new attack on the abuse of animals is *"I crave lamb coitus, save up fellatio poison."*

It would be in his Preface to *Sylvie and Bruno*, published one year after the Ripper murders, that Dodgson would "update" his feelings about "sport." The italics in the quotation are Dodgson's. The material in brackets and italics reflects the anagrams that derive from clues that they are present, reflected in Dodgson's use of italics and quotation marks to draw attention.

> [Apologizing for his treatment of the British passion for "Sport"] . . . . But I am not entirely without sympathy for *genuine* "sport" [*Urine! Sponge 't!*]: I can heartily admire the courage of the man who, with severe bodily toil, and at the risk of his life, hunts down some "man-eating" [*man-teaing -- tea* was slang for urine] tiger: and I can heartily sympathize with him when he exults in the glorious excitement of the chase and the hand-to-hand struggle with the monster brought to bay. But I can but look with deep wonder and sorrow on the hunter who, at his ease and in safety, can find pleasure in what involves, for some defenceless creature, wild terror and a death of agony: deeper, if the hunter be one who has pledged himself to preach to men the Religion of universal Love: deepest of all, if it be one of those *"tender and delicate"* [*Dean! Detect liar den!*, etc.] beings, whose very name serves as a symbol of Love — *"thy love to me was wonderful, passing the love of women"* [*"Few fellow dons give phony love to mouth man's wet arse,"* with two more variations] — whose mission here is surely to help and comfort all that are in pain or sorrow!

> *"Farewell, farewell! but this I tell*
> *To thee, thou Wedding-Guest!*
> *He prayest well, who loveth well*
> *Both man and bird and beast.*

> *He prayest best, who loveth best*
> *All things both great and small;*
> *For the dear God who loveth us,*
> *He made and loveth all."* [18]

Perhaps the most salient issue for Dodgson within the vivisectionist argument, including Gull's, was that the members of the medical community, including those in the universities, could police themselves. The argument was that students treated their subjects with dignity and respect, sensitive to the pain they were inflicting, and that they were in a way reluctant participants driven only by their desire to do good. It was Dodgson's experience as a member of that school system and the public schools that led to the university, that the sensitivity to the pain of others was far from the reality of the culture. At the lower levels it was clearly one of brutality toward the weak, oblivious to the pain and damage done. From his standpoint, himself a victim of that system, he knew that those who had succeeded in that environment were now laying a false claim to sensitivity.

I think it very plausible that in his assault on what he saw as respected society's hypocrisy he joined them and did them one better. He could not lose sight of the notion that killing the quarry as in "sport," followed by painless mutilation, in order to satisfy personal selfish needs (for revenge), and perhaps to accomplish a "scientific" study of the limits of human endurance for such acts, would make him certainly no worse than the practicing vivisectionist. "The game'll stop when we both faint."

These crimes would also prove him right in his argument that repetitions only increase the hardheartedness of the operator (argued under Fallacy 8) and that the practice as a pursuit of scientific goals would lead eventually to the inclusion of humans as victims (argued under Fallacy 13).

Coincidentally or not, on the sixteenth anniversary of the publication of Dodgson's first letter on vivisection, a killer was stalking Frances Coles. He would kill her one day later, in the wee hours of the 13th.

Chapter 7

The Medical Connection

Even if we accept the notion that in some way the Ripper crimes were efforts to pervert in an obscene distortion, with blatantly selfish goals, experimentation on "lower creatures," we are confronted with the question of whether Dodgson-as-suspect possessed adequate knowledge of anatomy and medical practice to even attempt such a venture.

From the time of Chapman's murder, the first one in which organs were removed, the issue of whether the Ripper possessed anatomical or medical knowledge has prompted discussion and heated debate among experts. Investigators have fallen on the side of the argument that supports their suspect, be it a slaughterman, Prince Eddy as a knowledgeable dresser of large game, court physician Sir William Gull, or, at the other end of the spectrum, J. K. Stephen or Montague Druitt, neither of whom appeared to have evidenced the possession of any such knowledge.

Philip Sugden concludes his work by suggesting the strongest suspect was George Chapman, nee Severin Klosowski, executed in 1903 for the murder by poison of several wives. Chapman had been Inspector Abberline's favorite likely suspect. Chapman had some medical knowledge gained in Poland, and the deaths of women seemed to follow him from England to America and back. [1] But if he had been the Ripper, he would have had to change his modus operandi from stabbing and mutilation to poisoning, the only murder method for which he was clearly known and convicted. And, his only known violence toward women was toward those with whom he had a relationship.

These theories were prompted not only by the apparent dexterity evident in some of the mutilations but because both mutilations and organ removal took place, except in the case of Kelly, outdoors in very dimly lit areas. Furthermore, they were all done in a very short period, from five to fifteen minutes. The killer would have had to operate primarily by feel, rummaging through the open and mutilated abdomen, identifying the organ he wanted, then removing it quickly with his knife, without cutting himself. The fact that there were many men roaming the streets with little black doctor-type satchels contributed to the plausibility of the theory.

The medical men who examined the victims at the scene and performed the postmortems differed in their opinions. This is well covered by Wilson and Odell. [2]   Dr. Ralph Llewellyn, who performed both services for the murder of Mary Ann Nichols, was of the opinion that: " The murderer must have had some rough anatomical knowledge, for he seemed to have attacked all the vital parts." [3]

Dr. F. Gordon Brown, who with Dr. George Sequeira handled both on-site assistance and the postmortem for the Eddowes murder and who was at the scene of the murder of Kelly, testified at the inquest that some anatomical knowledge was required but changed that assessment to "a good deal" when pressed, basing the opinion on the Ripper's knowledge of organ placement and means of removal.   Dr. Sequeira himself was of the opinion that the killer lacked professional surgical knowledge but was familiar with knives. [4]   Dr. George Phillips was involved in three crime-scene examinations and five postmortems; his opinions are given the greatest weight by both Wilson and Rumbelow.   He believed that the removal of organs with one stroke of the knife reflected the level of knowledge of anatomy and pathological examination such as would be possessed by an expert.

The dissenter among the group was Dr. Thomas Bond, who participated in both examination tasks with Phillips in the Kelly murder and who reviewed the postmortem records of the other victims. In his letter of 10 November 1888, he wrote that in his opinion the Ripper had neither knowledge of anatomy nor science, not even the knowledge that a "butcher or horse slaughterer" would have, nor even one who was accustomed to cut up (dress) dead animals. [5]   Wilson suggests that Bond may have been unduly influenced by the gross mutilation in the Kelly murder as reflective of lack of skill. [6]

One of the aspects of these murders not heavily explored except as Rumbelow touches on it is the deftness of the killing technique.   The sure and thorough slitting of the throats with relatively clean strokes, not quite to the point of removing the head from the body (even if limited by the strength of the spinal column), most likely preceded by strangulation (except perhaps in the Kelly murder) reflects extraordinary planning, control, and knowledge of the death process which would result from the effects of each act. For it was this technique as much as any that kept any victim outcry or struggle from disrupting the grisly task.

The weight of expert opinion — both medical and that of historical investigators — supports the notion that no one would be surprised to find that any final Ripper suspect was knowledgeable of anatomy, surgical technique, and ways to induce death quickly, even if he were not a practitioner by trade.

Did Charles Dodgson possess or have access to such knowledge? To answer that question, we again turn to the work of Jeffrey Stern, *Lewis Carroll's Library*, and draw the inference that the knowledge was readily available. We can also draw the inference that, voracious reader that he was, Dodgson possessed the knowledge.

That Dodgson was interested in medicine as well as preoccupied with concerns about his own health has been accepted by all biographers. Most attribute the interest to an early event in which he came upon a fellow Oxford student suffering from what was believed to be an epileptic fit and was unprepared to help. In his diary entry at the time he attributed the cause of his hesitancy to a lack of knowledge and promptly bought a book on health in order to be more prepared in the future. [7]   Later entries throughout his lifetime reflect that he was in fact able to offer assistance in such cases of fainting, which seem from the entries to have been his preoccupation.

As we examine Stern's work, we find over 120 books on health, medicine, anatomy, surgery, feminine psychology and anatomy, and venereal disease. The way the auction sheets were written, there may have been far more than those listed since the books were wrapped in bundles, usually by subject matter. The sheet would list one or two titles and then add, for example, "and 4 others." Among those lists we find Helmuth's 1873 work *A System of Surgery*, [8]   a bundle which includes "*Animal Physiology, Surgical Emergencies*, and 9 others*," (29), and another "*A System of Surgery, Acton on Prostitution, Lectures on the Progress of Anatomy and Surgery*, and 8 others" (27), Gray's seminal work "*Gray's Anatomy*" (46), and most interesting, "*Premature Death, its Promotion or Prevention*, with Lewis Carroll's markings in two places 1878" (81). These are but a sampling of what anyone would consider a very comprehensive medical library for a mathematician and writer of children's nonsense, even if we must admit that they could represent only a pursuit of knowledge in an era dominated by scientific investigation by a man of genius with many interests.

Perhaps the most curious auction sheet entry in the collection as it relates to the Ripper murders is that which describes in detail a book by J. W. Stapleton titled *The Great Crime of 1860* (70).   The sheet describes the work as a complete account of the infamous "Road Murder," that of a four-year-old boy by the name of Francis Saville Kent. The book includes an appendix which contains the evidence obtained from the inquest and investigations. The English fascination with this crime (a classic "who-done-it") lies in the fact that the youngster, having been last seen when put to bed in the evening, was found dead in the garden outhouse, outside his locked home, with his throat slit.

Stapleton wrote the work in defense of the boy's father, who was a prime suspect for some time, until finally the youth's sixteen-year-old half-sister, Constance, "confessed" from the convent home to which she had been sent. There were questions as to whether she had indeed confessed or whether she was coerced as a condition for her advancement. She claimed the murder of her half brother was an act of revenge against the woman, the family maid, who had taken her mother's place. Constance admitted that she had considered murdering her stepmother, but decided instead to target her cherished child. Constance served several years in prison until released due to public outcry and some lingering doubts that she had acted alone. Historically, Mr. Kent has remained a suspect, due in no small part to the relationships it was whispered he seemed to maintain with the hired female help throughout his life. Constance's stepmother had lived in the home as a nursemaid to the Kent children prior to their marriage. (Bernard Taylor implicates Mr. Kent in his 1979 work *Cruelly Murdered*. [9])

What is interesting is not just that the modus operandi mirrored the Ripper murders, but the amount of detail provided in that work by the doctor/author who was present at the scene and postmortem; for it describes the wounds and their effects in detail.

> [On examination of the bed-blanket in which the body was wrapped] . . . . In some places, and, for the most part, [the blood] was seen in large, irregular, stiffened patches, as if it had flowed over the inside of the blanket in an uninterrupted stream. In a few places it seemed to have fallen with the force, in the direction, and with the interruption, of arterial jets, as if sprinkled or thrown off from a shaken brush. [The nightdress was similarly stained.]
>
> . . . The child's body, stripped of its clothing, presented the following appearance: —
>
> One deep cut severed every structure in the throat — vessels, and nerves, and all — down to the front of the spine. It had been made from left to right; for the blood had gushed out upon the left side and arm — the right arm and side, on the contrary, being almost free of blood. It appeared to have been done by one clean sweep, leaving no notch, and presenting no irregularity in its outline, either upon the skin or upon any of the tissues across which it had been drawn. By its extent, and as to its inevitable and immediate results, this cut amounted, physiologically, to decapitation. It abolished at once all feeling, and prostrated all resistance.

Upon the left side of the body, below and to the outside of the nipple, a sharp blade had been passed diagonally over the fifth rib. Severing wholly the cartilage of the sixth, partially that of the seventh rib, it had been thrust into the chest, behind the membranous covering of the heart, which it had grazed without entering it. It then penetrated the diaphragm, and had grazed the stomach in a similar manner, and without piercing its cavity. In its passage, or during its withdrawal, this blade had been violently twisted or wrenched round, as was evident from the torn appearance of the muscular fibres, and the scraped, irregular appearance of the exposed rib, at the posterior angle of the cut. . . .

[Dr. Stapleton provided Mr. Kent with] assurance that the child had died an instant and comparatively painless death by the cut in the throat. On the part of both [he and a Dr. Parsons] this opinion was fully and unhesitatingly expressed. [10]

Although the cause of death was officially judged to be the cut to the throat, this was later changed, as part of a conspiracy theory, to one of suffocation. Dr. Parsons originated the strangulation theory on the basis that he felt there should have been much larger quantities of blood splashed about the boy's face and presumably the murder scene as well from the heart's pumping effect. Dr. Stapleton never concurred with this opinion, basing his stand on the detailed explanation he provided in the work on how the heart operates under the stress of such a trauma, and from the condition of the mouth and nose.

The parallels of this crime to the Ripper crimes and Dodgson's childhood emotional experiences are extraordinary. In her confession (not reproduced in Stapleton's work, so presumably not known to Dodgson, although he may have detected feelings of abandonment and betrayal in the narrative of events), Constance described how her hatred grew from the time of the marriage, which would have made her eleven years old, the very age in which Dodgson experienced his own felt betrayal in his abandonment to the public school system. The parallel to what I perceive as Dodgson's descent into a life of rage as described in *The Agony of Lewis Carroll* is striking.

. . . I vowed a deadly vengeance, renounced all belief in religion and devoted myself body and soul to the Evil Spirit, invoking his aid in my scheme of revenge. . . . From that time I became a demon always seeking to do evil and to lead others into it, even trying to find an occasion to accomplish my evil design. I found it.´

... Nearly five years have since passed away during which time I have either been in a wild feverish state of mind only happy in doing evil, or else so very wretched that I often could have put an end to myself had means been near at the moment. I felt hatred towards everyone, and a wish to make them as wretched as myself.´ [11]

The Scotland Yard handling of this crime would eventually end up in the politics of the Home Office, and it proved to be the undoing of the investigating detective Mr. Whicher, who doggedly pursued Constance as his suspect. He became the public scapegoat when he brought to public awareness the early police bungling in the case and again when Constance was convicted and punished for a crime which many believed she had not committed.

Is it possible that this sixteen-year-old girl, whose own emotional life had been destroyed at age eleven, became a model of both courage and method for Jack the Ripper?

When we examine the published and unpublished portions of Dodgson's diary, we find just a single snippet that adds to our understanding of the extent to which he knew surgical procedure. But, even more importantly, we can see how thirty years prior to the Ripper murders — on 17 December 1858 — Dodgson attended a surgical procedure which involved the amputation of a leg at the knee and recorded:

... I fully expected to turn ill at the sight, and be forced to go away, and was *much surprised to find that I could bear it perfectly well*. I doubt if I could have done this had the man been suffering pain all the while [he had been given chloroform], but it was quite evident that he felt nothing.

This is an experiment I have long been anxious to make, in order to know whether I might rely on myself to be of any use in cases of emergency, and I am very glad to believe that I might. Still, *I don't think I should enjoy seeing much of it*. (My italics.) [12]

Again, except possibly in the case of Kelly, we have a high likelihood that victims were rendered unconscious before mutilation and savaged in the dimness of secluded back-alleys in the middle of the night where neither police nor the Ripper could see the extent of the carnage. And we see again the self-testing of endurance, the ability to tolerate the penetration and cutting of the human body in a "surgical" procedure. It is the recurring theme of *willing* the self through the experience. In the case of Kelly, who cried out and was mutilated by the fireplace glow, a new testing may have been taking place. And, as we shall see, Jack may have fainted.

This diary entry follows by thirty days Dodgson's musings about the notorious criminal Jack Sheppard. Just what was being hatched that brought these two events together and made the coincidence of the anniversary of Sheppard's execution so noteworthy?

Perhaps the most chilling episode in this investigation occurred in the British Library's newspaper storage facility at Colindale. For, while searching the microfilm for Ripper coverage, I stumbled on a brief notice dated in early October 1888 that Inspector Marshall from Scotland Yard had been sent to Guildford to return with a human limb that had been found there. Investigators wished to determine if it was from the remains of a human trunk that had been discovered in the basement foundation of the new police station being built in Whitehall. Guildford was the town in which the Dodgson sisters lived from 1868 until at least 1898 and which the brother visited often. On 9 October Dr. Bond judged that the limb did not belong to the trunk and was not even of human origin. Pursuit of the notion that this or other body parts reportedly found in the Thames (downstream from Oxford University) might have represented "hands on" efforts at education were deemed beyond the scope of this work, my resources, or the likelihood that sources would grant me access.

As we have already seen, brooding and fantasizing over hurts and hurting are part of the psychological dynamic of killing and mutilation. Constance Kent acknowledged that her brooding search for revenge began from the moment her traumatic event began. Did Dodgson's explode in this form only when his forty-two years of brooding and alternative rage-filled activities failed to satisfy any longer?

Chapter 8

The Urge To Tell

Nowhere in the literature and discussion of the Ripper murders is there mention of those crimes as being "perfect." Yet if we conclude that they were the result of both skilled planning and execution, and not the act of a crazed lunatic acting in an out-of-control frenzy, then these crimes have all the elements of being perfect. One after the other, in the same area of a crowded city increasingly alert to the presence of danger, directed at the same population of women and with increasing savagery, i.e., involving women who became aware that they as a class were targeted, Jack the Ripper entered the scene, did what he set out to do, and disappeared without a trace. Police nets proved to be useless against him. To rub the wound, he taunted the highest level of government (including the Home Office) as well as his would-be captors with well-written letters, a modus operandi which *in itself* suggests a killer having some education, some wit, however perverse, and an obvious cunning.

These were not crimes done in secret, so secret that even the crime itself is not detected. These were not crimes of embezzlement. They were murders, brazenly performed, with clues, however bizarre, however obtuse, left behind. They were crimes committed by someone with all of his intellectual and emotional resources dedicated to one goal and one goal only, the commission of the most heinous violation of women and the psychic representation each victim played as mother-surrogate and a flaunting of that retributive act in the society which had tolerated his own destruction by sexual assault.

But if a perfect crime is committed, and committed repeatedly without detection, will the perpetrator be satisfied if no one knows of his cleverness? Is there an urge to tell? Indeed, is there a compulsion to tell? Did Jack the Ripper tell? And lastly, if we come to believe that Charles Dodgson "told" of the crimes, can we draw the inference in conjunction with a wealth of other circumstantial evidence that *therefore* he was Jack the Ripper? The appearance of a tell-all "diary" signed "Jack the Ripper" in 1993, even though it took some detective work to identify its writer and is considered by many to be a hoax, rides on the notion that telling became an essential dynamic.

There certainly may exist, as part of the same urges one has to share one's successes in a positive endeavor, the urge to share a success in deviousness or outrage. For some the self satisfaction that would come from the execution of criminal acts would be self-restorative; self-esteem would be intact based on accomplishment alone. Such a person, perhaps totally alienated, isolated, and without friends, would have little urge to tell.

However, someone with a few close confidants might be more tempted to seek the awe and admiration forthcoming from such accomplishment; such a person might not be so self-contained in his self-esteem, might need the enhanced social prestige to be gained from the group. The offsetting urge in both of these cases might be the need to protect the self from betrayal of the confidence and the consequences of detection and punishment. For the small group, just one member, might not react with awe but with contempt or fear of involvement due now to knowing, perhaps that this member has "gone too far." So there is the risk of being alienated from the group by placing members in the compromising position of either rejecting the behavior and the friend or of tolerating if not accepting the behavior and retaining the friendship.

There is the urge to tell that might come from lingering guilt and the need to confess and accept the consequences.

There could be an urge to leave the story in a hidden place for later discovery. This could reflect the need for posthumous admiration, condemnation, or the notoriety of both, or, it could satisfy confessional urges without the need to face the consequences in this life.

The urge could be to conceal the story in a place where discovery could occur at any time. This would satisfy the compulsive need for titillation, for continuing the "perfect" crime in a new form by increasing the risk of discovery as an arrogant statement of superiority over those responsible for solving it. This might apply particularly to a person whose already public notoriety in one aspect of his life would protect him from even the most compelling evidence of suspicion and implication.

And lastly, we have the urge written about in 1845 by Edgar Allen Poe, an American contemporary of Dodgson, in his short story "The Imp of the Perverse." This work was unquestionably in the collection of Poe's works which Dodgson owned at his death, as reflected in the library auction sheets. [1]

Poe describes the urge which has no motivation, the urge to do what one knows one should not, the urge to do what one knows will be self-destroying. He writes (in the voice of his character):

> It is impossible that any deed could have been wrought
> with more thorough deliberation. For weeks, for months, I
> pondered upon the means of the murder. I rejected a

thousand schemes, because their accomplishment involved a *chance* of detection. [Having finally committed the perfect crime] I would perpetually find myself pondering upon my impunity and security, and very frequently would catch myself repeating, in a low, under-tone, the phrases "I am safe — I am safe."

... One day, while sauntering listlessly about the streets, I arrested myself in the act of murmuring, half aloud, these customary syllables. In a fit of petulance at my indiscretion I re-modelled them thus: — "I am safe — I am safe — yes, *if I do not prove fool enough to make open confession.*"

No sooner had I uttered these words, than I felt an icy chill creep into my heart. (Poe's italics.) [2]

It was the Imp of the Perverse that had entered his consciousness and that chased him thereafter, a "formless shadow that seemed to dog my footsteps, approaching me from behind, with a cat-like and stealthy pace" until breathless and suffocating from holding in the words, he blurted out the confession that "consigned me to the hangman and to hell." [3]

Perhaps the one incontrovertible conclusion of *The Agony of Lewis Carroll* is that Dodgson used his entire body of literature to disclose in a concealed way his own sexuality, experiences, and the expressions of rage aimed at his parents and surviving family, a rage driven by the nature of those disclosures. He told how the sexual assaults began at age eleven when he entered public school and continued there for the duration of his stay. And he told of the "gay" prostitute-like behaviors that became so much a part of his inner world, if not his practice. And he told in vivid imagery of the contempt he had for his mother and women in general as he used the little girl friends to hone his skills.

It was in his character to tell. I believe it became his goal to tell all. It is clear that he worked with at least two others in the development of the material hidden in his books for he appears to have done all his other work with just two other people — Thomas Vere Bayne and, for a while at least, Henry Parry Liddon. [4] There is reason to suspect that he may have broadened this circle, however, and we will return to that question when we explore how and why the murder spree ended. But would he also work with others to disclose these murders if he or they committed them?

For Dodgson it would not be the Imp of the Perverse that would cause a "blurting out" of the story. He was already too sophisticated at hiding things in his literature. This practice and technique also served not only as a safe place in a hypocritical environment which required public denial of his sexuality but also as a means of self-titillation, in total defiance of the dangers inherent in being discovered. And it served as a constant reassurance of his continuing an abiding superiority over others. It was, above all, an arrogant assumption that the facade he had created in the *Alice* books would keep him above criticism even if someone discovered disturbing things in these works. It is, in fact, a facade that has kept him safe for over a hundred years despite the long-held interpretive conclusions that an ugliness lay beneath the surface. No one wants to believe anything about him other than the image that *he* created.

If we find the same self-disclosing anagrammatic constructions in the works Dodgson published after the murders, can we infer their veracity or is there the possibility that they represent a game he was playing with readers and researchers? If we conclude that the anagrams are not just this writer's creations and that the historical facts which appear in them were placed there intentionally, where did he get them? Was it necessary for him to be present? If he took them from published material — i.e., newspapers of the day — was it a fascination with the crimes that had him include them in his works? By including them as if he had performed them, would he be satisfying a wish to do them even if lacking the will or means?

The answers to these questions represented the focus of my trip to England to research a possible link between Dodgson and the Ripper murders. As we examine the material in his works in the next chapters, we must condition everything with the irrefutable assertion that everything found in them could have been found in the newspapers of the day.

This world of anagrams is certainly an unreal world and for it to become real, there is a demand for rigorous consistency in accepting the themes which emerge. But there is a very valuable "assist" which comes in the material to be examined as it relates to these murders. For, unlike the work done for *The Agony of Lewis Carroll*, when on just a few occasions there were illustrations to hint at the theme of the anagram, hints which insured that the theme was not just the creation of the solver, hints here seem to be more universally present.

In chapter II of *Sylvie and Bruno*, published in 1889, Dodgson the mathematician wrote in the words of one of his characters (characters and sentiments he always denied were his own) the suggestion that books should be treated like algebra. Each sentence should be reduced, i.e., rearranged, to its "least common multiple."

. . . if we could only *apply* that Rule to books! You know, in finding the Least Common Multiple, we strike out a

> . . . if we could only *apply* that Rule to books! You know,
> in finding the Least Common Multiple, we strike out a
> quantity wherever it occurs, except in the term where it is
> raised to its highest power. So we should have to erase every
> recorded thought, except in the sentence where it is expressed
> with the greatest intensity. [5]

This "search for intensity" will be the rule followed as we examine
Dodgson's nonsense — and some of the serious works — published after
1888. But there will be one variation on that rule, a rigid rule in
anagrammatic construction. While *themes* will be reduced to as few as
possible, the number of letters *must* not be reduced, must always be
used, must never be discarded. In this effort the intensity will be
obtained, not from elimination of material, but purely from rearrangement of the letters.

What we will find is a consistency of content. Most importantly, we
will often find thematic clues for the anagrams-to-be-derived in the clear
text. These clues allow us to answer nearly every open question from
the Ripper investigation. It will be left for the reader to conclude
whether what we find is truly self-disclosure, a game Dodgson was
playing with a notorious crime, exactly the game he had been playing for
years in his other books, or something imaginary on my part.

I categorically reject for one simple reason the notion that Dodgson
was playing a game with his reading public by implicating himself falsely
in the crimes. If the Ripper crimes had in fact been solved, with a
suspect captured, legitimately convicted and punished, such an elaborate
fabrication would have turned a private joke, a joke he *hid* in his works,
on himself. For Dodgson to have left open this possibility is totally
inconsistent with his thoroughness in detail, planning, and obsession
with assaulting society, not himself. That aside, however, the presence
and likely truthfulness of the material is only another piece in the totality of the argument which must include knowledge (which we have
seen), motive (which we have seen), and opportunity (which we shall
see).

Chapter 9

The Nursery "Alice"

While Charles Dodgson does not seem to have come under the spell of the Imp of the Perverse by blurting out his story, it appears he lost no time in bringing works to the public which I believe contain his version of the Ripper murders. The first and most primary of these is *The Nursery "Alice"*. This re-telling of his *Alice's Adventures in Wonderland* for children "nought to five" as he wrote in the Preface, to be read while snuggled in the mother's lap, provides the earliest evidence of hidden material on the Ripper theme.

The history of *The Nursery "Alice"* is an intriguing one. For while his diary of 29 March 1885, contains the first mention of plans to write such a book among a list of fifteen other projects, and his entry of 10 July of that same year notes that the selected illustrations from the original were in the process of being colored by their artist, John Tenniel, there is no further mention of the work until 28 December 1888, a week after the murder of Rose Mylett. He notes in that entry that he had begun the text, and on 20 February 1889, just two months later, that the last of the manuscript had been sent off to his publisher, Macmillan. Again on 18 April he notes that final proofs had been checked. Uncertainty remains as to whether Tenniel himself or someone else actually did the coloring of the illustrations. [1]

What happened after that reflects Dodgson's typical and obsessive attention to the details of production. He rejected the first edition of ten thousand copies off the press because the colors were too gaudy and finally disposed of them in America and elsewhere (despite American objections that they were not gaudy enough!). Subsequent covers were off-center, then the next batch cracked and curled. Finally, on 25 March 1890, a full year later, copies acceptable to him were in the hands of the public. [2]

Whether these diversions were intentional as part of an effort to keep his publisher distracted, reflected some hesitance at publishing the hidden disclosures, or merely personal pique, in effect they helped retain his public image as a perfectionist in all things. For just as no one had noticed that the title of one of his earliest adolescent publications, printed with his parents' guidance and approval — *The Rectory Umbrella* — was, by letter rearrangement, an anagram for "Re Rectum/Ball Theory," or that *The Nursery "Alice"* itself is an anagram for "Her cunt! Leer, I say!" neither did anyone notice that his dedicatory poem "A Nursery Darling" is an anagram for "Re Urinary Glands" or that its first line "A mother's breast" is an anagram for "A brother's meats" with *re* proper without the colon for "regarding" and *meats* Victorian slang for male sexual organs.

I had originally bypassed much of this work in the preparation of *The Agony of Lewis Carroll* after finding a continued presence of themes found in the other works. Without a doubt the pivotal event in this search for the Ripper occurred with my discovery of the poem "I'm not a butcher. . . ; But I'm your own light-hearted friend. . . ." and its anagrammatic re-working. It was a much later discovery in *The Nursery "Alice"* that brought about a change in theme search for I found what appeared a clear and intentional but easily dismissed inconsistency. This discovery was then followed by others.

Readers may find much of the following tedious, but this aspect of the evidence is built on nuances and subtleties in Dodgson's stories. They must be presented thoroughly to provide both credibility and tools for the use of others who may wish to pursue the search further.

The first inconsistencies are in the illustrations themselves. Several of them have undergone minute changes, changes not heretofore noticed or at least not mentioned by others if they were noticed. Whether these changes were made due to artistic considerations related to the addition of color or for other reasons, readers are left to decide as they are pointed out. Unfortunately first and second editions of *The Nursery "Alice"* are rare, and high quality reproduction of the illustrations was not possible in the preparation of this work, although an examination of a first edition copy was done. For ease of reference, chapter and page numbers for the quoted portions are in the text in brackets.

The pivotal inconsistency relates to the illustration which opens chapter XI of *The Nursery "Alice"* and chapter VIII of *Alice's Adventures in Wonderland*; it is the latter that is reproduced on the following page. Three worried-looking playing card gardeners, each holding a paint brush, are standing beneath a white rose tree, as they busily paint the flowers red. The Queen of Hearts is coming to inspect what she had ordered to be red rose trees and the gardeners are hastily trying to change the color of the flowers on this single white rose tree planted in error. A conversation is taking place between the gardeners as each blames the other for the mistake and for splashing paint on themselves in their haste. The cards (as gardeners) are each named by the number that is appropriate: Five, Two, and Seven.

In *The Nursery "Alice"* the sign of spilled paint which was represented by shading in the original has been removed from the playing card bodies, leaving them unstained. They are all clean except for a single drop of red paint which can be seen falling from the brush being held by Seven. As one would, the "paint" is dripping from the brush, or from "the painting instrument." Dodgson then adds a new paragraph which appears nowhere in the original version yet is deceptively familiar, because in the original "Five" is the first speaker.

> You see there were *five* large white roses on the tree —
> such a job to get them all painted red! But they've got three
> and a half done, now, and if only they wouldn't stop to talk —
> work away, little men, *do* work away! Or the Queen will be
> coming before it's done! And if she finds any *white* roses on
> the tree, do you know what will happen? It will be "Off with
> their heads!" Oh, work away, my little men! Hurry, hurry!
> [*Nursery "Alice"* Chapter XI, 43]

The italics which emphasize the presence of *five* white roses on the tree are Dodgson's. What the illustration clearly shows in both colored and original versions is that there are six roses on the tree with, as he says, three and a half painted red. (It is interesting that renditions by other publishers paint more red than the text supports.) What appears to be an apparent contempt for his readers and their historical acceptance of everything he says on its face value, is, I believe, a clue that the paragraph itself, is a construct, an extended anagram. For it was not five roses from the white rose tree that were being painted red, but five street whores. Not who were *being* painted red, but who, by the time this was written in late 1888, had already been painted red. Reassembling the letters we derive a familiar sounding but quite different paragraph:

> Dodgson and Bayne seethe, tune, hone a weird way —
> any way — to laud my father's holy work and let the hate
> vent. We plot how to kill dirty women, knife to throat. You
> see, to them it is such a large job to get five street whores all
> painted red.
> If I find one street whore, you know what will happen!
> 'Twill be `Off with her head!´"
> "Work away! Hurry, hurry! Or the Queen's little men
> will be coming before he's done!"

Painting the White Rose Tree

Source: *Alice's Adventures in Wonderland*, Chapter VIII.

This reconstruction of Dodgson's original paragraph responds to a number of the dynamics involved in his "personality and the Ripper murders. It suggests the search for the bizarre, a way that would provide shock and notoriety. It suggests cunning, plotting, preceded by a long-lasting brooding hate that had already seethed for a lifetime. And it identifies the object of that hate: women. In total disdain for his churchman father's efforts to reduce sin, we see the death of "sinners" chosen as a "holy" task. Finally, in a chilling reminder of the interminable cry of the castrating Queen of Hearts (Queen of Haters?), the near removal of their heads will be the method of destruction and, presumably, of psychological freedom from that metaphorical castration. The phrase "Queen's little men" reflects the disdain for government officials and police already evidenced by the Ripper letters.

If we were to capitalize *Father* in the anagrammatic solution, we would be touching the very limits of Dodgson's struggle with all-good and all-evil, with God and the devil. In many ways, drawing from what appears to have been his mythological model for survival, the Greek youth Orestes, who killed his mother in response to a command of the god Apollo, Dodgson may have brought himself virtually to that point of divine communication. In contrast to that, yet reinforcing self justification for his actions, he appears to have developed a religious belief that evil deeds, even the consummately evil deeds of the devil (who Dodgson's writings reflect he believed was potentially redeemable) worked to enhance the saving power of Christ's redemptive act. This anagrammatic solution suggests that he may have reached the point in his stress and need to rationalize his every act that these atrocities were not only justifiable, but positively good.

In the second inconsistency within this story and its illustrations, we examine Alice's visit with the Cheshire cat in chapter IX. Presented on the facing page are the portion of the illustration that shows Alice peering at the cat in the tree. The original from *Alice's Adventures in Wonderland* is on the left, the modified version on the right. Two things are different. Alice has been given a head-piece, most likely to add the touch of color, but her cheeks and nose in profile from the right side have been removed.

In an earlier illustration of Alice confronting a giant dog, Alice's left face half-profile is kept intact just a few pages prior, with just the bow added. So, it would appear that the needs of color were not the deciding factor for the change.

Alice and the Cheshire Cat

Source: Alice's Adventure in Wonderland, Chapter VI and The Nursery
"Alice," Chapter IX.

In chapter IX of *The Nursery "Alice"*, Dodgson describes Alice: "Doesn't Alice look very prim, holding her head so straight up, and with her hands behind her, just as if she were going to say her lessons to the Cat!" (Chapter IX, 33). But when he ends the chapter by suggesting that the corner of the page be lifted to reveal the same figure of Alice peering at the only part of the Cheshire Cat remaining in the tree — its grin — he writes: "If you turn up the corner of this leaf, you'll have Alice looking at the Grin: and she doesn't look a bit more frightened than when she was looking at the Cat, *does* she?" (Chapter IX, 36).

The inconsistency here, accentuated by the total removal of Alice's face from the illustration, is the fact that it is impossible to determine if Alice had been frightened at all, never mind "more" frightened in the second situation. (Of course there is humor in the fact that since the very same picture of Alice is there when the corner of the leaf is turned up, no change in Alice's demeanor could be possible anyway.) But why *frightened* when fright would require the observation of the face or a clearly defensive posture?

If we rework that paragraph, we can see that Dodgson is leading us, not to the two g-r-i-n-s of the Cheshire Cat, but to the two r-i-n-g-s that were removed from the body of Annie Chapman on the 8th of September.

> O, he hung a stiff twine tightly around the whore's neck
> like a ritual death, then as one last Voodoo Gehenna flourish
> he placed combs at her feet. I only took rings.

The mysterious symbols that surrounded Chapman's murder have baffled writers as much as they did the police and media people at the time. This could only be the work of the devil. Chapman, of all the victims, had had her intestines, by some accounts lifted, by others thrown, up to her shoulder and tied in place with a cord around her neck. Two rings had been wrenched from her fingers and taken away. Her combs had been placed at her feet in what appeared to be a conscious arrangement. Chapman was so poor it was believed the coins found among her possessions had been given to her by the Ripper. [3] What could it all mean?

The placement of Chapman's intestines on her shoulder was arguably a part of Masonic ritual murder; the cord was not, but served the purpose of holding them there, of completing the tableau. *Gehenna* was another word for *Hell*, and totally consistent with the "From Hell" letters. Dodgson had written on the subject of hell, including fine distinctions among the various words that had been used from biblical

times, including *Gehenna.* [4]   Turning again to his library, we find
items on the devil: an engraving by J. Noel Paton titled "Christ and
Satan," a work on demon possession, and "Magick, A system of, or, a
History of the Black Art; being a historical Account of Mankind's most
early Dealings with the Devil; and how the Acquaintance on both sides
first began." [5]

Dodgson did not have to turn to pagan ritual, however, to associate
this murder with the devil. What was good enough for the Prince of
Wales was good enough for an Oxford don. As a Royal Arch Mason, the
prince gave allegiance at his induction, not only to the Christian God,
but to Baal, the pagan god or devil in Israelite history. [6]   This oath
was one of many things revealed in Dodgson's source for Masonic
secrets. It may also have been an oath his father swore to even as he
served his church.

The Ripper's use of these symbols did not go unnoticed in the
media; and the notion that someone demon-possessed was at large in
London contributed to the panic, not only in the East End, but in the
West. As the *Times* editorialized on the 9 September:

> . . . malignant insanity. . . a monster is abroad. . . defy all
> rules of nature. . . utter absence of a moral sense with the
> most finished cunning in the adaptation of means to ends. . .
> suggests a mind completely off its balance — [then in
> somewhat Darwinian terms] that is quite undershaped on one
> side. . . . The police have to find for us one of the most
> extraordinary monsters known to the history of mental and
> spiritual disease, a monster whose skull will have to be cast for
> all the surgical museums of the world. [7]

There was, however, no mention of the symbolism as Masonic in nature.
Perhaps Sir Charles Warren began to put things together three weeks
later when the word *Juwes* appeared following the double event.
Stephen Knight put great weight on Coroner Wynne Baxter's testimony
that the rings had disappeared, part of his argument that someone did
recognize some significance and destroyed the evidence. [8]

The savagery as something beyond that conceivable in a civilized
society was noted further in the *Times* of 9 September:

> . . . The murders wreaked with an elaborate savagery,
> unheard of in cases where life-long misery has found sudden
> vent in homicidal fury, and only conceivable, heretofore, in the
> blood-thirsty orgies of cannibals. [9]

Is there a connection between Dodgson's inclusion of the illustration of the Cheshire Cat's "grin," "rings," and the third anagram (our Rule of Three appearing again) to be derived from the letter writer with the strange name of "P.S.R. Lunigi" — "Plus, I grin"?

There was much concern regarding the motives that caused the Ripper to leave the murder scenes with parts of his victims, especially the uterus. Although fairly quickly dismissed, there had been a rumor that the Ripper was selling them to doctors or laboratories for experimentation, possibly in response to an advertisement by an American which appeared in the newspapers. [10]   In the note to Mr. Lusk, the Ripper claimed to have eaten part of the kidney that he had returned with the letter. Did the destruction of womanhood that these crimes represented include the consumption of the symbol of womanhood, the oral incorporation of the at-once loved and despised representation of femininity and motherhood? Is it possible that the consumption of a uterus could represent the most distorted wish for the hated and loved feminine sexuality which would have saved Dodgson from the trauma of homosexual assault experienced at public school and a life of alienation which followed?

Even Martin Gardner wonders in his Introduction to *The Nursery "Alice"* why Dodgson had introduced a dull digression about a dog named Dash that didn't like his birthday treat of oatmeal porridge. This segment in chapter VI tells how some children tried to feed porridge to their pet, warning it not to be greedy, only to find that it refused to eat it at all, at which point they forced it down the dog's throat with a spoon. Is it any wonder that analysts see a great deal of sadistic violence in Dodgson's works, and this added apparently gratuitously for children "nought to five"? The paragraph which closes a discussion of how Dash deserves a birthday treat ends thusly:

> So we went to the cook, and we got her to make a saucerful of nice oatmeal-porridge. And then we called Dash into the house, and we said "Now, Dash, you're going to have your birthday treat!" We expected Dash would jump for joy: but it didn't, one bit! (Chapter VI, 24)

With a similar theme of cooking, of a rejected treat followed by a spiteful act against the integrity of the object of attention, we have, in an anagrammatic reconstruction of the passage:

> Oh, we, Thomas Bayne, Charles Dodgson, coited into the slain, nude body, expected to taste, devour, enjoy a nice meal of a dead whore's uterus. We made do, found it awful — wan and tough like a worn, dirty, goat hog. We both threw it out.
> — Jack the Ripper.

Hog appears to have been used by Dodgson for *penis* although this more modern slang meaning is not recognized by dictionaries of the day, in which *hog* meant "a dirty fellow." If this is real, and I believe there is too much coincidence in it for it not to be, both in theme and names, this scene would most likely have occurred during the estimated two hours with Mary Ann Kelly and represented a possible reason for the large fire in the fireplace. On the other hand, the autopsy report verified that only the heart was missing, with particular emphasis on the uterus as being present. [11] This would mean that the uterus used in this scene would have been from another victim.

Perhaps an equally likely scenario is that the entire scene is not based on reality, but was rather incorporated only for its shock effect and to meet needs of anagram construction of a fantasy or combination of time and events performed elsewhere, as in a safe haven.

A theme that recurs in Dodgson's works is that of the little baby boy who turns into a pig while in Alice's arms. This transformation becomes something else in his last work *Sylvie and Bruno Concluded* when the pig-like son of the Vice Warden turns into a prickly porcupine. We shall return to that symbolism in the following chapter.

The original version of this segment appears in chapter VI of *Alice's Adventures in Wonderland*. The Duchess has tossed the baby to Alice and told her to nurse it.

> . . . The poor little thing was snorting like a steam-engine when she caught it, and kept doubling itself up and straightening itself out again, so that altogether, for the first minute or two, it was as much as she could do to hold it.
>
> As soon as she had made out the proper way of nursing it (which was to twist it up into a sort of knot, and then keep tight hold of its right ear and left foot, so as to prevent its undoing itself), she carried it out into the open air. "If I don't take this child away with me," thought Alice, "they're sure to kill it in a day or two. Wouldn't it be murder to leave it behind?" (Carroll, *Alice's Adventures in Wonderland*, Green, ed., Chapter VI, 57)

Soon the baby began to grunt and became increasingly violent. Finally Alice realized that the baby had turned into a pig.

> So she set the little creature down, and felt quite relieved to see it trot away quietly into the wood. "If it had grown up," she said to herself, "it would have made a dreadfully ugly child: but it makes rather a handsome pig, I think." And she began thinking over other children she knew, who might do very well as pigs, and was just saying to herself "if one only knew the right way to change them — " [at which point she met the Cheshire Cat]. (Carroll, *Alice's Adventures in Wonderland*, Chapter VI, 31)

When we reach chapter VIII in *The Nursery "Alice"*, we get a slightly different telling, and the paragraph which describes the treatment of the baby boy before transformation is untypically awkward. It also drips with the sadistic method of holding a child (very different than depicted on page xvi from *Alice's Adventures*) and identifies the baby as ugly now, not something that would become ugly if allowed to grow.

> So she wandered away, through the wood, carrying the ugly little thing with her. And a great job it was to keep hold of it, it wriggled about so. But at last she found out that the *proper* way was, to keep tight hold of its left foot and its right ear. (Chapter VIII, 31)

The italics for "proper" are Dodgson's, and with a single letter replaced — an "*i*" for an "*o*" (using the game of Doublets) — we have an anagram for *ripper*, the Ripper way.

By rearranging the letters in the entire paragraph we have:

> She wriggled about so! But at last Dodgson and Bayne found a way to keep a hold of the fat little whore. I got a tight hold of her and slit her throat, left ear to right. It was tough, wet, disgusting, too. So weary with it, they threw up.
> — Jack the Ripper

Is this a less awkward paragraph than the original? Is it coincidence again that the appropriate names appear?

This would most likely describe the murder of Kelly, who was young and wholesome, unlike the others who were older and weakened from the wear and tear of street life. She was heavy, although not unattractive. Among all the victims, she was the one heard clearly to cry out "O, murder!" Perhaps there was a brief struggle in the dimly lighted room as she became suddenly aware that she was about to meet the same fate as the others. Observers at the scene were taken aback by the horror apparent in her eyes, virtually the only part of her body not mutilated nearly beyond human recognition.

This focus on the boy who became a pig would resurface on 2 July 1890, when Dodgson introduced *The Wonderland Postage-Stamp Case*. This little four inch by three inch contrivance for storing postage stamps of various denominations consists of an envelope with a picture of Alice and the baby on the front, the Cheshire Cat on the back. When one removes the contents, one finds the stamp holder which has Alice holding the pig on the front and just the Cheshire Cat's smile on the back.

Is it coincidence that the anagrams to be formed from the title during the period when the investigation had cooled are: "Don't stop case! The male nag's warped!" or "Don't stop case! Snag the warped male!" The theme of this anagram is totally consistent with the theme of the transformation into a pig that appears on the covers.

By this time the police effort, which had continued well into 1889, spurred on by the murder of Alice McKenzie on 17 July, had begun to die down. Some authorities were already convinced that Kelly had been the last Ripper victim, and, given the ghastliness of the mutilations, had without question driven the murderer to insanity and most probably suicide. Sir Melville Macnaghten's notes published well after his death indicated that he was quite certain that Montague Druitt's suicide in late December 1888 represented the end of the Ripper. As one still very much involved in the direction the investigation took in 1889, there certainly would be little life in any further police work at the top of the force. [12]

The Wonderland Postage-Stamp Case was accompanied by Dodgson's publication of "Eight or Nine Wise Words about Letter-Writing." [13] This short piece opens with an explanation for the possible uses of the postage stamp case and then proceeds to describe a number of ways to make letter-writing both easy, effective, and courteous. Williams, Madan, and Green, the editors of the *Lewis Carroll Handbook*, a volume that provides valuable insights into the details of Dodgson's publications, question the lack of precision in the title.

> It is odd that Dodgson the Mathematician should call the wise words "Eight or Nine," giving in some sense the impression of precision, and in some sense of doubt, for the rules are

precisely nine or thirteen, and the sections (in the first edition) five. [14]

Is it possible that the lack of precision is a clue that the title is in fact deceptive, that its true meaning lies in the anagram: "O, we grew tired of bowing. True, I slit nine throats."

It would hardly be unfair to characterize the relationship of don to Dean as one of subservience or to suggest that Dodgson and Bayne felt treated that way. While we have yet to examine fully the diaries kept by Bayne and Dodgson, Bayne recorded little of importance, but did include entries that possessed some sarcasm. He notes in his entry for Christmas Day 1888 that Dean Liddell, Alice's father, had paid him a compliment. When Bayne had told him he would go mad if he had to order dinner daily as they did at Radley (School), the Dean responded, "No you would do it `with admirable method and the imperturbable aplomb which is characteristic of you´" [15] As we'll see, there appear other references to "bowing."

But would "nine" have been correct in July 1890? It is possible, but from the historical count of victims not likely. The first two, Emma Smith and Martha Tabram were penetrated or stabbed, but their throats were not cut. The next five, considered to be certain Ripper victims, had their throats cut in the trademark fashion. This would leave Rose Mylett (20 December), Alice McKenzie, and an unidentified trunk of a woman found on 10 September 1889, which makes eight. So, we can only reach nine by the inclusion of all suspected victims, and then assume one more who was not found up to that date.

One possible alternative is the eight-year-old boy found in Portsmouth on 26 October 1888, five days after another "Dear Boss" letter was received, postmarked in Portsmouth. It indicated that Jack the Ripper would not be found in London. A young friend of the victim, whose bloody knife found near the scene was believed to link him to the crime, was tried but acquitted. A witness at the time reported seeing a tall thin man running away while another reported the fleeing man wore a top hat and carried a black bag. [16] The physical description fits Dodgson perfectly. Portsmouth is accessible by train from London. The diaries reflect that Dodgson was at Oxford during this period.

Another possibility is an eight-year-old boy by the name of John Gill who was murdered and mutilated in Bradford on 28 December 1888. The *Pall Mall* wrote on the 29th "WORSE THAN THE WORST OF THE EAST-END CRIMES." The *Times* on the 30th reported the mutilations in detail. Nearly every limb had been removed and the abdomen opened up with internal organs removed, some of them missing, some of them in quasi-ritual positions. The boy's ears were missing. There is no mention of whether or not the throat was cut or whether the head was also severed from the body. [17]

Another possible alternative is that the ninth victim was still forthcoming — Frances Coles. Or, yet again, unidentified victims may have been used to hone skills and experiment on organ location and removal may have been included in the count.

I have no definite explanation, and leave the anagram as derived.

The next anagram examined in *The Nursery "Alice"* occurs in chapter VI when Alice meets the puppy, Dash, much larger than herself since she has shrunk from eating a piece of the magic cake. She hides behind a thistle for fear of being run over. In the earlier *Alice* work, Dodgson leaves it at that — "to keep herself from being run over." But in *The Nursery "Alice"* he changes it by adding the sentence: "That would have been just about as bad, for *her*, as it would be for *you* to be run over by a waggon [sic] and four horses!" (*Nursery Alice*, Chapter VI, 22)

I am deviating from one of the rules for anagrammatic construction by selecting in this case an unmarked phrase, i. e., not a complete paragraph, sentence, or phrase in italics or quotes. But the fact that the added description "waggon and four horses" is an anagram for "four nag whores' gonads" could not be ignored given the other material and given the allusion in the story of what the dog would have done to Alice if it had attacked her or of having to experience being run over or over-run with them.

There are two other areas in the story that are worthy of note. In chapter IV Dodgson describes the Caucus Race as the way all the animals can increase their activity and dry off after swimming in the pool created by Alice's tears. When the race is over, all participants must have prizes. Alice searches in her pockets and distributes comfits to everyone, but there is then no prize for her. She did have, however, a thimble. The Dodo (long believed to be a Dodgson "self" character which played on his stammer on his name Do-Do-Dodgson) tells Alice "Hand it over here!" She does; then he hands it back to her as her prize. In the original *Alice*, Dodgson writes that "Alice thought the whole thing was absurd" but since the others were serious in cheering her, she just made a short bow and the scene changed.

In *The Nursery "Alice"* Dodgson adds a paragraph:

Wasn't *that* a curious sort of present to give her? Suppose they wanted to give *you* a birthday-present, would you rather they should go to your toy-cupboard, and pick out your nicest doll, and say "Here, my love, here's a lovely birth-day-present for you!" or would you like them to give you something *new*, something that *didn't* belong to you before? (*The Nursery "Alice"*, Chapter IV, 16)

At the inquest in the murder of Catherine Eddowes, Dr. Frederick G. Brown testified:

> The body was on its back, the head turned to left shoul-der, the arms by the side of the body as they had fallen there, both palms upwards, the fingers slightly bent. A thimble was lying off the fingers on the right side. . . [followed by a detailed description of the wounds]. [18]

Was there a thimble in Eddowes hand prior to and at the moment of death? And if so, why? Or, had a thimble been removed from her pocket and placed there intentionally as a clue? Was she in fact given a "gift" of her own thimble to replicate, to bring to real life, this addition to the *Alice* story?

Or, did this thimble answer to a much more sinister verse from *The Hunting of the Snark: An Agony in Eight Fits* which opens each of the last four "fits" or stanzas of the poem:

> They sought it with thimbles, they sought it with care:
> They pursued it with forks and hope;
> They threatened its life with a railway-share;
> They charmed it with smiles and soap.

In the poem, the Baker, among all the travelers considered to be the Dodgson "self" character by all critics, disappears without a trace from what appears to be a totally annihilating experience and what I believe is a veiled description of anal penetration committed by the Snark, a conclusion supported by the hidden material. Did Dodgson, in retribution for his mother's abandonment of him to the sexual assault of public school become the Snark, and visit his own penetration on these prostitutes as mother surrogates, as surrogates for the "baker" of the tarts in the *Alice* stories — the Queen of Hearts? Several of the Ripper victims were attacked in the rectum as well as the vagina. Rumbelow reports that Eddowes was "ripped open from the rectum." [19] But it is uncertain if this was the initial point of entry in a possible reenactment of the sodomy theme evident in the Snark.

The thimble was a common possession of the street women, who generally carried all their belongings with them, for this was an essential instrument for repairing the little clothing they had, often just what they were wearing. Mary Ann Nichols, the first victim receiving any real attention, had a comb, handkerchief and broken mirror in her pocket. [20]   Annie Chapman had her rings removed and the contents of her pockets had been emptied onto the ground — some muslin, a paper case with two pills, and a comb, the money most probably provided by the Ripper. We do not know the contents of Elizabeth Stride's pockets.   Catherine Eddowes was relatively well off as her pockets revealed clay pipes, some sugar and tea, a comb, some soap, a knife and teaspoon, two empty containers, some material and string, and a few pins and needles. [21]   For some reason the thimble had been removed from the pocket and was in or had been placed by her hand. Or, it had been given to her as part of the ploy of engagement.

We see a pattern emerge as we progress through the murders. Medical examination detected bruises around Mary Ann Nichol's neck, signs of a struggle, most likely during efforts to strangle her. Annie Chapman also had bruises on her chin and throat. [22]   Elizabeth Stride had no neck wounds but was still clutching "a small packet of cachous wrapped in tissue paper." [23]   Catherine Eddowes was found with a thimble next to her hand. Had the Ripper found a way to occupy his victims hands and avoid the struggle? Had he given them something to be clutched and treasured, something maybe even more valuable than the immediate protection of their own lives? Did the "comfits" and thimble have another purpose as well, that of providing a clue to Ripper identity? Was this thimble the "curious present" that had been taken from Eddowes's pocket or "toy cupboard" and returned to her as a gift? Or had the Ripper asked if he could borrow it and then given it back? I suggest it might be stretching credulity too far to believe that among all the items in her pocket this could have been identified and removed in those hasty moments in the dark, without removing any of the other contents.

But it is curious that both victims of the "double event," which we shall see had a curious relationship with Dodgson's "Rule 42 of the Code," first introduced in *Alice's Adventures in Wonderland*, had the very gifts from the *Alice* stories in or by their hands.

Before leaving *The Nursery "Alice"* there is one additional difference in the story worthy of note (although I suspect more could be found with additional work). Chapter XIII opens the finale to the story which focuses on the trial of the Knave of Hearts for having stolen the queen's tarts. Interpretations of this ending focus on the search for identity as the primary theme of the entire story. This interpretation is seen in the evidence produced at the trial, which is a lengthy nonsense poem that totally confuses identity. It is seen in the Queen's call for punishment before a crime is even committed, never mind proven, a most likely reference to the extremely restrictive childhood Dodgson experienced and also to his homosexuality, whose practices were crimes at the time, and whose acknowledgement was therefore risky, even though secretly condoned. As we have seen, Colin Wilson particularly, as I do, views these murders as existential in nature, as an effort to break a smothering and self-destroying mother-bond. Contrary to Wilson, however, I see them as crimes of rage, with the sexual content a means of manifesting rage, but not as out-of-control carnal desire for a woman.

Having noted similarity in motive and ending, let us return to our story. In the original version (Chapter XI, 146), a parchment-scroll was presented that contained the written charges:

> The Queen of Hearts, she made some tarts:
>   All on a summer day:
> The Knave of Hearts, he stole those tarts,
>   And took them quite away! [24]

In Dodgson's new version of the story, there is no parchment scroll; instead there is a *song*. [25]   I believe the reason for the change to a song points to another crucial work which was also published in 1889, the first of the *Sylvie* works, *Sylvie and Bruno*. (This title, too, appears to have been an anagram, one which reflected a difficult life finally concluding — "O, sly, vain burden.") This song, "The Gardener's Song" becomes the focus of the next chapter.

Tarts also has a number of meanings appropriate for Victorian times, meanings which include "fag students from public school" (especially those chosen for or who provided sexual services) as well as "loose women." (It is even possible that Dodgson had been called a "harsh demented tart" by the illustrator of his *Sylvie* books, Harry Furniss, as the anagram formed on a phrase from Shakespeare's *Hamlet* already discussed suggests. [26])   Did this crime of the Knave of Hearts take on a new meaning as the tarts were taken "quite away on a summer day"? The Ripper spree was at its height in the late summer of 1888. Coincidentally, Furniss was writing about them for his newspaper.

Is the sexual nature of these crimes against womanhood reflected in the mother-killing symbolism of masturbation which emerges when the two sentences that refer to the charges as a *song* are rearranged? Are Dodgson's italics in these sentences clues that they should not only be examined more closely, but an indication that the word does not really fit with the story, which never had any music? He writes in chapter XIII after presenting the song:

> Well, yes, the *Song* says so. But it would never do to punish the poor Knave, just because there was a *Song* about him. (*The Nursery "Alice"*, Chapter XIII, 49)

But in its re-working we have:

> O, yes, the gay son swells so! But as blood gushes out, even I shun a view, masturbate onto the wound. — Jack the Ripper.

This imagery is totally consistent with theories on sexual crimes already reviewed. In such crimes, sexual arousal derives from the killing and consequent mutilation of the bodies, at its worst in the handling of belly contents and inner organs. Rage at powerlessness in the face of the overwhelming but betraying mother-image kills, and, as Wilson points out, these murders were compulsive, [27] driven by spite. And it is spite that mutilates. [28] Sexual stimulation is the feeling state that is used to restore the sense of power, of self.

As Dodgson had foretold, hidden in the message of "Jabberwocky:"

> Bet I beat my glands til
> With hand sword I slay the evil gender.

Chapter 10

Sylvie and Bruno

The *Sylvie* books were made up of the two-volume novel titled *Sylvie and Bruno* and *Sylvie and Bruno Concluded*. The former was published in December 1889, the latter in December 1893. They were the last of Dodgson's "children's" books. The works never met with critical acceptance or commercial success, have been deemed far inferior to the already famous *Alice* books. Both involve a continuing story that shifts between several "eerie" states, one inhabited by two little fairies, one by their child counterparts, and another by their adult counterparts. Hidden beneath these eerie states is another that takes place in Dodgson's anagrammatic world, where he discloses his own sexuality and continues the incorporation of gay sexual practices in the hidden imagery. Strange and deemed humorous for a novel, both books contain an index; I found that most entries point to pages where the hidden themes can be found. This is much like the eleven-volume Victorian pornographic novel *My Secret Life*, whose index explicitly guides the reader to the location of erotic vignettes of every variety.

In the middle of our discussion and presentation of anagrams with Ripper themes, we should recall that it was in *Sylvie and Bruno* that Dodgson put into the words of Bruno the changing of *live* into *evil* merely by "twiddling the eyes." A third word which he did not have Bruno find but left for his readers is the word *veil*, and a fourth *vile*. This word brings us to an interesting coincidence when we examine the organs removed during the Ripper murders, words, and anagrams. Acknowledging that the removal of uteri has far more symbolic meaning than any which word games could represent, is it purely coincidence that the word for each organ found to have been removed and taken away or placed in a ritualistic position as if to draw attention to it forms an anagram? For *uterus* becomes *suture*, *heart* becomes *hater*, *ears* becomes *arse*, *liver* becomes *viler*, and even *left kidney* becomes *felt kid yen* (a theme of bestiality from *kid*, not one of pederasty at the time). Were there nine murders because *intestines* forms the anagram *test is nine*?"

But *Sylvie and Bruno* contains a much more important clue in solving these crimes. In what appears to be nearly an addition to the story, inserted throughout at rather odd intervals in nine (that number again) verses, is "The Gardener's Song." It is a "song" of pure rhyming nonsense, where every verse begins with the same "He thought he saw. . ." Significantly, as we shall see, the last and ninth verse appears in *Sylvie and Bruno Concluded*, not published until 1893, well after the murder of Frances Coles.

It would be only after I suspected this poem to be a construct for Ripper disclosures that I realized the game Dodgson was playing with the title. In 1879 he had introduced to the public a word game which I believe he had created many years earlier, in fact, with the *Alice* theme of the boy turning into the pig. This was the game of Doublets, in which words of equal length are modified letter by letter, position by position, creating with each change a new valid word until a "target" word is reached. To turn *boy* into *pig*, one would move through the sequence BOY, bog, big, to finally arrive at PIG. The stated object of the game, for which there were published contests in *Vanity Fair*, was to make the transformation with as few interim words as possible. When he defined the rules, Dodgson emphasized that only proper English words should be used. In fact, however, it appears that he was creating a hidden dictionary which allowed him to write with hidden meaning. For example, he could write about love when he meant hate, knowing that *love* could be turned into *hate* (LOVE, lave, late, HATE). Is it love or hate that "makes the world go round" when he quotes the Queen of Hearts? Likewise, *tree* could be turned into *cock* (TREE, thee, them, teem, seem, seam, ream, roam, room, rook, rock, COCK). In the latter case he wrote some very explicit masturbatory material in *Sylvie and Bruno* around the word *tree*, which we shall see below, as it provides a clue to a Ripper anagram. In his diary entry of 11 May 1885, he noted that he had established a list of over five hundred seven-letter words capable of doublet conversion. [1]

With that introduction, combined with the clue regarding the *Song* Dodgson indicated *they* had written about the Knave of Hearts in *The Nursery "Alice"*, "The Gardener's Song" can be turned into "The Murderer's Poem" by converting *garden* to *murder* — GARDEN, harden, harder, hurder (obsolete form of herder), MURDER, and *song* to *poem* — SONG, long, lone, bone, bane, bare, pare, part, port, poet, POEM. Is it purely coincidence that gardeners were the very characters who were "painting" red the *five* white roses on the rose tree in *The Nursery "Alice"*? The song is reproduced below so that it can be seen in its entirety before analyzing each verse. Page numbers from first and facsimile editions are in brackets; all but the last are from the first volume, *Sylvie and Bruno*. Coincidentally, Dodgson identified the location of each verse in his Index under the entry "Gardener's Song."

The Gardener's Song

"He thought he saw an Elephant,
  That practised on a fife:
He looked again, and found it was
  A letter from his wife.
`At length I realise,´ he said,
  `The bitterness of Life!´" [65]

"He thought he saw a Buffalo
  Upon the chimney-piece:
He looked again, and found it was
  His Sister's Husband's Niece.
`Unless you leave this house,´ he said,
  `I'll send for the Police!´" [78]

"He thought he saw a Rattlesnake
  That questioned him in Greek:
He looked again, and found it was
  The Middle of Next Week.
`The one thing I regret,´ he said,
  `Is that it cannot speak!´" [83]

"He thought he saw a Banker's Clerk
  Descending from the bus:
He looked again, and found it was
  A Hippopotamus:
`If this should stay to dine,´ he said,
  `There won't be much for us!´" [90]

"He thought he saw a Kangaroo
  That worked a coffee-mill:
He looked again, and found it was
  A Vegetable-Pill.
`Were I to swallow this,´ he said,
  `I should be very ill!´" [106]

"He thought he saw a Coach-and-Four
  That stood beside his bed:
He looked again, and found it was
  A Bear without a Head.
Poor thing,´ he said, `poor silly thing!

It's waiting to be fed!'" [116]

"He thought he saw an Albatross
   That fluttered round the lamp:
He looked again, and found it was
   A Penny-Postage-Stamp.
'You'd best be getting home,' he said:
   'The nights are very damp!'" [164]

"He thought he saw a Garden-Door
   That opened with a key:
He looked again, and found it was
   A Double Rule of Three:
'And all its mystery,' he said,
   'Is clear as day to me!'" [168]

"He thought he saw an Argument
   That proved he was the Pope:
He looked again, and found it was
   A bar of Mottled Soap.
'A fact so dread,' he faintly said,
   'Extinguishes all hope!'"
                    (Sylvie and Bruno Concluded, 319)

Most significantly, following the last verse published in 1893, Dodgson has the Professor confess that the entire song is a history of the Gardener's life.

Certainly a fair criticism of using anagrams as evidence of reality is that there is a projective process on the part of the solver. Theoretically one could derive any of a number of possible themes or solutions by rearrangement. This is a particularly applicable criticism in dealing with "The Gardener's Song" because of the total nonsense which it involves. As presented, the verses appear to have no relationship whatsoever with the surrounding plot theme. Therefore, it is especially relevant in the use of the technique here that the themes for the derived anagrams come from each verse itself or from material surrounding its placement in the original text. Perhaps it is only in the anagrammatic solution that justification for each verse's placement is found. In nearly all cases, the theme was chosen from clues provided, with even more supporting clues found as the theme seemed to evolve. In some cases the clues could be found to support an anagram solved first by the projective technique (before I realized there were clues in the text). As we will see, the references to Jack the Ripper are to "he," which could reflect that they were written by someone else, that they reflect a depersonalization, a split between Dodgson and the Ripper persona, or that they just fit the needs of anagrammatic construction. I do believe, however, that the anagrams were sketched out first, then honed in what a mathematician would call a "simultaneous solution" to contrive the nonsense poem.

We will now proceed to examine each verse in sequence.

The clue to the verse beginning "He thought he saw an Elephant" (65) is taken from the last line regarding "the bitterness of Life." The text preceding indicates that Sylvie and Bruno could tell the Gardener, covered with straw from head to toe, was "maddest of all, by the shriek in which he brought out the last words of the stanza!" That he was mad at all harks back to *The Nursery "Alice"* where Dodgson described the March Hare (an anagram for "reach harm") as mad because he had straw in his hair.

> The straws showed he was mad — I don't know why.
> Never twist up straws among *your* hair, for fear people should think you're mad! [2]

Dodgson appears to be anticipating the Mad Gardener/Murderer. By reworking the entire first verse from The Gardener's Song as an anagram, we obtain:

> Ah, bitter with his fate —
>   life of stuttering, sadness, and hate —
> He designed a heinous act that he felt three people here
>   now might look on as a "wild affair."

Dodgson did, of course, stutter for all of his life, as did his sisters. While he and they, with his financial assistance, obtained the help of the best doctors available at the time, his sisters made little progress while he became capable of planning the avoidance of troublesome words. This allowed him to return to preaching with some confidence, coincidentally during these years. Remarkably, no doubt due to his comfort with and sense of control over the many young girls whom he entertained, the stammer disappeared in their presence. [3]

He had very much become a fatalist, in secret, however, as on the surface he appeared to be a devout Christian. This was part of his way of reaching justification for what he did. His own self image was one of having been damaged at birth from hereditary taint deriving from the consanguineous relationship of his parents as first cousins. On one occasion he even used "destiny" to justify his choice of an artist for a particular illustration — the Magic Locket in *Sylvie and Bruno*. The description of a "heinous act" fits with the "wild affair" or escapade that I believe this sequence of acts represented for their perpetrators. That there may have been a third person involved will become evident.

The thematic clues from the second verse "He thought he saw a Buffalo" [78] derive much from the presence of the words *sisters, house,* and *police,* and the paragraph which follows the verse in which the Gardener says

> ... "But I always loves my *pay-rints* like anything."
> "Who *are* oor *pay-rints*?" said Bruno.
> "Them as pay *rint* for me, a course!" the Gardener replied. [4]

In this solution we can perhaps confirm one of the suspicions held by some officials and investigators, that the Ripper was not a native Londoner and had a place in or near the East End to which he could retreat. Verse two becomes:

> Abused as by a mother hen,
>   he'd hug his faithful, icy sisters —
> so naive. Then
> he'd lie awake,
>   use wiles, fuel his hate.
> He has a house up in London —
>   to confuse inept police —
>
>   C. L. Dodgson

We have already seen the "mother hen" description which Dodgson provided of his mother, but which solves to an anagram.

Dodgson visited his sisters often at their home in Guildford, called "The Chestnuts," whose acquisition he had arranged after their father's death in 1868. While he maintained what anyone would conclude was a continuing close relationship with them, there appear hidden even in his letters to them the same kinds of hate-driven structures that are found in his published works. He had described them at one point as "children of the North" and photographs of them reflect a great lack of related-ness. As already noted, prior to the publication of the *Snark*, he had considered renting a place in London to use as a studio. The notion that he would have an entire house is not unreasonable. He could afford it, as he had by this time become quite financially independent as a result of the royalties from his books, and was in London often enough on a regular basis to be seen as "coming and going." A house would have given the Ripper the seclusion required to be able to return unseen in the middle of the night, with no chance to disturb anyone or risk being seen in what must have been bloodied attire. He could have washed clothing easily or even have disposed of it. Even more grotesquely, he could have done with impunity any of a number of things with victims or organs that had been removed and taken from the scene of the crimes.

Ripperologist Colin Wilson's notion of the importance of brooding in these crimes is evident.

"C. L. Dodgson" was his standard signature on nearly all of his nearly one hundred thousand letters written over his lifetime, as reflected in the register that he kept. He even used the formal signature when writing to family members. While he was an "unknown" Oxford don, for all intents and purposes, and made great attempts to separate his Oxford identity from the notoriety provided "Lewis Carroll," there could be risk in the name being used for apartmental rental. In 1890 he criticized the *St. James Gazette* severely for identifying "Lewis Carroll" as Charles Dodgson in print.

He may have used any name for rental registers. In an early short story with the same masturbatory themes that appear throughout his works, a story published while he was an adolescent at home with the unwitting support of his parents titled "The Walking Stick of Destiny," he created right under their noses a character named "Baron Slogdod" (an anagram for "Dodgson labor") and a second "Signor Blowski" (an anagram for "I blow gross kin" with *blow* meaning "to destroy" in Victorian usage). Perhaps the house would be under that name — "C. N. Slogdod," an anagram for "C. L. Dodgson."

But did he have a house? That is an area where more research could be done in the Census Registers for the period. I did find he used 29 Bedford Street as a mail return address on 3 December 1888, when he was searching for a printer for his "Wonderland Postage-Stamp Case," but that turned out to be the offices of his publisher, Macmillan. It was in the middle of the Covent Garden district, the theatrical and bohemian center of the city. Its proximity to the East-End is startling, and its even closer proximity to the workplace of Montague Druitt is more startling. This aspect of the case is covered more fully in chapter 14, which explores the significance of geography in the Ripper crimes and chapter 15 which identifies Druitt as a possible third suspect.

In any event, the weight of this anagram, like the others, lies in its biographical and characterological consistency, their connectedness to material surrounding the verse interpreted as clues, and to the valid if mostly neglected hypotheses regarding the Ripper murders.

In examining the third verse "He thought he saw a Rattlesnake" (83) we find two clues in the text that follows the verse. There is reference to an *open letter* regarding the transfer of *sovereignty* to the young Bruno; but then the Vice Warden and his Lady connive to place their own pig-like son Uggug on the throne in Bruno's place.

The anagram that we find reads

> I think Dodgson wrote a fake letter
> asking the pig-like queen I hate that,
> to hush murder-shaken,
> to cage a foe in the East End,
> she tithe West End women
> an additional high tax.

With apologies to Queen Victoria, in these her later years, one would have to allow that her short, heavy appearance could cause one to make the allusion, especially if one felt ill toward her. There is no evidence in Dodgson's diaries that he expressed or had any such feeling. She met him on one occasion on a visit to Oxford, although he appears to have been very much one of the crowd. He had some interaction on photography with the Prince of Wales while the prince was a student at Oxford. And she had commented favorably on his *Alice* works. On one other occasion he recorded in his diary he had been passed by her on the street as she rode in her carriage and that she had acknowledged his bow personally. He seemed to believe that she recognized him, which may or may not have been true. What feelings he had for her underneath can only be surmised; she was one who could generate strong dislikes in people because of her controlling ways and lifelong public disdain for her son, whom she blamed for her husband's death. She was extraordinarily intrusive in the life of her grandson, Prince Eddy, who became a Ripper suspect in the later literature and who was featured in the BBC broadcast and again in David Abrahamsen's 1992 work *Murder and Madness*. Dodgson could very well have included her in his overall feelings toward powerful titled women. Her treatment of family males may not have been at all obvious to the public of the day. Of course, the wording in the anagram suggests the feelings came from someone other than Dodgson, possibly Bayne.

The taxing notion is totally consistent with the feelings of the time. The women of the West End were becoming increasingly fearful for their lives. Fanned by the press, it was becoming apparent that women were the target, whether it be women alone anywhere on the street or just prostitutes in the East End. Of course, the West End was not without its own potential prostitute targets if the Ripper decided to move a few miles further west as the police net tightened in Whitechapel.

George Bernard Shaw used the events as a forum for calls for justice and equity, when he wrote to the *Star* on 24 September 1888:

> ... Indeed, if the habits of Duchesses only admitted of their being decoyed into Whitechapel backyards, a single experiment in slaughterhouse anatomy on an aristocratic victim might fetch in a round half million and save the necessity of sacrificing four women of the people.
> [McCormick adds] This typical Shavian extravaganza infuriated the police and magistrates. [5]

Even closer to home, however, the Reverend Samuel Barnett was writing letters during the same period from his mission in Whitechapel, which, as we have seen, had its Oxford contingent that included Thomas Vere Bayne if not Charles Dodgson personally. While I found nothing which suggested a direct women-to-women tithe, Barnett did seek more public monies for police, lighting, and housing, but especially for better control over the slaughterhouses, which he felt provided an environment of violence as the brutalization of animals was a common sight. In the same letter, he noted that the crimes were not without their bright side as the media focus was providing for the first time public attention on the horrible conditions in the East End. [6]

Historically, police have defended their actions during the period as very much limited by the budget allocated. Public debate on the costs of police protection and general surveillance as well as the dragnet established to catch the Ripper was considerable and did often raise the question of sources for the funds. That such a letter might have been written (indeed, might still exist) is not at all unreasonable and would be totally consistent with both Dodgson's feelings toward women and his facility with sarcasm when claiming the high road.

The verse which begins "He thought he saw a Banker's Clerk" [90] occurs in perhaps the most critical section of the *Sylvie* books. It is here that we find the two anagrams which Dodgson called attention to in his Preface, anagrams which disclosed his support of pederasty and his "gay" victimization and behavior. Of course he did not identify them as anagrams; he described them as having come to him "in a dream."

All of these self-disclosures precede by a single page this verse of "The Gardener's Song." The Vice-Warden, whose involvement in "vice" is clear in the hidden material (supported in clear text by his emergence flushed and out of breath from a session alone with Uggug), assures the Baron that the gardener was not directing the verse to him, and that he in fact meant nothing by it. When asked for reassurance of that fact, the gardener just stood balanced on one leg with his mouth open.

Zeroing in on *clerk*, *bus*, and *dine*, along with the other anagrammatic themes that involve suggestions of oral sexual behavior, this verse becomes:

> Dodgson, disguised as a clerk,
> bought a knife, took trains,
> stayed in his London house.
> He'd help the Fates.
> How?
> Hump from behind,
> cut a whore in the face,
> masturbate,
> wash up.

There is no question that Dodgson could have effected such a clerk's disguise. Although strong from exercise with dumbbells and walks of up to twenty-five miles, he had none of the toughness that comes from hard work. If one were to guess his occupation, not aware that he was an Oxford don, one would choose clerk. He was a frequent train traveler, not just between Oxford, Guildford, Eastbourne, and London, but throughout England. [7]

Rumbelow above all believes that an intent to sodomize was the method of approach which placed the Ripper behind his victims. [8]   I believe strongly that there may have been a pretense of sodomy, that penile penetration was never intended or carried out, at least in the crimes committed in the open. Faces were cut; there are many expert suggestions that masturbation in response to the stimulation of the murders and mutilations is the sexual release in murders of this type. "Wash up" totally depersonalizes the experience and reflects the action believed to have occurred after the murders of Stride and Eddowes in the hallway sink where the "Juwes" message was found. The gardener's standing with his mouth open suggests that perhaps the Ripper masturbated in the face, perhaps in the mouths of his victims in a reenactment of his own school experience, an allusion that emerges repeatedly below.

The clues to the next verse "He thought he saw a Kangaroo" (106) lie in the word *vegetable* and the suggestions of illness that would take place if something were eaten. The material that follows this verse finds Sylvie suggesting "`We don't want him to swallow *anything*.´" Then there follows the true identity of the Magic Locket as Bruno proposes that Sylvie kiss it, then rub it this way and that; finally, right and left rubbing creates the desired effect:

> For a number of trees. . . were moving slowly upwards, in solemn procession: while a mild little brook, that had been rippling at our feet a moment before , began to swell, and foam, and hiss, and bubble, in a truly alarming fashion. [9]

As we have seen, in the world of anagrams, the "Magic Locket" becomes "Me, a gilt cock" and *Bruno* turns into "Rub on!" And in the world of Doublets *tree* converts into *cock*. So, in effect full blown oral/penile imagery follows this verse as we find Sylvie kissing and Bruno rubbing the Magic Locket until "trees" begin to rise and mild brooks begin to foam and bubble.

Solving the verse as an anagram we find:

> How full of hate I was.
> I, a thin, a vile, a naked C.L. Dodgson,
> looked into the whore's vegetable-like eyes.
> I masturbated;
> I had her swallow a frig —a whole, a hot gulp.

The sequencing of this solution offers a number of alternatives. If the vegetable-like eyes were the result of death there certainly would have been no real swallowing. My suspicion is that this may have comprised the ultimate retributive thrill for Dodgson as the Ripper. Having most likely been subjected to this felt assault repeatedly in public school, perhaps he subjected Mary Ann Kelly as mother-surrogate to it in the room before killing her. She was the only one with whom he lingered indoors. The scene does not fit with any of the other murders committed outside in the dark with only moments to escape. Oral sex certainly fell into the category of "gay" behavior for which she might have been engaged with consent. If, as I believe, the Ripper was not aroused by feminine sexual stimulation, he may very well have produced semen by masturbation, still unable or unwilling to penetrate a woman by any means other than a knife. The "vegetable-like eyes" may have properly described the vacancy of the woman's stare as she engaged in the acts quite impassively. This view of the prostitute is inconsistent with Victorian belief regarding the psychology of prostitution, i.e., that prostitutes were insatiable nymphomaniacs who enjoyed the work, a not uncommon male perception which helps justify the degradation, even today. For most East End prostitutes it offered a bed for the night or something to eat or drink. Several researchers, including Wilson, believe that the Ripper was naked at the scene of Kelly's murder.

We reach a pivotal event in the Ripper murders as I envision them when we analyze the verse that begins "He thought he saw a Coach-and-Four" (116). The material which surrounds this verse is filled with violence, including "razor," "blow after blow," a panting Sylvie, a whimpering Bruno, and finally the acquisition of a "DAGGER" by the "Conspirator" as a birthday present for "my Lady." "DAGGER" is capitalized in the original, the usual clue that the word is suspect. Is it a coincidence that *DAGGER* is an anagram for *RAGGED*, characteristic of some of the wounds, but more significantly, it becomes *RIPPER* by Doublet conversion (DAGGER, bagger, bagged, barged, barred, burred, burped, bumped, dumped, damped, damper, dapper, dipper, RIPPER). The anagram which is derived from the verse is:

> O, I gasped;
> I was choking at her wounds — the blood.
> As I sobbed uncontrolably,
> aghast at the thought of what I —
> I —
> heinous rat, a pig,
> had done to the dead whore,
> I hid.
> Safe, I fainted.

This anagram fits nearly perfectly with all of the hypotheses reflected in the modern literature on the Ripper regarding the Kelly murder. He is believed to have consumed some of her blood, the ultimate blood-thirsty orgy of mutilation. If he had, it would have caused him to choke, and from other material, to vomit, as human blood is a natural emetic. [10]   Colin Wilson identifies this event as pivotal because of a fetus found within the carnage, that Kelly was pregnant and that the killing of a fetus would have been an ultimate thrill, based on a psychosis related to the "horrors of birth." [11] But Sugden argues convincingly that this "pregnancy," first reported by Donald McCormick in his *The Identity of Jack the Ripper*, is part of Ripper myth, that there is no documentation to support such a claim of a fetus. [12] I believe this sudden confrontation with what he had done, not just to woman-as-object but to woman-as-human, was overwhelming to the core. And it would not be just from what those entering the room observed, but included all that he had done physically and psychologically in the orgastic process for which there was no lasting evidence.

Of course, this murder also represented the first opportunity the Ripper had to visually encounter and contemplate the extent of the damage done to his victim, and it was the worst of the mutilations. If the anagram is correct, for the first time the Ripper internalized, personalized the act; "I was responsible; this is what I did." The allusion to self as a rat or pig in these circumstances is characteristically appropriate in terms of the way both animals approach the feeding process. Dodgson's lifelong view of himself as a boy who turned into a pig is again apparent.

If he did indeed faint, did indeed reach this psychological limit he had set for himself, was this the last of the murders? Contrary to what earlier material suggested as the event that would end the murders, I don't believe so, but I believe strongly that it explains the change of pattern in subsequent murders, as abdominal mutilation, although at times furtively attempted, was not completed. There was still an uncontrolable compulsion to kill, but as we shall see, a fear that would become overwhelming as the last murder was indeed committed. This fear reached critical proportions during this event.

The clues for the next verse that begins "He thought he saw an Albatross" (164) derive from the albatross as the foreteller of doom and "tracker" of ships at sea and the story references to postage stamps and dampness. In the text that follows the verse, the dampness is described as sticky while the Gardener is seen watering the garden with an empty watering can (he claims it's less work that way). In her 1955 work *Swift and Carroll: A Psychoanalytic Study of Two Lives*, Phyllis Greenacre viewed this scene as a screen memory of a young Dodgson having possibly viewed a Daresbury or Croft gardener masturbating. I think Dodgson left it intentionally for the "adult" reader to fathom. The anagram reads:

> Thomas Vere Bayne penned,
> posted a "Dear Boss" letter to the papers in a red ink.
> He laugh'd with a fit at the thought of getting hounds
>   to bag us.
> We dandy, gay sons hump, hate all, Mama!

The first of the "Dear Boss" letters was written in red ink and was in the same schoolboy handwriting style that is so evident in Bayne's diaries. It is in his diary entry of 1 August 1888, that the word "Bosses" appears (in a context I am ashamed I cannot recall except that it seemed innocuous). The "B" in the diary was somewhat different than in the letter, more similar to that on the envelope. But on 31 August, the night of Mary Ann Nichols's death, Bayne reports that he had met Liddon on the train to Dover where they spent the night before leaving for France in the morning. This letter was not received by the Central News Office until 29 September, and it is the only one in the files written in a schoolboy hand. Bayne reports that he was exchanging letters with his mother, who was ill in London, and with Liddon, who by late September had left him and gone separately to Germany while he remained in France. If the diary is correct, if he was really in France the entire time, any argument that he wrote the letters would require that he gain his knowledge from the papers or from Dodgson in a communication to him. A Ripper letter could have been sent by Bayne to Dodgson for forwarding using a domestic post office. He could have used any of a number of enciphering methods he possessed.

The reference to *hounds* is totally out of context with the letter having been written before November. It would not be until then, when Bayne was back at Oxford, that there was serious consideration of using bloodhounds for tracking the Ripper. Many others were amused at the suggestion, which proved unworkable, and led to Warren's resignation. Of course, there is no requirement that the statements in the anagram reflect coincidence in time.

Mama was the name used by the Dodgson children when they referred to their mother as evidenced by early letters.

The last of the verses that appears in the first volume *Sylvie and Bruno* begins "He thought he saw a Garden-Door" (168). The clues to the anagrammatic solution lie in the text which precedes the verse. It describes the inability of the children to get through a locked gate. The gardener arrives and finally is able to find the correct key to open the door. The text that follows the verse references a nervousness which one of the adult characters has about dogs. The following anagram can be derived from the verse.

> He had no key to a whore —
> Marie Kelly's — door,
> opened it through a window.
> He dug a fist in and feasted as a dog,
> a leech —

really a Satan —
at her mutilated body.

Again we find historical accuracy regarding Marie Kelly's door. When the police arrived to enter the apartment, they found it locked, with a broken window within reach of the inner latch mechanism. There was and has been much speculation as to whether the Ripper indeed escaped with the key. Investigation proved that the door had been without a key for some time. Is it possible that Kelly's quarters had been scouted out beforehand? Had he entered alone and confronted her from his hiding place when she returned? Or, had the Ripper learned the technique when he observed her as they both entered together either at this time or an earlier one?

The feasting at the body returns us to the psychological dynamics of such mutilations and the same theme as the earlier anagram, the blood-thirsty sucking of mutilated remains. Yet, there is a realization that the activity is satanic by someone who had sources of such knowledge in his library.

Magnus Hirschfeld writes in his seminal work *Sexual Anomalies and Perversions*, a book which was judged obscene when published, but was later reclassified after court proceedings:

> In genuine cases of sexual murder the killing replaces the sexual act. There is, therefore, no sexual intercourse at all, and sexual pleasure is induced by cutting, and slashing the victims' body, ripping open her abdomen, plunging the hands into her intestines, cutting out and taking away her genitals, throttling her and sucking her blood. These horrors. . . constitute the — so to speak — pathological equivalent of coitus. [13]

As we move to the last of the verses in "The Gardener's Song," we find ourselves in *Sylvie and Bruno Concluded*. It is relevant that this work was published in December 1893, well after the last of the Ripper murders. And in it we find a strong suggestion that it was in fact Frances Coles, murdered on 13 February 1891, who was the last victim, not Marie Kelly, as most hypothesize.

In the text of the story, more than three hundred pages into this second *Sylvie* volume, the children find the gardener still humming the last part of the previous verse.

"He looked again, and found it was

A Double Rule of Three:
And all its Mystery,´ he said,
`Is clear as day to me!´"
                        (*Sylvie and Bruno Concluded*, 319)

Then, sadly, in tears, he sings this final verse which begins "He thought he saw an Argument" (*Sylvie and Bruno Concluded*, 319) In anagrammatic reconstruction we have:

Though he had proven the argument
that he was a pig,
able to hate,
strike again,
and stop,
he was so anxious a fool
he fainted cold dead away,
found himself,
later stopped.

Here we have suggestions that there was an intellectual argument involved in these murders, that there was something to be proven. What it appears to have been was the ability to start and stop, to have even the most base emotions under the control of will. And, again, we have the allusion to fainting, not only as what would stop the murders, but what did finally stop them. But why this time?

Could this represent a restatement of the scene at Kelly's murder of 9 November 1888, or had "destiny" brought the Ripper back for one last murder, or perhaps one last murder with mutilation as mutilation had not been consummated after the Kelly murder. During February, the Greek month of expiation, on the 13th, the "Ides" of February, on the sixteenth anniversary of the publication of Dodgson's article on vivisection, the anniversary of the beheading of Catherine Howard (Henry VIII's fifth wife), a woman whose first name was *Frances*, the same as his mother's, and whose last name *Coles* is derived from the Greek and Latin words for *vagina*, was murdered in Ripper fashion. Had he spotted a woman whose murder he just could not resist?´ Was he fearful of an inability to carry it out, that the same thing would happen as occurred at the murder of Mary Ann Kelly, that he would faint?

Dodgson's diary entry for the 6th, one week before the murder of Coles, an entry corroborated in Bayne's diary, reflects that he found himself on the chapel floor in a pool of blood following morning service.

He had lain there for more than an hour after fainting cold dead away. He would record himself still recovering in April, not having ridden in a train "since February." He described the incident in more detail in a letter written to his child friend Edith Blakemore on 26 April. [14] He tells her his doctor had found him in quite poor health in general, that the attack might have come from a digestive problem and of too many late hours with too much "brain work." (It was this brain work related to the preparation of *The Nursery "Alice"* and *Sylvie and Bruno* that I had attributed as the cause of Dodgson's migraine symptoms having peaked in 1888 in my first book. I now suggest there were other stressors.) He also described the amount of "vital force" the preparation of sermons took as he responded to the fact that the College Servants were suspending invitations to preach for a while in consideration for his health. ("Vital force" was commonly used in medical and church literature as a euphemism for *semen*, the loss of which in heterosexual intercourse was believed to weaken the male, or, in masturbation, to cause mental illness.) Interestingly, as he lists all the possible causes, he emphasizes the words *might* and *may* in his speculation. Is this because he *knew* what the cause was?

Having written nearly all of his letters for many years in purple ink, all letters, manuscripts, and notations known to have been written after the 5 February 1891, were written in black ink. [15] Why?

There are many people in 1888 just as there are many today who wish to make the murder of Marie Kelly the last of the Ripper crimes. They believed and wished to believe that the orgy of mutilation that occurred in that room in Miller's Court must have been a last step in the mad descent to suicide. What I would like to leave open is the notion that the murder of Kelly was a psychological turning event based on the immediate proximity to overwhelming gore and that the nature of any subsequent murders could now have changed for a very good reason. It is partly this change, this decrease in intensity and the lack of or minimal mutilation in subsequent murders which tends to classify them as not of Ripper "quality." But if these murders were also acts of will and driven by distorted notions of "chosenness" and "destiny," not totally uncontrolled lunatic emotion, which I think they were, then they could very well have continued. But the emotional peak of the total event, the mutilation, could very well have become inhibited by the Miller Court experience. Mutilation, not murder, is what the Ripper would avoid in the future, perhaps not due to the fear of killing but controlled by the fear of knowing that he might indeed faint and be caught.

Despite the fact that many might consider the following observation bizarre and grotesque, I offer it anyway. There were four doctors who spent six and a half hours handling Marie Kelly's mutilated remains as they attempted to perform an autopsy and reassemble the severed and mutilated parts. [16]   In order to do so, they placed their emotions under the control of their wills *to do the jobs they were assigned to do.* For the Ripper to have done so, adequately enough to escape, is totally reasonable, especially if he were acting under the delusion that he, too, was on a mission.

Before turning to an examination of the diaries kept by Dodgson and Bayne for more clues that might corroborate involvement in these crimes — i.e., provide opportunity — let us end this chapter by examining a scene which occurs very close to the end of *Sylvie and Bruno Concluded.* In chapter XXIV something significant happens to Uggug, the despicable boy, and I believe, a self character for Dodgson. (Writers historically have identified only the good, benign characters in his works as "self" characters. I go further and identify both the good and bad as aspects that Dodgson recognized exist in everyone.) While Bruno mis-hears what the excited crowd is saying, believing they are calling Uggug *preoccupied* (which the Ripper certainly was during this time), what they are shouting is

> "... Porcupine! Prince Uggug has turned into a Porcu-
> pine!"
>   "A new Specimen!" exclaimed the delighted Professor.
> "Pray let me go in. It should be labeled at once!"
>   ... "Never mind about Specimens, Professor!" said the
> Emperor, pushing his way through the crowd. "Tell us how to
> keep him safe!" [17]

They brought in a cage with a portcullis on one end, placed it against the door of the room Uggug was breaking down, and then opened the door.

> ... with a yell like the whistle of a steam-engine, [Uggug]
> rushed into the cage.
> ... The Professor rubbed his hands in childish delight. "The
> Experiment has succeeded!" he proclaimed. "All that is needed
> now is to feed it three times a day, on chopped carrots and
> ——."
>   ... "See the fate of a loveless life!" [the old man] said to
> Bruno... to which Bruno made reply, "I always loved Sylvie, so
> I'll never get prickly like that!" [18] Immediately on things
> settling down, the Professor is incapacitated by an attack of

Uggug Becomes a Porcupine

Source: Sylvie and Bruno Concluded, 388.

"My old enemy!" groaned the Professor. "Lumbago __
rheumatism — that sort of thing. I think I'll go and lie down a
bit." [19]

Psychological interpretations of this passage have made reference
to the penile allusions to the "prickly" transformation undergone by
Uggug. [20]   But if we examine the rather indiscriminate slashing
motion made by the porcupine when it attacks, the result of which is
both quill penetration and cutting, if we relate the comment of the
Professor (long considered a Dodgson "self" character) with the notion
that an experiment has been completed, and the newspaper editorials
that suggested that the Ripper's skull should be preserved for study, we
have the screen of a Ripper story. And, the experimenter-Professor was
immediately confined to his bed for a lengthy stay. Dodgson was also
confined for a lengthy period, but not with lumbago, with what at the
time he thought was an old enemy — epilepsy, his doctor's diagnosis for
his having fainted.

Dodgson's development of the evil boy began in *Alice's Adventures
in Wonderland* when he had the Duchess's baby boy turn into a pig
when held by Alice (see illustration on page xvi). The adolescent Uggug
transforms into a very angry porcupine. It was in adolescence that
Dodgson experienced what I believe were sexual assaults (exactly what
Uggug seems to be participating in in *Sylvie and Bruno*) which
destroyed him and turned him into a child bent on revenge and locked
him in a life as a man-child.

The conundrum from the quoted passage, if indeed it does reflect
the conclusion of the Ripper spree, is why the author had the prickly
Uggug caged by others since the Ripper was never captured.   Did
friends put a stop to him? Investigators have often thought that a few
close friends of the Ripper were aware of his activities. Or was he caged
by other aspects of himself — the benign Professor and the playful
Bruno?   In a "looking-glass" reversal of the Robert Louis Stevenson
story, did the kindly Dr. Jekyll finally contain the evil Mr. Hyde?

Chapter 11

The Diaries

It is not my intention to examine the entire range of Dodgson's or Bayne's diaries in this work. A number of references have already been made to them, and *The Agony of Lewis Carroll* discusses those written by Dodgson in some detail. What we shall do here is examine the diaries of both men for all of 1888 and for selected periods through the end of 1891. The purpose of this examination is to identify entries that might be directly or indirectly relevant, but also to establish as best as possible an essential element in any circumstantial case — the one so far not covered, the presence of opportunity. Is there anything that places Dodgson at the location of the murders, or, lacking that, is there anything that conflicts with the notion that he could have been there?

I have already suggested that Dodgson's diary entries may have been intentionally deceptive. There is a risk of being quite arbitrary in making that claim, as it certainly would be done only when it supported an author's argument. So, despite that lingering suspicion, this examination will make no such specific suggestion; nor will any evidence regarding opportunity be based on such a claim. A much more likely scenario regarding the diary and Dodgson's overall motive in keeping it is that he intended it for the use of biographers and recorded a number of obscure but revealing things in it quite intentionally. There is no reason to believe he acted any differently in this document than he did in his books and letters, although I found only one instance where he used an anagram. But there may also be things in it that were not intended. This analysis integrates the handwritten manuscripts that reside in the British Library with *The Diaries of Lewis Carroll*, edited by Roger Lanclyn Green and published in 1954, and the unpublished handwritten manuscripts of Thomas Vere Bayne from the library at Christ Church, Oxford. All diary references are to date of entry, not the page numbers, which are at times inconsistent in the manuscripts. Dodgson's diary manuscripts are referenced only for material that was not published. Since the date of each entry is in the text, there are no references in the notes section of this work.

Several general comments are in order. Bayne's diaries contain very little of substance. While much more dedicated to making an entry each and every day, he often commented on only the weather or what he took for meals. Significantly, they also reflect his health, every ache and pain. Both he and Dodgson, the latter acknowledged by biographers, indulged themselves when feeling ill, usually confining themselves to bed. We will see a pattern of stress-related afflictions in both cases, but in Bayne's entries we will also see the effects of excessive alcohol, especially wine.

A pattern that emerges in Dodgson's diary is a noticeable deterioration in handwriting from January 1888 onward. Except as they reappear on occasion, the remnants of a "schoolboy" hand virtually disappear, even though the writing remains for the most part very legible.

Dodgson could be said to have "resumed" preaching from 1888 to 1891. He had given it up for many years. At the very least he made more reference to it in his diaries than he had done previously. He had claimed he had given it up because of his stammer, but there may well have been other reasons. I have deemed it relevant that he resumed the activity, and have quoted the content of the biblical passages he chose as his themes, something he rarely did as he provided only the reference.

January 1888

The year began at Guildford as usual. The Christmas holidays were nearly always spent there with the family, with Dodgson returning to Oxford for the resumption of his teaching duties. As he often did, always in the earlier years, he recorded a prayer asking God's help to spend the year according to His will. The published diaries rarely reflect this or other prayers, whose urgency clearly reflects inner conflict.

Notice now and in later entries the traveling flexibility. On the 10th he returned to Oxford by way of London. On the 14th he went from Oxford to London, then in the evening to Guildford, where he preached on the 15th at the local parish, St. Mary's. He chose for his sermon Isaiah VI, 8, which reads:

> Then I heard the Lord say, "Whom shall I send? Who will be our messenger?"
> I answered, "I will go! Send me!"

His manuscript indicates that on 3 July 1887 he had preached on the same theme, this time quoting the passage in his diary "Here am I; send me." There seems to have been a building up toward a year or time filled with God-directed, destined activities.

On the 16th he went to London, then proceeded to Guildford in the evening, and returned to Oxford on the following day. Except for some detailed activities, the month ends with an entry that he had completed his favorite eighteen-mile afternoon walk and that he had averaged three and three-quarters miles per hour.

Bayne's diary reflects concern for his mother's health. Widowed now for several years, she lived alone in London but spent 1888 with a live-in nurse. She would be ill for most of the year, finally dying on 6 December. Bayne appears to have been the dutiful son in visiting her throughout this period.

He notes that Dodgson's fifty-sixth birthday (on the 27th) was celebrated in the Common Room with some fine Madeira.

February 1888

In a lengthy, rambling, angry unpublished entry made on the 4th, Dodgson sounded extremely betrayed by Bayne when he discovered that the latter, after the Common Room Curator's stipend had been made a voluntary contribution years before, had continued taking money from those new students who still believed that it was a mandatory fee. He had no respect for Bayne's explanation that new students were "beings incapable of choice," and that therefore the failure to disclose was not "cheating." In their discussion, Bayne claimed that one of the reasons he had given up the job (in 1882) was due to the number of students (three quarters) who stopped paying the fee once they knew it had become voluntary. Dodgson notes that he would insure that he would make proper disclosure in the future and that he had learned of the fraud only "with pain and shame." By this time Dodgson had been curator for six years, and had accepted the money as a gift under what he now learned were false pretenses.

This is a disturbing entry regarding the integrity of his relationship with his close friend, whose name comes up repeatedly in the Ripper anagrams. They were constant walking companions throughout their adult lives.

As it turns out, with no visible source of wealth, Bayne left an estate of £145,000 on his death (compared to Dodgson's £4,000), [1] although perhaps it (also) came from a secret sharing of royalties from the "Lewis Carroll" works or from his "fraudulently obtained" Common Room fees. Subsequent entries indicate that they remained friends, although there are some lengthy lapses in the diary entries in terms of mentioning one another, often at critical times.

On the other hand, given what we can now see was the flagrant inclusion of explicit anagrams in the body of what may very well have been "their" works, this entry, even if he felt deceived only because his friend had not disclosed this to him, may represent just a temporary falling out, more reflective of Dodgson's eccentric pique.

There are few additional entries for February, but the manuscripts indicate that he was involved with Stuart Collingwood, his nephew and future biographer, who had matriculated to Oxford and whose progress Dodgson followed throughout the year.

On 6 February, Bayne writes that he had come down with an attack of gout on his left wrist and spent several days treating it. He also reports that Edward Sampson, their close friend from Oxford student days, had collapsed from some unspecified "nervous weakness."

March 1888

March contains few entries. On the 6th Bayne reports that he and Dodgson had walked through a "Slough of Despond." One could only wonder what that was, but no clue is offered by Bayne, and Dodgson does not mention it.

While Bayne notes that he had tea with the Liddells on the 10th at which the famous "Alice" (now Mrs. Hargreaves) was present, Dodgson made no note of any visit with his now grown-up child friend and long considered inspiration for the "Alice" works.

Dodgson notes and Bayne confirms on the 29th that the former developed a problem with his knee, diagnosed as "synovitis" and that he remained "condemned to sofa" until the 8th of April. Bayne's manuscript indicates that Dodgson was still there on the 13th. The published diary reflects that he was still walking with difficulty until 6 May. On 11 March Bayne reports that he had dined with Liddon, who was suffering from a throbbing headache.

April 1888

Emma Smith was murdered on the 3rd, during which time Dodgson and Bayne were at Oxford, with Dodgson writing that he was unable to walk.

On 29 April Bayne writes that he heard a sermon at "the Cathedral" (most likely St. Paul's) by an H. S. Holland regarding the Christ Church mission in East London. This is no doubt referring to Toynbee Hall and the Reverend Samuel Barnett's activities in which both Christ Church and Montague Druitt's alma mater, New College, were involved.

May 1888

Mrs. Bayne was recovered from her illness on the 11th. Bayne "lionized" (showed the Oxford sights to) thirty men from East London on the 21st, a clear indication that he was actively involved with the mission, although there is no indication that he performed duties in the East End. Bayne also reports that Dodgson was still having difficulty walking.

June 1888

On the 12th Dodgson reports having an optical attack of "seeing fortifications" in his right eye, without a headache (implying with the entry that usually headache accompanied them). This was an attack of migraine, from which Dodgson is known to have suffered. The psychology of migraine sufferers is explored fully in *The Agony of Lewis Carroll*, indeed as evidence of the inner world of extreme stress. Causes for these attacks are considered now nearly always based on psychological factors such as extremely conflicting feelings toward people to whom one professes love, the inability to manage feelings, perfectionist tendencies, and extreme inner conflict over sexual and moral issues. [2] In Victorian times causes were deemed to be dietary, and may have contributed to the reasons Dodgson kept such a sparse diet. While he makes no note of seeking medical help, he does write that he had found discussion on the symptoms in a book by a Dr. Latham on "billious headache," a note that reflects his tendency to self-diagnose and treat. Particularly during the Victorian period, the symptoms of migraine were often confused with those of epilepsy. [3]

On the 18th he went to London for the theater; the manuscripts indicate that on the 19th he went to the beach at Eastbourne for the day. On the 20th he visited London for medical advice on his knee and exhibitions with the children. Again on the 28th he was in London at the theater.

July 1888

Dodgson was in London on the 2nd, where he stayed overnight at the Great Western Hotel (right by Paddington Station which served the line to Oxford), and was there on the 4th, at which time he discussed the revival of *Alice* on the stage with Savile Clarke, noted producer of children's theater. This would eventually open on 26 December, Boxing Day, produced by Richard Mansfield, who had thrilled and chilled

London theater goers with his performance in *Dr. Jekyll and Mr. Hyde* during the time the Ripper murders were taking place. On the 3rd, he met Isa Bowman at Paddington Station. She was one of his favorite child friends and would be featured in the revival. She remained as his guest at Oxford until the 16th. He wrote as a gift for her his rendition of "her" diary of the visit. [4]   This short piece is one of the most delightful among his body of works. On the 20th he went to London, then to Eastbourne on the 21st to begin his vacation. On the 16th and 21st he records viewing several delightful pictures of nude children. He notes on the 29th that he was working on *Sylvie and Bruno*, an activity that had appeared occasionally in the diary earlier in the year.

Bayne writes that he was taken again with gout, this time from some unknown cause. He continues to report on its progress, showing improvement by 1 August.

August 1888

On 4 August, Dodgson's handwriting deteriorates noticeably. He reports a "curious piece of Eastbourne statistics" which places him there. He visited fourteen shops unsuccessfully in search of a pair of cloth gloves. It was his practice to wear gloves always when outside. He continued his work on *Sylvie and Bruno*.

On 7 August, Martha Tabram was murdered.

On 10 August Dodgson complained that he was lonely for childhood company at the beach and was pleased to make friends with two children that day. On the 20th he was in Margate, a town nearly a hundred miles east of Eastbourne, beyond Dover, where he stayed for the night. The entry for the day is a long, rambling one on minutia. On the 21st, his handwriting reflects long wavy lines and is very much opened up, not as tight as it had become. On the 24th he reports that Savile Clarke has gotten over a "hitch" that threatened a Christmas opening for the *Alice* revival.

Bayne had stayed over at the Great Western on the 1st. The word "Bosses" appears in the diary between the 1st and the 16th (*mea culpa* for the lack of precision) at which time his heretofore perfect handwriting becomes poor. He writes "Can barely move — pain great." He identifies the cause as lumbago. He writes that Liddon visited him on the 23rd and they settled on 1 September for their departure to France. On the 31st he indicates that a friend told him there was no reason not to go abroad with anything but a peaceful mind. This may very well constitute or include a reference to concerns about leaving his mother. However, she was doing well at this point. He may very well be playing on his own preoccupations, perhaps making a note of sarcasm at the friend's presumption regarding his private thoughts, while his friend was referencing his mother. He found Liddon on the same train to Dover in the evening, an entry that reflects the rendezvous on the train was not planned.

On the 29th, Dodgson met Isa Bowman at Victoria Station in London and returned to Eastbourne in the afternoon. We enter a difficult period in the analysis of Dodgson as a Ripper suspect because later diary entries report that Isa was there with him for the next five weeks, until 3 October. For him to have left Eastbourne at night or for an overnight stay would have required that he find some accommodation for her during the period, someone whom he knew he could trust. While it is certainly possible that she "stayed over" with a family both of them knew — many of the families returned each year — there is nothing to indicate that any such thing happened. There may be a clue to this in entries for 1889, however, as we find some people quite suited for the task and what appears to be an effort by Dodgson to conceal the fact and their identity.

On the very next evening (30th) Dodgson accompanied Isa and her friends Muriel and Ida Weddell to a concert at Devonshire Park in Eastbourne. He also began writing his diary in black ink; all previous entries had been written in purple. In 1889, he returned to purple ink for all but one entry.

Later that night, in the wee hours of 31 August, Mary Ann Nichols was found murdered.

September 1888

Bayne continues to keep his diary while in France for the entire month. He includes entries which reference letters from his mother and Liddon, who had gone his own way to Germany, a country which Bayne preferred not to visit. He spends much of the time at public or private "baths" in France; bathing in special waters is mentioned frequently in Bayne's diary, just as it was a favorite activity of Liddon.

On the 2nd, Dodgson attended church twice, once with Isa; but attending twice was not an unusual practice on Sundays. He was also in virtually daily attendance at chapel services. The remainder of the entries for September are for the 4th, 6th, 14th, 18th, and 22nd, all of which reflect activities with Isa.

Annie Chapman was murdered on the 8th.

On the 18th the manuscripts indicate that Dodgson wrote a very angry entry regarding the rudeness of a Mr. Murley, who had apparently treated him very badly when he had visited the Murley home. He wrote Mrs. Murley that he would not let Isa accept her invitation to visit again "and that she probably could guess why." But the diary offers no clue. On other occasions he had responded similarly when either mothers or fathers openly or by implication questioned his involvement with their daughters.

On the 28th the first "Dear Boss" letter was received by the Central News Office, followed three days later by the postcard that referenced and added authenticity to the first letter.

On 30 September Eddowes and Stride were murdered. Dodgson was in Eastbourne; but there were no diary entries from the 22nd of September until 3 October during which the murders occurred. Isa was still with him in Eastbourne.

October 1888

On the 3rd, Dodgson notes that he had returned Isa to her family and that she had visited longer than anyone had in 1887, during which time he had five child guests over a period of twenty-five days. On the 4th he records feeling lonely without Isa, certainly a natural reaction, but notable, none-the-less.

Bayne writes that he returned from France on the 5th.

On the 11th, Dodgson returned to Oxford, stopping off in London for several visits.

On the 14th Bayne notes for the first time the subject of a sermon. He was one to avoid them, rarely attending any except those given by Liddon, who was renowned at Oxford and St. Paul's Cathedral as a preacher. On Easter Sunday just passed, he had gone to early service expecting there would be no sermon, and walked out as soon as the priest started one. The subject worthy of today's diary entry was: "May it be my blessed lot to live the life of a *Taylor* and die the death of a *Bull!*" (Bayne's italics). Again we could question what he meant and just whether he had a plan to achieve what heretofore no one would perceive as a bull-like existence.

On the 15th Mr. Lusk received a package containing a letter "from Hell" and a piece of Catherine Eddowes's kidney.

On the 27th, Dodgson sees Dr. Burnett, a practitioner of homeo-pathic medicine, who diagnoses a spleen disorder as the probable cause of "eczema and varicosis."

On the 29th, he records in the margin that he has invented the "Wonderland Stamp Case," which would later be produced as "The Wonderland Postage-Stamp Case," although few refer to it by its full name.   Dr. Thomas Openshaw, who had examined the kidney and declared it likely that of Mrs. Eddowes, receives his letter.

November 1888

Throughout November and into early December Dodgson's handwriting further deteriorated.

On the 1st, he visited for the first time with Alice's husband, Reginald Hargreaves, and reminisced about the difficulty in linking the adult Alice with the young child he once knew so well.

On the 7th the poem "Eight little whores" is received.   Two days later Marie Kelly is murdered.   Dodgson was at Oxford.

On the 13th he hears from Savile Clark that Richard Mansfield will produce *Alice* and open on 26 December.

On the 25th he writes that he preached again in Guildford (first note of having preached since January) on Paul's Epistle to the Romans VIII.8.   That verse reads: "Those who obey their human nature cannot please God."

On the 30th he records thoughts regarding *Sylvie and Bruno*, that separating them into two volumes might be a good idea, and he tentatively targets December 1889 for the first, the following year for the second (it would not appear until 1893).

December 1888

Mrs. Bayne died on 2 December.   Bayne had been in close touch with her during her final decline and was with her when she died. Despite the fact that Dodgson and Mrs. Bayne were close friends — the diaries reflect that he often accompanied her to museums and shows in London — he did not make any mention of her death or attendance at her funeral except for a brief note on the 7th.   And then it was only in parentheses as he referenced Bayne "(whose mother died last Sunday)" while on a social call to a lady friend.

On the 3rd Dodgson records that he had experienced "optical fortifications" again, this time losing vision in a large portion of the left eye. The remainder of December's entries focus on works involving logical problem-solving, as if he had buried himself in work.   Despite all the planning and earlier references, there is no mention of the opening of *Alice* on the 26th, while he does note that he began working on *The Nursery "Alice"* on the 28th.

On the 8th Bayne made his first reference to Dodgson since his own return from France on 5 October.

On the 20th, Rose Mylett was murdered. On the 22nd, Dodgson records traveling from Oxford to Guildford (for the holidays).

On the 30th Bayne attended Liddon's sermon "My life is in thy hands" and indicated that despite a deafness that he was experiencing he could hear every word. He also reported that Liddon was in ill health.

On the same day Dodgson preached at Guildford on Matthew XX.6, the parable of the workers in the vineyard, which reads:

> It was nearly five o'clock when he went to the market-place and saw some other men still standing there. "Why are you wasting the whole day here doing nothing?" he asked them.

January to December 1889

On 7 January Dodgson noted in the manuscripts that Mansfield was "*excellent*" in the role of Prince Karl. This is obviously not a character in *Alice*. There was still no mention of the *Alice in Wonderland* revival until he noted on the 10th that he had heard from Mrs. (Savile) Clarke that Mansfield had been particularly harsh with Isa: "one could not hear it without indignation." (For some reason these entries were never published.) He still does not mention whether or not he had seen it.

In May he attended the funerals of two friends, and noted them in his diary. This leaves one wondering whether he attended Mrs. Bayne's funeral in December or if there were other things occupying his mind — recall Uggug being "pre-occupied" — that left it unmentioned.

For all of 1889, all diary entries are in purple ink except for the one in black on 26 June, Commemoration Day (in prior years the day of the Masonic fete). It was a "white stone day," Dodgson's diary note for wonderful days, usually those spent with children, as this one had been.

On 17 July Alice McKenzie was murdered in the wee hours of the morning. Dodgson's diary places him in Eastbourne.

Later that morning, at 11:40, Dodgson took the train from Eastbourne to Croyden to visit friends, then went on to London to pick up Isa Bowman for her vacation with him. They left London at 3:00 P.M., arrived at 5:00, and spent the evening with friends. For the first time we see that the London to Eastbourne trip takes just two hours.

It is in this entry where we find what may very well be a slip which will help answer a question from the summer of 1888. For in returning to Eastbourne, Dodgson's manuscript entry indicates he visited "the other house," while, on the 20th the published diaries indicate that "they" had taken care of Isa while he had been away. Dodgson does not tell us who "they" are. The manuscript indicates only: "After tea I took Isa to the other house, for her to see her. (They have Miss Helen Lewis with them.)" Note the awkwardness. There is no reference to the second "her" except as an afterthought. But Roger Green expands on the published entry, telling us that "they" are Louisa and Margaret (his sisters), Alice (his sister-in-law), and Alice's three children. He no doubt obtained his information from the family as he was their choice to be editor of the diaries.

In the summer of 1889, Dodgson's sister Louisa had a place at Eastbourne; she was there with their sister Margaret and their brother's wife Alice and her children! Is it possible that they had rented a place there in 1888? Dodgson vacationed there every year for nearly twenty years. Is it possible that he had used his naive sisters to care for his guest while he was off in London the year before just as he acknowledged he had done on the 20th? Did his family and closest child friend Isa provide the window of opportunity to spend a night or two in London?

On 21 August we have a different scenario reflected in the manuscripts. He declines another family's request to take the children, indicating that "3 consecutive nights is too much." The question of whether sleeping over was a practice at the beach is answered. Had Isa slept over with them or some other family in 1888 for one or more nights?

Dodgson's emotional dependence on the children becomes increasingly evident in 1889. In another unpublished entry that reflects his emotional life, on 22 and 23 July he refers to Isa and her sister Nellie as "my children" on two occasions and describes walking with them in "my `Paradise´" (Eastbourne, more specifically Beachy Point).

On 2 September Dodgson was suffering from a number of maladies whose origins lie in stress, including boils, synovitis, and another attack of moving fortifications. On the 10th, Henry Parry Liddon died. On the following day, Dodgson's entry is in black ink; then he returns to purple.

On 9 November he preached at the College Servant's Service on Mark XVI.7. This time he quoted the passage: "Go your way, tell his disciples, and Peter, that he goeth before you into Galilee; there shall ye see him." Dodgson's underlining of the words is curious. As we have seen *Peter* had a special meaning to him. In Victorian slang it meant *penis*, or, in another slang word, *prick*. It figured in the first game played on him within a day or two on his arrival at public school, "Peter, the red lion" and in his secret message to his brother Skeff. I believe it was the beginning of the ordeal that turned him against his parents because of their abandonment of him, an ordeal that made the nights a terror for him throughout his life. This may have been the reason that the middle of the night was chosen to wreak vengeance on both mother figures and father-like authority figures, the police. Was "and Peter" italicized to emphasize that he identified himself in an obscene distortion as "me, the gilt cock," a special apostle with a special message? Was this the "prickly" figure, the transformation of Uggug, going forth to do the Lord's work, yet wreaking his own vengeance as he stabbed and mutilated anuses and vaginas, a reworking of the homosexual assaults he experienced?

Dodgson made another biblical reference to the same theme on 22 April 1877, an entry not included in the published diaries. It is clear that such associations as that made in underlining "Peter" were in his conscious mind. In the entry he noted that he had heard a striking sermon on

> . . ."a narrow place, where there [sic] was no way to turn either to the right or to the left." Such "narrow places," where one *must* meet God face to face, come in sorrow — in disgrace — in temptation — in the hour of death (Dodgson's italics). [5]

This is a pivotal entry. It is as clear a reference to the horrors of oral sex or sodomy to him and his conflicting association of them with God as one could expect to find. What was the nature of that meeting which took place with God? I suggest he came away from it with a mission and a justification for it. The affinity between this entry and the theme of *The Hunting of the Snark: An Agony in Eight Fits*, which some analysts and critics believe focuses on existential annihilation [6] is remarkable.

It could also be a screen for the murder of the prostitutes in the same existential confrontation in the dark, narrow alleyways of the East End.

January to December 1890

The entries for this year are routine, with a great deal of work on writing, especially *Sylvie and Bruno Concluded*, theater-going, and socializing. The summer was again spent at Eastbourne.

From 24 October until the 31st he kept to his rooms, suffering from "ague, cystitis, and lumbago."

If there was one thing on which Dodgson rarely made comment in his diaries, it was the subject of politics. On 29 November, however, he wrote "History is moving briskly just now!" What he describes as "history" is a divorce scandal in Gladstone's government and the more serious "Home Rule" bill and the political shenanigans going on behind the scenes.

It was on 6 December that he took such offense at *The Saint James's Gazette* for identifying him with his pseudonym "Lewis Carroll." He had written to them condemning as profane a stage performance at Queen's College, Oxford. In response to his letter, someone wrote accusing Lewis Carroll of being himself profane in parodying the Book of Proverbs in his poem "'Tis the voice of the sluggard." In his letter Dodgson begged the *Gazette* never to make the association again and he persisted in his wish for privacy. He never wrote to that paper again.

January to December 1891

1891 began at Guildford. All entries for the year are in black ink. On 25 January he preached on Acts 9.6. This text reads: "But get up and go into the city, where you will be told what you must do." On 2 February he preached again on Romans 8.28, whose theme is "chosenness" and the need to accept the purpose for which one is chosen even if it is not understood: "We know that in all things God works for good with those who love him, those he has called according to his purpose."

On the 6th he fainted "cold dead away" and speculates that the cause might have been epilepsy. The manuscript indicates that his doctor felt it was just a fainting spell. On the 12th he writes that the doctor has changed his diagnosis to an epileptic fit that "passed off" into sleep. He also notes that the only other time it had occurred was on 31 December 1885.

I do not know the circumstances of the 1885 episode, or, with apologies to readers, if he recorded it at the time. Although Green published this occurrence, he omitted the reference to any episode in 1885; in fact, there is no published entry for that date in 1885.

On the 12th he writes that he feels better, but still has a headache.

On the 13th Frances Coles was murdered.

Dodgson's next entry is on the 19th and is routine. On 5 March the manuscript reflects that this is the first time he had been on a train "since February," but there is no entry to identify when in February it was.

On 24 September he notes that he had invented the "Typhlograph," later to be renamed the "Nyctograph." As we have seen, this appears to have striking similarities to Masonic cipher encoding.

There are no other entries worthy of note. His life resumed its routine, filled with social engagements, the theater, the children, and writing.

After 1891

There are only a few episodes beyond the publication of *Sylvie and Bruno Concluded* in December of 1893 that deserve mention. Throughout 1892 and 1893 the manuscripts indicate that Dodgson preached at least four times on the same theme, in one entry noting the frequency, it was on Luke XI.4, the portion of the Lord's prayer that reads "lead us not into temptation."

In the middle of January 1892, he was again suffering from pains in the knee which lasted into March. On the 30th he noted his sixtieth birthday (which was actually on 27 January) and recorded how "ill spent" his years had been; he prayed for forgiveness and help for the future. It had been some time since such an entry had appeared in the diaries, a theme that filled them in earlier years although they rarely appeared in the published *Diaries*.

While at the beach in October 1893, he was forbidden by a Mrs. Richards from ever dining with or even walking with her daughter again. While Green does not mention the incident more than once, the manuscripts indicate that Dodgson brooded on it in his diary for several days. It seems that there had been rumors about him circulating among the mothers, rumors he blamed on Mrs. Richards. Another woman explained to him that Mrs. Richards had not originated the gossip but that she was concerned about the one-on-one hospitality, which Dodgson interpreted as meaning "in his rooms." On the 10th he met young Marion on the street, spoke with her briefly, thanked her for a note she had sent him, but refused to walk with her, piqued, but also no doubt protective of the child's relationship with her mother.

What is interesting about this passage is the noticeable deterioration in Dodgson's handwriting during the few days until he became reconciled to it on the 10th. It represented further evidence to me that his handwriting did change during stressful periods. Unfortunately, through an error in notation, I was unable to obtain a copy of those portions of the diary from the British Library. I had sought them because the writing was remarkably similar to some of the worst of the Ripper letters.

Conclusions

What conclusions or inferences can be made from these diary entries? Except for a claim that he was unable to walk in March and into early April 1888, when Emma Smith was murdered, there is nothing that excludes the possibility of Dodgson having visited in London on all of the dates in question. Whether he was "home based" at Oxford, Guildford, or Eastbourne, however, he was intimately familiar with the public transportation system and just a few hours away. There is no question that he would have been required to find someone to take Isa for the nights in August and September, which included the "double event." Certainly further investigation could be done to determine if the family was an actual or possible source of such care in 1888.

We can note the pattern of stress in both health and handwriting. The experience of optical fortifications in early December 1888 could have been a delayed response to the 9 November murder of Kelly or in anticipation of the upcoming murder on the 20th. The fainting spell in February 1891 could very well have been the result of a building anxiety for something he felt compelled to do, a compulsion evident in the themes chosen for his preaching. That he would experience anticipatory stress after November would be totally consistent with the orgy that occurred there and what the anagrams suggest might have been his response.

If there is a pervasive characteristic of Bayne's diary throughout the years he kept it (five volumes from 1886 to 1990, with one volume missing), it is of unmitigated boredom. His reference at age sixty to exiting this life as a *bull*, after having lived it very much as a *taylor* is suggestive, as he certainly appeared to live it as a taylor. Dodgson's, on the other hand, is thoroughly filled with social activity. But this can often be a compulsive effort to avoid the boredom, and the torments, of being left alone with oneself.

When Dodgson died on 22 January 1898, Bayne noted the passing in his diary, also that Charles's brother Wilfred had come to visit; but he made no mention of having attended the funeral which was quite a public event filled with praise for the author.

Of particular relevance in the theories regarding the Ripper murders as driven by a religious monomania, the biblical themes chosen by Dodgson (at least those recorded in the diary) from 1887 to 1891 are universal in their reference to chosenness, chosenness for an unspecified but God-given task, about going out and doing God's will. Then, following the murders, the themes are inner-focused, about avoiding temptation. If he were Jack the Ripper and were preaching on those themes, it is highly likely that he would find both sermon preparation and delivery stressful, beyond the stammering which he and others identify as the likely primary reason he avoided the task.

Perhaps the nonsense that ends "The Gardener's Song" — "He thought he saw an Argument / That proved he was the Pope" — is not nonsense after all, but the truth hidden in clear, but not well known history. It was in 1870 that the doctrine of papal infallibility had been proclaimed by the church in Rome. There had always been a special relationship with the divinity claimed. Dodgson was unquestionably aware of papal history in his studies of the church and the Oxford Movement in which his friend Liddon was involved. As Robert De Rosa describes the horrid lives lived by some of the popes in his *Vicars of Christ*, published in 1988, [7] it would not have been difficult to draw the parallel between the hypocrisy of the Masons which allowed murder and treason at its highest levels with the hypocritical contradiction between papal lives lived and the Christian message for which infallible authority as messenger was claimed. Papal murder and treason (in a religious sense) for the perpetuation of the organization and preferred members certainly occurred over centuries. For Dodgson to have interpreted any felt chosenness in a similar fashion would have been no more unreasonable than the allusion made in the nonsense.

But beyond these perhaps subtle and at times opaque suggestions, there is absolutely nothing in the diaries or letters to definitely place Dodgson or Bayne at the scenes of the Ripper murders. Neither is there anything to place them elsewhere in the hours just preceding or following them.

Chapter 12

Handwriting Analysis

In the years since they first appeared, the letters believed to have possibly been written by Jack the Ripper have been subjected to a number of analyses. These efforts were aimed at providing answers to two investigatory questions. The first involved understanding the psychological profile of the letter writer and whether that profile fit into a hypothesized "Ripper" profile. The second was to determine if any of the letters received had been written by the same person. All of these efforts were hindered by having no suspect to use as a base of comparison. To my knowledge no effort was made to analyze them against the readily available handwriting of historical suspects as they emerged — Montague Druitt, William Gull, J. K. Stephen, or Prince Eddy.

As part of this investigation I returned from London with facsimile copies of several pages from the diary manuscripts of Charles Dodgson and several Ripper letters from the Metropolitan Police microfilm records. These included the letters and postcard considered most likely to be authentic. All of the material was submitted to a forensic handwriting analyst, Rose Caterino, recommended to me by the Massachusetts State Police, who use her services as an expert witness in investigations involving documents and possible forgeries. Caterino, a member of The World Association of Document Examiners and the International Graphoanalysis Society, Inc., also does extensive handwriting analyses for purposes of describing personality characteristics of employees of business organizations who contract for her services.

The process involved in providing Caterino with the material deserves examination. The contracted engagement was explicitly identified as a research effort into the identity of Jack the Ripper and that the suspect in the investigation was not one who heretofore had appeared in the literature. This was done for two reasons: to interest her in the effort and to identify the items as Victorian in nature so that period-specific differences in writing and writing instruments would be incorporated into the analysis. The identity of the writer of the diaries was not provided until I had received her report, read it, and completed interview questions regarding elaboration on some aspects of the findings. The specific diary pages were identified only as "from the suspect's age twenties, two from his forties, and several from his fifties," and included one identified as having been written at the height of the spree and the diary entry that records his "fainting cold dead away" the week before the murder of Frances Coles. From those pages I requested a personality analysis of the writer and her opinion as to whether that writer was capable of murdering and mutilating several women. We agreed that no other information about the writer would be provided and that she would avoid "corrupting" her analysis by reading any of the literature on Jack the Ripper. Most explicitly and succinctly, I requested that all inferences come from the analysis of the handwriting.

The Ripper letters were divided into two groups, those that were historically believed authentic and the remainder of the group I had selected. Unfortunately, the "conundrum" letter was not included. Caterino was to render an opinion as to whether the writer of the diaries was the writer of any of the letters. I did not submit for examination any other letters that had been published in facsimile by others.

In retrospect, this approach is subject to the very valid criticism that it depends too much on the integrity of the analyst to remain objective. A better procedure would have been to identify the diaries only as Victorian in origin without identifying them as the work of my Ripper suspect, to provide no lead as to what I thought the profile might contain based on suspecting very violent homicidal behavior. Then, once the personality analysis had been completed, the letters signed "Jack the Ripper" could have been introduced and analyzed. As the process unfolded, however, I became convinced that the integrity of the engagement had not been compromised, but in fact benefitted from Caterino's enthusiasm to dig deeper into Victorian handwriting. Be that as it may, in the end we return to both credentials and integrity as the ultimate test in the analysis because the source material used here is available to anyone who would wish to do an independent analysis. A condition of the engagement was that the findings would be incorporated into a published work. My own commitment was to publish the findings whether or not they supported my hypothesis.

Letter Findings

The findings from this analysis were mixed, very disappointing in one case, quite confirming in the other. To take the disappointing finding first, the analysis indicates with considerable certainty that none of the Ripper letters presented were written by the writer of the diaries. This means also that there is equal certainty that the letters were not an effort by the diary writer to disguise his handwriting. The technical reasons for those conclusions were provided to me but presentation of them here is not authorized.   On the other hand, Caterino suggested that it is quite possible that the first group of letters — the historical "most likely valid" Ripper letters — were written by the same writer and that some of the other letters were written by the same writer.

This latter suggestion begs for a comparison with the handwriting of Dodgson's close friends if samples could be obtained.   Thomas Bayne's writing is clearly available from his own diaries at Christ Church, Oxford; and to the eye of this amateur his writing is extraordinarily close to the primary Ripper letter written in a schoolboy's hand. Comparison with the writing of Montague Druitt and perhaps Henry Parry Liddon could yield interesting results.   Both Bayne and Liddon were very stressed during this period.   And we know that Druitt was. Given the condition of the letters before they were microfilmed, an examination of the originals, if available, might help the effort, especially if a chemical analysis of the ink can still be done to determine if the letters are done in the same ink as diaries or letters.

Diary Findings

The analysis of the diary manuscripts, on the other hand, represents an extraordinary and independent confirmation of the profile provided here and in more detail in *The Agony of Lewis Carroll*. It also confirms and extends the handwriting analysis performed by Dr. Mannheim for Derek Hudson's biography of Carroll and it also confirms the very unresolved issues in my earlier work, issues that led me to question whether this writer of rage-filled anagrams could move from writing as a means of rage expression to action.   It especially confirms questions which lingered regarding the integrity of Dodgson's avowed religious convictions.   The remainder of this chapter summarizes the findings from this analysis and quotes liberally from Caterino's report. [1]   Those portions in parentheses are my own inferences from her comments.

The writer's character was a complex one reflecting strong and conflicting forces.   The strength of these forces created a management process within the writer's personality so that he presented only those aspects which he wished to be seen and hid those that he wished to hide.   In reality, it was those negative forces which most drove him. (What we see is a conscious, not an unconscious, Jekyll-Hyde personality.)

The writer was a "fastidious and most sensitive individual. . . [with] discriminating tastes."   He was "idealistic," concerned with propriety, and felt deeply about right and wrong. Words such as *"indoctrinated, infused, affected,* and *colored dramatically"* describe the way his emotional life was experienced. (These words suggest a rigidity in position, an inner rather than an outer drivenness, and strong emotions.) When "touched" emotionally, he was driven by a "strong moral pressure to be exact, accurate, precise, selective, and astute. . . [he was] a thorough and remarkable critic." This appearance of dignity, however, was a facade "which enabled [the writer] to function well in the realm of the upper-crust in society."

The diary writer "had an active interest in the cultural and literary fields." He was by nature interesting, "had worthwhile interests about which to talk; and he would most certainly hold the interests of others who related well to his interests." The enthusiasm found in his writing was an infectious attraction that carried others along with him. With a strong intuitive sense, he possessed an "awareness of everything that was going on around him." This sense, (perhaps driven by a vigilance needed for facade maintenance), was supported by an enormous capacity for detail such that he could achieve "perfection and thoroughness in all of his accomplishments." His memory for such details was excellent (although we know from other sources that his memory for names and dates, those things which reflect a true relatedness to people and events-in-time, was poor).

The writer possessed a great "fear of the judgement of others. Acceptance as an individual was very important to him." Indeed, he was "obsessed with a desire for approval. . . . [He] was basically insecure. He felt unable to cope with a situation or situations which others handled well. . . . He was uncomfortably conscious of himself. . . may have felt [himself] an object of the observation of others with whom he felt less comfortable." (This has long been considered a major dynamic in his involvement with children, by whom he felt adored. It is also a part of the psychological profile of a stutterer.) "He had an aversion toward criticisms concerning his ideas, theories, and philosophies. His self-conscious state made it rather difficult for him to truly enjoy the company of others who differed in their points of view from his. He was selective about his acquaintances." When the approval of others was not forthcoming, his own "self-righteousness and self-approval" were effective substitutes in restoring self-esteem.

Driven by great "pride" and "vanity," the writer "hid from others that which runs counter to approved or conventional conduct. He was not above-board, open or candid when he spoke. The traits of acquisitiveness and tenaciousness combined indicated self-interest, no matter how generous he appeared to be toward others (the historical biographical conclusions). He had a grasping nature. He would appear to others as a dignified and considerate individual."

In conjunction with this trait, he was a jealous man, "hostile toward anyone whom he believed enjoyed an advantage over him. . . vigilant in guarding anything he tenaciously possessed." This trait was constant and very strong throughout the range of diary samples.

Always thinking, the writer "excelled in learning about theories and philosophies," an activity he approached with an eager mind. But, quite importantly, Caterino labels him a skeptic in all of its meanings — one who "*habitually* doubts, questions, or suspends judgement upon matters generally accepted. . . one who doubts religious doctrines, *especially those of Christianity* (my italics)." He was not easily persuaded and "doubted the fundamental doctrines of religion" although there are signs that he may have been a churchman.

The writer was possessed with great determination that drove him to complete all of the tasks he undertook; and they "would be done well. He was well organized and persisted in accomplishing his goals. He would take the initiative to explore all areas of a given task. He was keenly analytical. . . direct. . . cautious." Within this dynamic, he had "an avid disregard for authority." (This trait of possessing a "rebellious mind" was detected by M. J. Mannheim, handwriting analyst for biographer Derek Hudson, from a letter written while Dodgson was a student at Oxford.)

The personality trait that appears the strongest and most subject to being hidden was that of "sensuality." The writer was "preoccupied-engrossed in things of a sensual nature. Sensuality predominates. This trait has a superior strength and exerts control over the writer. He had a preoccupation with sensual expression. This was a side of his nature which could not be seen by others. . . [This hidden influence, like others] betrayed those around him." Here again, Caterino is explicit about her use of the term *sensual* — "fondness for or indulgence in sensual pleasures, lasciviousness, lewdness. . . . [Such feelings] enveloped most of his being." All of this was despite the fact that he was seen by others as a strict moral man.

Caterino posits that the writer may have been raised by a very domineering mother. She sees a "strong desire for fulfillment with the opposite sex [but that] due to his strict upbringing [he was made to feel] that such feelings were wrong and immoral to be felt; and therefore, those who brought about such feelings in him and others like him should be banished from society." In response to questioning, Caterino indicated that the writer was not comfortable with his own sexuality, and that there was a "strong possibility that he was homosexual."

Very evident in the early diaries is evidence that the writer had felt spurned by someone "he admired immensely, [with whom he was] strongly in love. . . [with whom he had] an unbelievable deep devotion." When queried, Caterino insisted on *spurning*, being pushed away, not *abandonment*, as the operative feeling.

Departing briefly from Caterino's analysis: Phyllis Greenacre, author of the earliest complete psychological study of Dodgson, *Swift and Carroll: A Psychoanalytic Study of Two Lives*, pointed to the quick succession of siblings that followed his birth and the likelihood that he was "pushed away" by a busy mother at barely one year of age. Such a child often continues to pursue the mother's attention and love (which he not only believes he has lost, but has lost due to some defect in him). [2] In the case of Dodgson's mother, it appears (biographers agree) that he was her favorite throughout his childhood, but by this time no amount of adoration was enough to outweigh the hurt of feeling spurned. In *The Agony of Lewis Carroll*, I suggested that the young boy sacrificed his sense of self by becoming the perfect child for his parents in a desperate attempt to gain (or in this case regain) their approval, to measure up to what they wanted, to be a clone of his father. Then he experienced extraordinarily traumatic feelings of abandonment when he entered the sexually assaultive life at public school, a life totally in conflict with what his parents had taught, yet an environment they sent him into, most likely not forewarned. This could have been felt as a second spurning, a turning out from what was to him a safe world of home. There is also the possibility that at some point he sought relief from the school experience from his parents and was rebuffed, told to deal with it, to "grow up" as it were, but the early "Dear Skeff" letter suggests he was and felt very much alone with the experience from the beginning.

From the diary sample written in the middle of the murder spree Caterino sees:

> The corroding influence of the traits, sensuality and jealousy are found throughout these writings. His emotional responsiveness becomes unpredictable. His defiance against authority is very strong. He becomes highly aggressive and is driven by his feelings. The writing indicates that he is intent on a purpose and persistent in his pursuits. His outlook on life is bleak. Pessimism has set in. (Recall that Bayne had reported that he and Dodgson had gone through a "Slough of Despond" in April 1888.)

(At this time, in addition to the self-satisfaction the Ripper would have been experiencing as he continued the spree undetected, the reactions of the press and public would only serve to support a hunger for approval.   Yet we can never forget Dodgson's ability to satisfy himself secretly.)   Caterino continues, indicating that the writer was carefully measuring the consequences of his acts and decisions.

> A deliberateness is also indicated in the writing. . . a due attention to the arguments within himself which were for or against a stand he may have taken.   He took the time to consider carefully and fully the consequences of an outcome. He was no longer sudden or rash in his thinking.   He was very self-conscious of every move he made.   He was under an emotional ordeal.

From the diary page written in 1891, when he was fifty-nine, just before the murder of Frances Coles, Caterino sees:

> The writings take on a stabilized appearance.   The corroding influence of the traits, sensuality and jealousy still prevail.   The trait of defiance still persists; that is, his avid disregard for authority.   Distrust and a lack of faith in the authorities in his life encouraged boldness and a continuing resistance toward any opposition.   Any authority offered him a challenge to defy it.   Past hurtful experiences still hover over [the writer].   The trait of persistence found in the writing [reflects] the writer [had] a hard time in ridding himself of the hurtful experiences of the past.   Nothing in his behavior pattern has changed.

There was nothing in this last diary entry examined to indicate that the writer's then current behavior would change, so imbued in his character were the strong negative traits and forces.

In response to the specific question: "Could the writer of these diaries have murdered and mutilated several women?"   Caterino provides a confident and unequivocal "Yes."

Conclusion

What we have here is confirmation by an independent analyst of a person who harbored deep resentments toward a primary love object — the mother, a resentment which still was as strong or stronger at age fifty than it had been at age twenty. With a sexuality in total conflict with a rigidly and forcefully taught moral code, he had the potential for an explosive release of built-in rage which used distorted sexual release as the means of expression. Here was a man obsessed with detail and thorough planning, defiant of all authority, self-satisfied with his own grand accomplishments even if ignored or disdained by others.

We see an independent confirming source for a profile of a hater of at least one woman, driven by very early feelings of having been spurned by an adored object of his love. He was a man able to hide, who had, in fact hidden from public view the most negative of the forces that drove him in life, especially those represented by sensual pleasure. Yet he was a man with an extraordinary ability to plan, with uncanny awareness and attention to detail, an extraordinarily complex operation which would allow him to revel in secret over his successful defiance of the highest authority in the land.

Chapter 13

Dates, Names, and Numbers

There has been much written over the years about the dates on which the Ripper murders occurred, not only the specific days and their possible symbolic meaning but the patterns involved. It is useful to examine dates as they might apply to Charles Dodgson because he was a Latin, Greek, and church scholar, all areas steeped in the historical and symbolic meaning of dates. There is risk, however, in drawing too much from them because one is left with the inverse question, not of why certain dates were "chosen," but why certain others were not. We must also be sensitive to the issue of security and victim availability, for any of the murders might not have taken place on the precise day planned.

Perhaps the first thing noticed at the time was the extent to which the murders occurred on week-ends.

Emma Smith	3 April	Tuesday
Martha Tabram	7 August	Tuesday
Mary Ann Nichols	31 August	Friday
Annie Chapman	8 September	Saturday
Elizabeth Stride	30 September	Sunday
Catherine Eddowes	30 September	Sunday
Marie Kelly	9 November	Friday
Rose Mylett	20 December	Thursday
Alice McKenzie	17 July	Wednesday
Frances Coles	13 February	Friday

As can be seen, the pattern is true for the traditional five murders and again for the oft-rejected murder of Frances Coles. It is certainly not true of the others. Despite the fact that the papers classified (retrospectively) the murder of Smith as the first of the Ripper victims, only after Mary Ann Nichols was killed, the emerging pattern which followed in subsequent murders captured the imaginations of the police, papers, and even Queen Victoria. This weekend pattern led to suspicions that the murderer might come from a profession that brought him to London on the weekends, a search that settled on the sailors from ships whose arrivals and departures fit the pattern. Considerable investigation ensued, perhaps fanned by the line from the Ripper poem "Nor yet a foreign skipper." The notion that it would fit the pattern of an out-of-town schoolteacher was not heavily weighed, if at all, until Druitt began to emerge as a suspect in the more recent literature.

As far as Dodgson is concerned, any pattern is quite meaningless, although in at least three of the four murders which occurred during the week, Dodgson and Bayne were on school break. In addition to possibly having a rented house in London, he often stayed over at hotels there. But an overnight stay was not necessary as the trains ran through the night between London and all three of his homes — Oxford, Guildford, and Eastbourne. He records in his diary often taking an overnight train, especially to distant points. Even his work schedule allowed for great flexibility. He had a light academic schedule teaching very basic mathematics; he had taught it for a number of years and extensive preparation was not required. While he was curator of the Common Room from 1882 until 1892, those duties allowed for great control of his own time. He chose when he performed clerical duties. The flexibility in his schedule was enormous, one of the characteristics listed by some Ripper analysts as a most likely part of a suspect profile.

Those who favor Druitt as a suspect focus on the observed pattern that the murders had been committed on weekends which spanned month beginnings and endings. This is certainly true of the central five, with a gap of a month in October. This is also true of the first two but is not true of the murders of Mylett, McKenzie and Coles, which occurred in the middle of the month. Again, from the standpoint of Dodgson as a suspect, patterns in date placement here are meaningless as he was generally free to do as he pleased.

As we examine the symbolic meanings of the murder dates, however, we find some interesting coincidences and patterns. Unfortunately, one aspect of the research which I have not been able to pursue (none of the several biographies lend any support) is whether any of the murders coincide with birthdays of Dodgson's parents or siblings.

All of what follows notwithstanding, it is difficult to believe that the Ripper went out on specific nights and was universally successful in bringing together a victim and a safe situation in which to perform his task. There must have been nights when he was unsuccessful and put things off for a day or more. However, it would be easy to believe that this consummate planner met the women in public before the fateful rendezvous and set an agreed-upon time to meet in the dark, perhaps enticed to do so with a small gift along with friendly, disarming conversation.

Before proceeding I should provide for reemphasis a summary of an important piece of *The Agony of Lewis Carroll*. It is my belief that Dodgson virtually assumed the identity of the Greek mythological figure, Orestes, which we have already seen. To refresh briefly, believing he had received a command from the god Apollo, but fueled also by resentment at his mother's abandonment of him to unspeakable acts in the Greek school system, Orestes put his mother to the sword. Dodgson updated the story by holding his father also responsible for his experience, that being off "fighting the wars" (involved in his own church work) was not an adequate excuse for turning over his upbringing totally to his mother.

The thesis of *The Agony of Lewis Carroll* was that Dodgson took on the Orestes persona, incorporated it into his real/fantasy life, and devoted his entire life to destroying his mother primarily, but also his father, with *words*, the anagram for *sword*. When he found that battle lacking in its ability to satisfy his retributive obsessions, it is the thesis of this book that he perverted his father's clerical effort of ministering to sinners by making his task a "holy" one and further destroyed his image-of-mother by returning to the Orestes-Jabberwocky theme, but this time with the *sword*. In that light, Dodgson was very much tied to Greek myth and its influence on his life.

Let us run down the dates.

Dates

3 April

This is one of the most significant of all of the dates and one reason among several why I believe Emma Smith was the first victim. It is the birth date of Cybele, the Greek, Roman, and Oriental "Great Mother of the Gods." This feast crosses all cultures. Cybele was the symbol of all motherhood — gods, man, and lower creatures. She was especially the mother of wild creatures, and festal celebrations were characterized by orgiastic activities, the themes of the God Dionysos. She was attended by creatures who were half demons and she was ministered to by eunuch priests. The celebration rites ended with self-abuse to the point of exhaustion. [1]   This is exactly the theme of "Jabberwocky" in which the act of masturbation preceded and followed the slaying of the "evil gender." It also coincides with themes found in many anagrams in *The Agony of Lewis Carroll* and touches every aspect of what I believe constituted Dodgson's self-perception.

I doubt there could be any closer symbolism than that surrounding this goddess. Served by heterosexually impotent priests, symbols of the psychologically castrated and heterosexually impotent gay son, an orgy of the symbolic self-abuse of masturbation ensued, not in celebration of the birth of the mother-symbol, but in celebration of her destruction. Even though it is uncertain whether the Ripper masturbated during or after these murders and mutilations, the accepted theory on sexual murder assigns sexual symbolic value to the orgiastic handling of mutilated viscera. It is this handling that arouses the sexual impulse, which may then be released by masturbation. Within his assumed persona, this symbolic Orestes destroyed this mother of mothers.

But within the Christian tradition in which he was raised, 3 April was Easter Monday in 1888, one day after the celebration of Christ's resurrection. Was Dodgson beginning his own felt "resurrection" with a series of murders which he hoped would free him from his compulsions and urges by sating them?

6 August

Philip Sugden, Colin Wilson and Robin Odell place this murder on the 6th [2] while others place it on the 7th. Martha Tabram's body was found at about 3:00 A.M. The 6th coincides with the birthday of Clarence's uncle, the Duke of Edinburgh. [3] But perhaps more significantly 6 August is the Feast of the Transfiguration in the Roman Catholic calendar of feasts. This feast celebrates the New Testament story in which Christ's special relationship with God the Father was made manifest in the presence of his Apostles. If the Ripper were operating on the basis of some delusion of connectedness to the Divinity, the very theme of the Orestes story, then this date could represent a partial confirmation of that story in Christian terms.

31 August

Wilson identifies the 31st as the birthday of Princess Wilhelmina of the Netherlands [4] but attaches no significance to it. While Mary Ann Nichols was found at 3:45 A.M., her body still warm, the Ripper may very well have been stalking her earlier in the evening of the day in which Roman Catholics commemorate the beheading of John the Baptist. It was John who was the Messenger, the precursor to the Messianic message of salvation, the impending arrival of the Redeemer.

August itself has a meaning in Greek tradition. It derived its name from festivals to Eros, which included festivals that focused on children and the spirits of the unknown world [5] and rituals to Orestes.

8 September

On this date the first serious mutilation occurred and the first uterus was removed (from Annie Chapman). Again turning to Roman Catholic Christian tradition we have another Feast dedicated to a mother, this time Mary, the Blessed Virgin, mother of Jesus Christ, and honored as mother of mankind and the Church.

30 September

This was the date of the "double event." No one suggests significance to this date but again if we look at the stalking as having begun earlier in the evening, we are on the 29th, the feast day of Michael, the Archangel, who in Christian tradition confronted the devil with his sword and drove him and his rebellious cohorts out of heaven, another messenger doing the work of God to defeat the evil one.

Looking into the Greek world, we find this date to be the birthday of the playwright Euripides (480 B.C.), [6] who, like fellow Greek Aeschylus, wrote a version of the Orestes story. Were these murders a fitting memorial to the origins of Orestes, the mother-slayer?

The Greek word for September derives from a title of Artemus, the "Shooter of Deer." Was there a "sportsman's" costume being worn as part of the Ripper murders? The deerstalker hat was seen among suspects near the victims.

9 November

This is the date of Marie Kelly's murder. Wilson identifies this as the birthday of the prince of Wales, Clarence's father. Within the England of the day, there could probably be no other person who so represented the symbol of self indulgence in sexual matters than the prince. His appetite appeared to be insatiable and notorious. There could be no symbolically better day to "use" a woman in the most perverse way to dedicate the day to the so evident monarchical hypocrisy. The Prince's behavior was such that it prompted a most telling comment from his mother, Queen Victoria, when she said twenty years before these murders that the behavior of the Royal household was no less decadent than that which led to the Revolution in France one hundred years before. [7] Her fear was that the socialist claims were not totally without merit; her government was already fearful of the growing unrest, so much so that they would later reorganize the police department into a quasi-military force to quell the riots.

On this particular date in 1888, London was celebrating Lord Mayor's Day, certainly no better day to choose for a ghastly murder. For the police were quite preoccupied with crowd control, never mind being on the lookout for a possible murderer. And what better way to insult the authorities than to usurp the attention of the city again?

Two days previous to this, the Greeks celebrated a feast dedicated to Apollo, who Orestes claimed had commanded him to murder his mother.

17 July

This is the date of Alice McKenzie's murder. I find no religious significance to it, but it is preceded in Catholic tradition by another feast to the Virgin Mary which dated from the eighteenth century.

Perhaps of some significance, it was on 13 July 1880, nine years before this, that Dodgson's child friend Alice Liddell consented to marry Reginald Hargreaves. [8] Was there a reminder of a spurning, betrayal, or abandonment? Had overwhelming feelings overcome the fear that had emerged after the Kelly murder? Is this why a mid-July victim was named "Alice?" Nine years later, was Alice his nineth victim?

13 February

What I believe to be the last of the Ripper's victims, Frances Coles, occurred on a date which has by far the most coincidences of any of his victims. February was the month of expiation. The 13th was the Ides (night) of the full moon and fed right into the belief that a lunatic had been at large. It was the eve of the feast of St. Valentine, on which day Victorians exchanged Valentine Day gifts to loved ones.

It was also the anniversary of the beheading of Catherine Howard, fifth wife of Henry VIII, in 1542. [9] This creates a fascinating "looking-glass" allusion and parallel, for Catherine had been, prior to her marriage to Henry, what would be called a "courtesan" in the society of her day but a "prostitute" in the Victorian East End. When suspected of continuing her infidelity in the marriage, she was judged guilty of treason by the Parliament on the basis of her lack of chastity and was beheaded with Henry's assent. In 1888, do we have another person, with a quite different sense of chosenness, who struggled for a lifetime with issues of hypocrisy, taking the same restitution against a mother-figure seen as unfaithful and a betrayer of her most likely favorite, first-born son? In one case we have the foundations of the modern monarchy and the Anglican Church in which Dodgson lived and served, in the other, a most heinous crime. Is it coincidence that on this anniversary day, Frances Coles was murdered at Chamber Street and Royal Mint Street, an area that is the virtual gateway to the Tower of London, the site of Catherine Howard's execution?

Perhaps drawing on Harrison's work (rather than his own sources) that pointed to J. K. Stephen as the Ripper, and Harrison's need for ten and only ten victims to fit into Stephen's poem about the ten "Harlots of Jerusalem," Rumbelow indicates that 13 February was significant also because it was dedicated to Terminus, the Roman patron of boundaries and endings, thus signifying the end of the spree. [10]   This is not correct, however; the Feast of Terminalia is on the 23rd, not the 13th. [11]

As we can see, there are a number of symbolic interpretations that one can give to the dates of the murders, especially within the context of symbols deemed important to Charles Dodgson. They form just another link in a mass of coincidental evidence regarding the identity of the Ripper.

The Significance of Numbers

It is in the area of numbers that the greatest symbolic relevance can be found. This should be no surprise when we recall that Dodgson was a mathematician and consummate gameplayer with numbers.

There were two significant numbers in Dodgson's world as reflected in his literature. There was the number 42, which appeared as "Rule 42 of the Code" and which represented his manifesto to bluff the world, creating a totally false image, as his life's goal, his road to immor-tality, and there was the number 3, which appeared as the "Rule of 3" or the "Double Rule of 3." Three was also of great significance in Greek, Masonic, and Christian traditions.

As we examine the frequency of certain numbers in these murders, always conscious that there is enormous potential for contrivance in any such pursuit, one wonders if the appearance of these significant numbers is purely coincidence. For example, I am inclined to see something possibly meaningful in the "double event." If Dodgson were attempting to incorporate the number "42" into his real life events as well as into his literature, there could be no better way to relate these murders to that code than to follow murder number four, not with a routine fifth and sixth, but with an emphatic "2" following the first "4." While theorists tend to believe that the second murder on 30 September was a madman's response to unsatisfied lust following interruption during the first killing, were two in fact planned or was the second one planned "on the fly" when a target of opportunity appeared? Two could have been planned even if the first was interrupted before mutilation could take place.

In another coincidence, "42" appears in the murder of Martha Tabram, stabbed thirty-nine times. Assuming the autopsy results were correct, was the repeated stabbing the result not of frenzy, but of careful calculation and execution? Was there a goal to combine both the "Rule 42 of the Code" *and* the mysterious "Rule of Three" by finishing just three strokes short of forty-two? Was it coincidence that thirty-nine also was Martha Tabram's age? Had the Ripper determined her age in the course of disarming conversation? Was the frenzy a counting frenzy, an obsession for precision, not that of a lunatic out of control? Was there a meaningful selection process going on? Was there a subtle message to the police to pay attention to numbers in efforts to solve the crimes?

Is it coincidence that Emma Smith was forth-five years old, again a difference of three from forty-two? Mary Ann Nichols, possibly the third victim, and possibly the first murdered without assistance, was exactly forty-two years old and was killed exactly twenty-four days after Martha Tabram. The pattern fails with Annie Chapman, who was forty-seven; but on the night of the double event, the first victim, Elizabeth Stride was forty-five, while the second, surely not "selected" as she had just been released from the jail house, was forty-three. But when we come to Marie Kelly, the number appears again. For if the double event occurred just after midnight on 30 September, and Kelly's on 9 November, we have the latter occurring exactly forty-two days after *stalking* Elizabeth Stride on the 29th of September. A lapse of forty-two days between murders had been missed by just moments. Could that be the reason why in flight from detection, someone fixated on the number "42" remained fixated and had to commit another murder?

There is some question regarding Kelly's age. Rumbelow, Wilson and Odell both have her twenty-four years old when she was murdered but the death certificate indicated she was twenty-five and was most likely the source used by Howell and Skinner. Given the quality of both researchers, the certificate may be incorrect. Did the Ripper believe she was twenty-four based on disarming casual conversation? Did he choose her because her age is the reverse of forty-two? Or is it all just coincidence?

Knight places Rose Mylett/Davis's death on the 26 December. [12] Rumbelow places it on the 28th/29th. [13]   But the *Daily News* of 26 December was already reporting during those days that it had occurred on Thursday, the 20th.   She is not mentioned in the works of Wilson and Odell or Howells and Skinner; most do not believe she was a Ripper victim, although Sugden is so inclined. I add her as a possibility *only* because of the symbolic meaning of 20 December. For Rose Mylett was murdered exactly forty-two days after the murder of Marie Kelly on 9 November.

Is it purely coincidental that these murders began exactly forty-two years after Dodgson entered Rugby, the boys' school where the sexual assaults appear to have reached an intolerable level, a level which most likely brought on a psychotic break? Was this the forty-second anniversary of when the "perfect child" became a confirmed psychopathic killer who would spend the rest of his life brooding and plotting his revenge? Is this why the spree *had* to take place in 1888?   Had destiny so declared it?

Names

But if the murder of Alice McKenzie and that of Frances Coles in 1891 were indeed the last of the Ripper murders, the names of the women were coincidentally the same as the two historically most important women in Dodgson's life, Alice Liddell (at whose request he wrote *Alice's Adventures Under-Ground*, later expanded to the famous *Alice's Adventures in Wonderland*) and his mother, Frances Lutwidge. Did these "extra" murders represent compulsive wishes to satisfy a bringing to climax his rage at the object of his earliest love and betrayal and the object of his love and betrayal as a man-child? Yet were they ineptly executed because the fire had been quenched in the mutilation of Kelly?

On at least one occasion Dodgson had identified "destiny" as "having spoken."   It was when he notified Lucy Walters [14] that he was rejecting her and choosing instead "Miss Alice Havers" to draw the mysterious "magic locket" in *Sylvie and Bruno*. And it was that locket which when rubbed created the masturbatory passages which followed and which tie us into the same imagery as "Jabberwocky."

Perhaps "destiny" had paid an earlier visit when Dodgson's pseudonym "was chosen" (as he wrote in his diary at the time) from four suggestions he had offered his editor, who had rejected his first choice, "Dares." "Lewis Carroll" forms two anagrams that become significant when we explore in depth his life and works. Having spent a lifetime bringing the first, "Lore will scar," to life in his writings, was he bringing the second, "Role will scar," to life in these murders? [15]

Chapter 14

Geography

Just as there is a reason to examine the dates of the Ripper murders for what might be considered coincidental clues or symbolic meanings, the geography of the murders — where they took place — is also worthy of examination. As with dates, however, care must be taken not to draw excessively on meanings, as there were certainly other forces than possible symbolism active in site selection.

There is another good reason to describe the areas involved, however. It is to understand the modes of public transportation available at the time. For many readers are totally unfamiliar with the geography of England, London, the East-End, and the public transportation systems used by Dodgson and usable by the Ripper.

Unquestionably, security was of utmost importance in the Ripper's choice of location for both murdering and mutilating his victims. Prostitutes, however and wherever chosen, had to be enticed at least a short distance away, into the shadows, where the agreed upon activity could presumably be consummated for the agreed upon fee. Except in the case of Eddowes, killed in what should have been a very much deserted Mitre Square and Kelly, killed in her room, the other women were apparently approached unobtrusively on the street by someone who was either able to fool them with a totally disarming manner, or who offered them something that overcame any fears they might have had as to whether they should accompany him during what became "dangerous times" in the neighborhood. So, as we proceed with the examination, we need to be aware, not so much of the specific location, but of what was in the immediate vicinity.

But there is also another possible dynamic in the murders, one which appeared occasionally in suspect reports — that is an arrangement to meet could have been made some time prior to the murderous rendezvous, and the meeting could have been assured by the offering of some money or gift with the promise of more to come.

Before proceeding with additional narrative regardiing the influence of geography on these crimes, several maps are reproduced on the following pages with explanations facing. They include rail maps of England for the time and detailed street maps of various parts of London.

The Railway System Operating
In Southern England In 1894.

The extent of the network that existed in 1894 is startling. Although not shown, the density continues northward to Scotland. I have highlighted the areas of interest in a Ripper/Dodgson connection: Oxford, Guildford, Eastbourne, Brighton, Bournemouth (Druitt's family home), Blackheath (the location of Druitt's school), and Dover (from which Bayne and Liddon departed for France). With London as a hub, any of these destinations could be easily reached within hours. Even the notion that Druitt was more than a day away from London when he visited Bournemouth is highly questionable. Oxford, Guildford, and Eastbourne trains ran all night long.

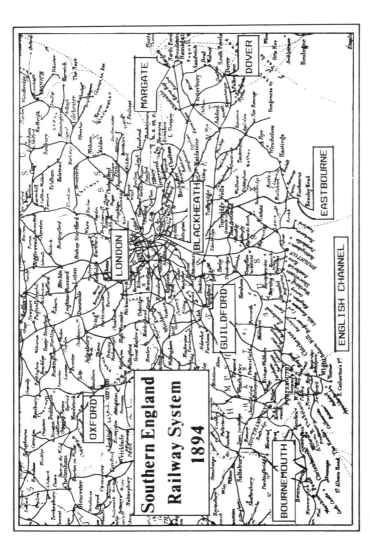

Source: *Baedeker's London and its Environs*, K. Baedeker. Leipsic: Karl Baedeker, Publisher, 1894.

The Combined Surface And Underground Trains
In And Around London
1894

The inner circular line that went as far east as Aldgate (right by Mitre Square) very much comprises today's Circle Line, co-used by the Metropolitan Line, which branches out to provide extended service to the suburbs, including Whitechapel. A branch at Kensington to the west ran to Hammersmith, which can be seen against the left edge of the map along with the Thames River and the Hammersmith Bridge. The station is less than half a mile from the bridge.

Moving clockwise around the loop from Kensington, we see Paddington Station, the station that served Oxford and the location of Great Western Hotel, much used by Dodgson. Three miles further we see King's Cross Railroad Station, then the loop proceeds to the edge of the East-End, with a stop at Bishop's Gate (300 meters west of Dorset Street), then to Aldgate (200 meters from Mitre Square).

Continuing on its westward loop, it passes a station at The Temple (Druitt's offices), then to Charing Cross and the theater district that Dodgson frequented. Bedford Street, site of Macmillan's offices, is there.

Just below the Aldgate Station, one can see Church Station on a rail line that heads east. This runs right to the Poplar district, two miles away, the site of the murder of Rose Mylett.

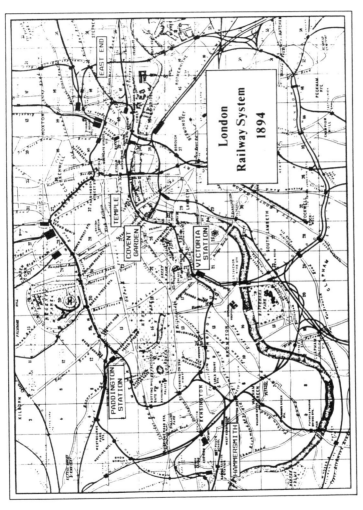

Source: *Baedeker's London and its Environs*, K. Baedeker, Leipsic: Karl Baedeker, Publisher, 1894.

Fleet Street and the Strand east to St. Paul's
1894

Trafalgar Square, scene of public demonstrations and "Socialist" riots in 1886 (which Dodgson heard with annoyance from his hotel) is in the lower left corner. Moving northwestward, through the theater district, the Garrick Club (meeting place of Sir Melville Macnaghten and Sir William Gull) can be seen, then Bedford Street (location of Macmillan Inc. to which Dodgson wanted some mail sent), then the Covent Garden Market.

Continuing up the Strand from Bedford Street about two-thirds of a mile, a right turn down Mitre Court leads to King's Bench Walk, site of Druitt's offices, and below that The Temple on the edge of Victoria Embankment. As Howells and Skinner point out, it is a much more convenient place to fill one's pockets with stones and plunge into the Thames if one wanted to drown oneself, than to take the train to Hammersmith.

Approximately one and a quarter miles further east, down Strand, Fleet, and connecting streets, one reaches Mitre Street and Mitre Square in Aldgate, which can be seen in Map No. 4.

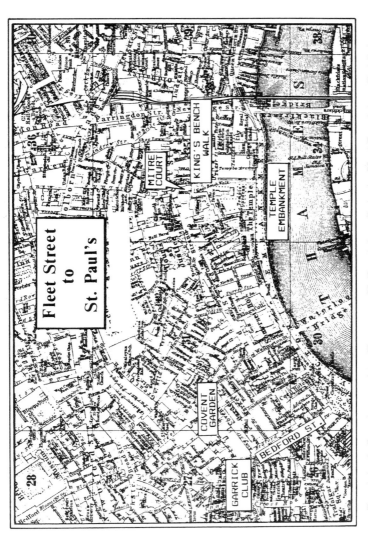

Fleet Street
to
St. Paul's

Source: *Baedeker's London and its Environs*, K. Baedeker, Leipsic: Karl Baedeker, Publisher, 1894.

The East End
(connects with prior map in scale)
1894

The name of each Ripper victim is shown near where she was murdered. Hanbury Street (site of Chapman's murder) is at the top, then moving two blocks south, we see Christ Church, Spitalfields, at the corner of Fournier (renamed from Church) and Commercial Streets. Dorset Street (the location of the Kelly murder in Miller's Court) is diagonally across the street from Christ Church. Then moving further south, we see Fashion, Flower & Dean, and Thrawl Streets in which numerous Common Lodging Houses existed and in which many of these particular women lived or had lived at one time or another.

George Street, the location of the Smith murder, can be seen crossing Thrawl Street. George Yard, where the body of Tabram/Turner was found, is further south, and, right behind the yard, both Toynbee Hall and St. Jude Church. The latter was the Rev. Samuel Barnett's parish. Toynbee Hall was the school operated by Barnett as a missionary extension of Oxford University. Many students set out from the school in search of the Ripper. Bayne was a participant in the outreach program.

Moving west from the intersection of Commercial Street and Whitechapel High Street, we pass Castle Alley, the location of the McKenzie murder, then past St. Botolph's Church to Mitre Street, with Mitre Square, the location of Eddowes murder, branching off to the right half way up Mitre Street.

Northeast of The Tower (by the Thames) we see Royal Mint Street and to the north, Chamber Street; it was in this vicinity, beneath the elevated tracks, that Frances Coles was found.

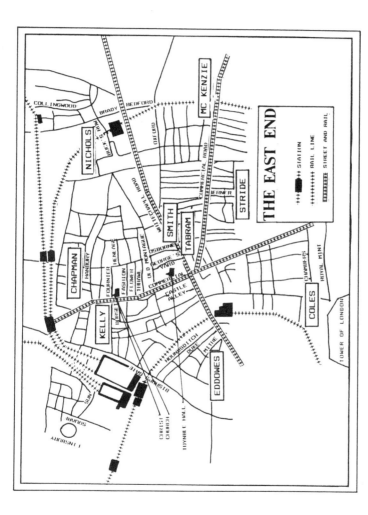

Source: Author's rendering, drawing on: *Baedeker's London and its Environs*, K. Baedeker, Leipsic: Karl Baedeker, Publisher, 1894.

For those with access to current maps, Dorset Street had been renamed to Duval Street, but no longer exists. Everything from Fashion Street south to Whitechapel Road has been changed. Castle Alley no longer exists.

Moving from Aldgate at the bottom left, east up Whitechapel High Street, we move on to Whitechapel Road and the Whitechapel Station on the rail line. Just north of that is Durwood Street, which in 1888 had been named Buck's Row. This is the approximate location of the Nichol's murder.

Three things should be noted. First, one can see the proximity to the rail station, which would have allowed for a quick ride north to Liverpool station, then, if one wished, a one block walk to the Metropolitan line and on to anywhere in the city from there.

Second, the intersection of Durward and Brady Streets is two blocks away from Collingwood Street to the east. Collingwood was Dodgson's sister Mary's married name, and it was her son Stuart (who would become his biographer) that he was guiding through Oxford in 1888.

Third, Durwood Street is just one block north of Bedford Street, which is the continuation of Brady Street south of Whitechapel Road. This is not the Bedford Street that housed Macmillan's offices. It was during these murders that Dodgson referenced Bedford Street as the mail drop for a response he wished regarding the printing of *The Wonderland Postage-Stamp Case.*

Berner Street, the site of the murder of Stride on the night of the double event, intersects in the middle in its north/south direction as it ran from Commercial down toward the railroad yards at the lower end. The walk north from there to Commercial Road, then west to Mitre Square, the most direct route, is just under a mile.

Midway up the left edge of the map one sees Finsbury Square with Sun Street emerging eastward at the base of the square and Worship Street at the top. As can be seen it provides an excellent "base of operation" with access to both surface trains and Underground at Liverpool Station.

Is it coincidence that two of the murders were committed within a stone's throw of Christ Church, Spitalfields, a church having the same name as Dodgson's college at Oxford? The worst of them was virtually right across the street.

One reason that the murders might have been committed at familiar locations could be the wish to leave a clue, certainly the Dodgson modus operandi in all his "works." Equally important, however, are the unconscious factors that bring one near to things familiar, things about which one might have been consciously aware at some point, but were not consciously chosen in the time of stress. In the latter case, motive is unconscious. Either could contribute to the existence of "coincidence."

For example, Knight [1] suggests that Eddowes was taken to Mitre Square, that she had told the police on leaving the station that she was heading home to Spitalfields, the opposite direction from where she was found. His argument is that she was brought to a location with Masonic significance, where in 1530 another woman had been murdered right in the church that backed up to the square. Of course, Knight's argument needed that assumption. But was there another reason?

Is it coincidence that one of the victims was found barely a block from Collingwood Street? Is there a connection between that victim being murdered in Buck's Row, Dodgson's writings on "sport," and the deer-stalker hat seen in the area?

Beyond the Masonic symbolism evident in "Mitre" Square, there is also Christian symbolism as both Anglican and Catholic bishops wore the mitre in ceremonial events as symbols of their office. If the line "He thought he saw an Argument / That proved he was the Pope" is no accident, did Dodgson leave a clue, knowing full well that the pope also wears a mitre as part of ceremonial costume? But even beyond that, is it purely coincidental that Montague Druitt's legal offices were at the end of Mitre Court? Was there an effort, not just to leave a clue, but to play with words and the police at the same time?

Is it coincidence that the two victims found in George Street and George Yard were nearly on the back doorsteps of Toynbee Hall, the Oxford Mission in which at least Bayne was involved and active at the time? Were one or more "Cheshire cats" leaving their victims on the stoop for display of their hunting prowess? Or is it a clue implicating Montague Druitt or just coincidence that both victims were but one block away from Old Montague Street in the other direction?

In the poem believed to be an authentic communication from the Ripper (already analyzed in chapter 4), we have the line "One stays in Henage Court, then there's a killing." There is no "Henage Court" on any of the maps, but there is a Heneage La. one block further down Mitre Street, and the 1834 map shows a Heneage Street as the continuation of Fashion Street when it meets Brick Lane. This was most likely a living area, just as Fashion Street was, and may have had a "court" much like Miller Court existed (unmapped) off of Dorset Street. Assuming that my sources for the poem reproduced it correctly, why is *Henage* misspelled? Was it accidental or was it done to meet the needs of anagrammatic construction?

A question already raised: Is it coincidence that Frances Coles was found nearly on the doorsteps of The Tower of London on the anniversary of Catherine Howard's death by beheading?

And lastly, is it purely coincidental that all of the murders except one (Stride) were committed within a short dash to public transportation which could have taken the Ripper either into London proper or further away to the north, south, or east if he feared there were police in pursuit? Always cognizant that the portion of the East End in question was a small geographic area, the fact that transportation might be nearby would not be an extraordinary coincidence. But a Dodgson Ripper, as one who knew the rail system intimately, certainly could have used it to his advantage. There is little question that he would have needed to clean himself of the blood stains beforehand, even change clothing. But with an overcoat, hat, shoes, and trousers stashed nearby, he could have changed in less than five minutes, wiped off his hands, stuffed them into his pockets, and disappeared into the system. Clothing left behind, however dirty, would have been salvaged quickly by the poor on the streets. Even if trains were not running, or running only infrequently at the late hour, he could have disappeared into the tunnel and emerged later at the same or another station. Or, he could have walked off in any direction on the surface, totally unnoticed.

As we can see, there are a host of potential clues which add their little piece to the totality of the coincidental case against Dodgson as the Ripper.

Chapter 15

The Druitt Connection

There are a number of reasons to explore the perennial Ripper suspect — Montague John Druitt, the thirty-one year old barrister whose body was found in the Thames on 31 December, 1888, and whose death was ruled a suicide. He was on Sir Melville Macnaghten's list of suspects, the first of three, and the one toward whom he leaned. He was the subject of a television program put together by Daniel Farson in 1959 and has been the subject of three books, the first in 1965 by Tom Cullen titled *Autumn of Terror*, by Farson in 1972 titled *Jack the Ripper*, and the third by Martin Howells and Keith Skinner in 1987 titled *The Ripper Legacy*. Knight thought he might have been a scapegoat, but not the Ripper himself. Both Colin Wilson and Donald Rumbelow judge him to be perhaps the most viable suspect but consider the evidence as totally inadequate to close the case. In their 1987 work, Wilson and Odell do not address the case that Howells and Skinner were preparing at the same time, but, consistent with their other comments, I believe they would still find their argument speculative, particularly lacking in hard evidence of his "sexual insanity."

Nowhere in my research in London did I address Druitt as a suspect. It was never my intent to make a point-by-point rebuttal of the case against Druitt, which key "Ripperologists" already thought was weak. Rather, it had been to show that many of the arguments *for* Druitt as a suspect based on his presumed psychological condition of being "sexually insane" are even more compellingly applicable to Dodgson than they are to Druitt. For Dodgson leaves far more visible evidence of both his rage and the part which sexuality played in it than Druitt did. The latter left nothing.

As my work proceeded, however, there emerged an even more interesting twist. It seems there may be a historical connection between Dodgson, Bayne, and Druitt. In the end, I discovered a most bizarre and chilling possibility.

The evolution of Druitt's involvement in these murders is itself an interesting one. The material presented is a composite from Rumbelow, Wilson and Odell, and Howells and Skinner. While Druitt's name first appeared in notes written by Sir Melville Macnaghten, who did not join the police force until July 1889, six months after the murder of Kelly, it would not be until seventy years later, in 1959, that those notes with the

Druitt name would come to public attention. Dan Farson, a television interviewer and writer, quite accidentally mentioned his interest in the Ripper murders to a Lady Rose McLaren, whose mother-in-law turned out to be Dowager Lady Aberconway, Macnaghten's daughter. In turn she made available transcriptions of those notes that had been typewritten after her father's death and kept in the family. Eventually further examination of Scotland Yard files located what is believed to be handwritten "facsimiles" of the original material, discrepancies and all. (What good mystery would be without them?) Those few words from Macnaghten, a minor player in the Ripper investigation, have led to an enormous investigatory effort extending from London to Australia.

Montague Druitt was born on 15 August 1857, the second of seven children; his brother William was firstborn. His father was the prominent local surgeon in Wimbone, Dorset, and his own brother Robert and nephew Lionel were also doctors. It is considered highly likely that the quick investigation done by the newspapers at the time the body was discovered in the Thames led to the belief that Montague was himself a doctor, a belief that carried over to the Macnaghten file. At the age of thirteen, he was awarded a scholarship to Winchester College, where he spent six years succeeding in sports and debating, and did well enough in academics to receive a scholarship to New College, Oxford, in 1877. He excelled at Fives (a variation of handball) and was Winchester champion in 1875. In 1876 he was on the starting eleven in cricket, a sport in which he continued to excel until his death. He received his B.A. degree in 1880 after taking Second Class Honors in Classical Moderations in 1878 but barely "scraped through" with Third Class Honors in the Classics. In 1883 he paid the required fee and received his master's degree. [1]

Rumbelow speculates that Druitt may have begun studies in medicine because it would not be for another two years that he enrolled at the Inns of Court to begin the study of law. In any case there was a delay before the Oxford graduate settled on a career quest. In order to enter the Inner Temple, the required entry point for a successful career in law, on 17 May 1882, Druitt was required to pay £500, a sum he borrowed from his father, who deducted it from the legacy intended for the children on his death. A further advance was made, but the limit of advances was set at no more than half of what would be bequeathed. In order to supplement his income, Druitt took a position as teacher at a "crammer" school (offering intense preparation for the university) in Blackheath, a "suburb" southeast of London. He was a master there in 1883 and remained until he was released for unspecified reasons just days before his death. It is speculated that he had gotten "caught" in homosexual activities with the boys, which, consistent with Victorian hypocrisy regarding sexual behavior, would have made him "sexually insane." The "insanity," which appears to have applied only to homosexuals and criminals, seems to have derived from the inability to keep one's appetites in control enough not to be caught. In a hypocritical application of that rule by the privileged, the Prince of Wales, renowned during his lifetime for his heterosexual excesses and "caught" on a number of occasions, was not sexually insane, just "indiscreet." In fact, he was implicated and called to the divorce trial of Lord and Lady Morduant in 1869, after which Lady Morduant was deemed insane and institutionalized until at least 1890.

Druitt joined the bar on 29 April 1885, and his father died the following September, leaving an estate valued at £16,579. [2] Montague and his two younger brothers were virtually excluded from the will, with William receiving the family properties, his mother the income from the estate until her death, and his three sisters the remainder. (Rumbelow claims £6,000 each, but there must be an error.) The family dynamics that created this situation are not known. William was already an attorney practicing in the home town; whether he was selected to manage things and then trusted to some more equitable distribution after their mother's death could have been a reason. His sisters' inheritance is understandable because the will stipulated that they would lose their portion if they married before reaching age twenty-one. In any case, for their father to have protected the women as incapable of acquiring their own wealth except through marriage would be totally consistent with Victorian custom. The boys would be expected to earn their own way.

On a deeper level, however, whether Montague's alleged homosexuality was part of a mother/son or father/son dynamic that had him rejected by his father is a possibility. [3] There are signs that things fell apart for Montague beneath the surface of normality that participation in team sports and sociability suggest. He had attended Winchester School, one of the notorious public schools in terms of the homosexual experiences encountered by the younger boys. Dodgson had attended Rugby beginning in 1846 and appears to have been destroyed by them. While by any measure Druitt succeeded there, things began well at Oxford, then declined, and we find him somewhat adrift for a year or more after gaining his degree, then moving on to law. Oxford may very well have provided him with a continued need to pursue private compulsions as homosexual behavior among students and a clerical faculty was rife.

While Druitt set up his practice at 9 King's Bench Walk, Temple, in 1885, it is believed that in the following three years he never had a single client, a not totally untypical experience in an environment that saw only one fledgling barrister in eight able to earn a living, but a devastating one, nonetheless, for one whose brother was successful and whose father had been a doctor.

In July 1888, Druitt's mother was admitted into an asylum for the insane, where she was diagnosed as suffering from "melancholia" and "brain disease"; she remained there until her death in December 1890. Among her fellow inmates was Lady Morduant. Druitt was dismissed from his school position on or about 1 December 1888, the end of Michaelmas term, and was last seen alive on the 3rd. While we can see further decline in his fortunes, certainly enough to be moving him toward depression, more "like mother," we hardly can see on the surface, at least, serious suicidal potential.

His body was found in the Thames on 31 December; an inquest was held on 2 January during which his brother William testified that he had not seen him since Montague had visited at his home in Bournemouth on the south coast, and that he had been alerted to possible trouble on 11 December when he was informed by Montague's friends that he had not been seen in more than a week. When William searched his brother's London apartment, he found a note addressed to him that became the prima facie evidence that he had committed suicide. It read: "Since Friday I felt I was going to be like mother and the best thing for me was to die." [4] Found in his pockets were two checks, some coin, a watch, gloves, a white handkerchief, and most curiously, a return ticket from Hammersmith to London. His death was quickly ruled a suicide and matters were closed.

Early newspaper accounts identified him as a forty-one-year-old doctor, but this later was modified to reflect his correct age of thirty-one and his occupation as barrister. The notion that he was a doctor would linger in the police department, however, where it appears Druitt was quickly embraced as the Ripper, not by name, but as "the body that was pulled from the Thames." Inspector Abberline disagreed totally, claiming that this death proved absolutely nothing. [5] But it appears that for whatever reasons, upper echelons, perhaps in the Home Office as well as Scotland Yard, were under intense pressure to solve the crimes one way or another. Howells and Skinner decry the lack of police investigation into the circumstances surrounding Druitt's release from the school and other aspects of his background. Apparently there was none done.

In March 1889, Donald McCormick, a leading member of the Whitechapel Vigilance Committee, complained about the complacency that had crept into the police effort after the Miller Court murder. Police brought him into their confidence, swore him to secrecy and told him that the Ripper had died, had been pulled from the Thames at year end, and that there would be no more murders. Feeling betrayed that he had been sworn to confidence and given no credible evidence, just optimistic reassurances based on conjecture, he responded that if there were another Ripper-like murder, he would not remain silent. They threatened that they would arrest him for inciting a riot if he became vocal about the Ripper still being at large. When Alice McKenzie was murdered on 17 July 1889, there were quick denials by all the experts that this was another Ripper murder.

It was not until 1959 that Druitt's name came up again. But in 1973, in response to the work of Farson and Cullen, Irving Rosenwater published the results of his research into Druitt in *The Cricketer*. What he found has been used to negate earlier claims that Druitt had in fact been living in Bournemouth and could not have murdered Nichols and Chapman. For in the case of the former, Druitt was playing cricket in Canford, Dorset, just three days after the murder. At 11:30 in the morning, just six hours after Chapman was murdered, he was playing cricket at Blackheath. And on 19 November Blackheath records show that he was acting in his capacity as honorary secretary and treasurer of the club making recommendations about expanding the size of the field. [6] Could he have made the trip between Canford and London in three days, or the trip from the East End to Blackheath in three hours? Certainly. Could he have played cricket after such carnage without showing telltale signs of distress? Possibly. It is not unknown that the continuation of social and physical activity would be sought by one deep in depression, possibly more true in Victorian England where maintaining the facade of well-being was expected of a child, never mind an adult. My own belief, however, is that at least the Chapman murder was committed by Dodgson alone, with Bayne now in Dover, heading for France.

Perhaps one of the most curious connections in the Druitt affair is presented by Knight and supported by Howells and Skinner. It is the close geographical proximity in which Druitt and other suspects as well as Victorian notables lived and worked. Within doors of one another we find Sir Melville Macnaghten, Oscar Wilde, and the artist James Whistler, who was Walter Sickert's mentor. It was Sickert who, due to his lifelong fascination with the crime and propensity to weave stories, may have "talked" himself into being Knight's one-of-three Ripper murderers. And it was Sickert who belonged to the Garrick Club, just a block away from Bedford Street, Macmillan's offices, along with Macnaghten. Also close by were Herbert Stephens and Frank Miles. Miles was reportedly Oscar Wilde's lover and Prince Eddy's equerry, who, in turn, may have had a homosexual relationship with J. K. Stephen (Herbert's brother), who was Prince Eddy's tutor and himself a woman-hater if one can judge by his poetry. Sir William Gull was physician to both Eddy and the Stephens. The Prince of Wales, Eddy's father, was known to attend parties in which Wilde, Sickert, and Miles were present. [7]

While Farson developed a connection with a Lionel Druitt in Australia and developed considerable research based on a letter from someone who claimed to know the identity of Jack the Ripper, Howells and Skinner's research (which consumes much of their book) identified the gaps in Farson's work and determined that there was no credible Australian-Druitt connection.

Where Howells and Skinner take the Druitt story is interesting. Pursuing the notion that Druitt was a scapegoat, they draw links between Druitt's acquaintances and a small group of homosexuals centered at Trinity College known popularly as the "Apostles" but carrying the full title "Cambridge Conversazione Society." This group of Christian scholars who focused on debate, was formed at Cambridge University about 1820 but in the intervening years had not only moved to Trinity but was now pretty much a clique of homosexuals. Their focus was on the Greek ideal that championed the love of man for man as a higher form of love than that for woman, "a philosophy known to the apostles as `the Higher Sodomy´" [8]

> . . . But such sentiments were not confined to debate, and manifested themselves in more obvious expressions of a homosexual and misogynistic kind. [9]

J. K. Stephen had been a member until 1882, when he resigned. The group slowly became extremely powerful in its influence within government circles, eventually birthing several spies in the mid-twentieth century. In a fascinating parallel to the Royal Arch code within the Masonic Brotherhood, Howells and Skinner quote prominent Apostle E. M. Forster:

> "If I had to choose between betraying my country and betraying my friend I hope that I should have the guts to betray my country." [10]

In their argument that Druitt was murdered by fellow Apostles who feared that he was the Ripper and would threaten their organization, Howells and Skinner add to the number of notables living and working in close proximity to one another. [11] There was now Harry Wilson, a friend of Eddy's, and a very active member of the Apostles and friends with many of the Winchester, Eton, Oxford, and Harrow cricket crowd in which Druitt operated. Furthermore, several of the Apostles were headquartered in Blackheath.

That Montague was involved in these circles becomes quite evident in mid-December 1888 for he and his mother were invited to a ball at Wimborne hosted by the Lord and Lady Wimborne, who were still quite unaware of his disappearance and demise, a ball that was to be attended by Prince Albert Victor — Prince Eddy. Howells and Skinner suggest that proper protocol would have directed the invitation to the then head-of-household, brother William, unless friends specifically wanted Montague to attend on the basis of his friendship with the prince.

If there is any connection between Druitt and Dodgson, quite outside of these social circles (no biography supports his involvement with any of them), Dodgson would certainly have had access to fact and rumor and the opportunity to create fact and rumor at the highest levels of influence.

It would seem that we can conclude from the material researched by others that Druitt was possibly a homosexual, socialized with homosexuals when there was some risk in doing so, and was headed downhill in terms of career. An Oxford graduate, trained for law at the "right" place, having no success in his field, just recently released from what had to be considered a temporary line of work at Blackheath, maintaining an active social and sportsman's life as he extended the glory of his school days, there is every likelihood that he was a vulnerable young man. But, there is precious little evidence that he hated women with any of the passion that might have him taking on the character and activities of Jack the Ripper, especially in an August/September time frame.

Were Dodgson, Bayne, and Druitt connected in any way? There are only two tenuous hints of a connection.

We find a possible connection to Dodgson and Bayne at Oxford, for Druitt was elected by fellow students to the position of steward of the Junior Common Room, where the students ate and socialized. Since New College is a short walking distance from Christ Church, the "home" of Dodgson and Bayne, and is administratively separate, it would be highly likely that they would have become acquainted. Bayne had been curator of the Common Room at Christ Church since 1861 and would hold the position until 1882, when Dodgson was elected to succeed him. Dodgson would hold it until 1893. It would not be an unreasonable inference that on at least one occasion during his tenure in the position that Druitt would meet Bayne in a meeting or social function as part of his official duties, perhaps as part of his training.

Dodgson's diary entry of 12 December 1878 indicates that he provided a bed for a fellow by the name of "Drewitt" following a Censor's dinner. This same man spent a few hours with him on the following day and sat to be photographed. In a rare instance when Dodgson's handwriting was somewhat indecipherable, the first name "looks like" *Mowtnay*, enough of a variation from *Montague* to make things questionable. The distance between Christ Church and New College is short, less than a mile; an overnight accommodation would not be required unless Drewitt was quite drunk. The entry is crossed out in the manuscript by what was probably the family (their way for signaling to their editor Roger Green that they wanted something omitted from publication) and does not appear in the published Diaries. Most likely this is because no one in the family could identify the person. In general, they tended to "lionize" like Dodgson did by including the acquaintance if the person was a notable. On the other hand, they were very protective of the privacy of many friends, especially the children and their families. Had Dodgson spelled the name phonetically and chosen a similar spelling "ew" as had occurred when *Lewis* was chosen in favor of *Louis*? The published books do not indicate when Druitt was steward of the Junior Common Room, but 1878 seems a little early. If he were in the position, he might have been eligible to attend a Censor's or supervisor's dinner.

A very thin thread.

But, when we examine a curious poem purportedly received from Jack the Ripper, published by Michael Harrison in his 1972 work *Clarence: Was He Jack the Ripper?*, in which he pointed to J. K. Stephen, not Clarence, as the Ripper, we find a possible answer to this and other questions. Harrison analyses the poem in the context of its meter and rhyme, whose similarities he compares to some of Stephen's poems. He also notes that George McCormick, in his 1959 work *The Identity of Jack the Ripper* referenced the poem and its allusion to the popular police theory regarding the Ripper as having drowned in the Thames. It reads:

> Up and down the goddam town
> Policemen try to find me
> But I ain't a chap yet to drown

In drink, or Thames or sea. [12]

Harrison gives no indication as to when the poem was received by the police. From its contents, if it does indeed allude to Druitt's drowning, it might have been received before, thus predicting the event. If it is an "as if written by Druitt" poem, he seems to deny that he is the Ripper. And it references being drowned in drink, or, if found soon, in the Thames. But if discovery is not done quickly, the body will have been carried all the way to the sea. (Incidentally, it would be interesting to find the original to determine if "ain't" was spelled as Carroll would have done — "ai'n't.")

There is no need here to do a poetic analysis of this work against the poems of Lewis Carroll. There is no question that we can find the kinds of meter and rhyming schemes that Harrison was seeking in J. K. Stephen's works in the works of Lewis Carroll. But look what we find when we subject the poem to anagrammatic analysis!

Hint to police: To take a ripper now, you can find M.
Druitt, drowned, at Hammersmith towne.
Dodgson and Bayne.

Here we have possibly another "perfect" anagram. Not only does the subject of the anagram conform to the subject of the original, but it adds knowledge, identifies Druitt as "a ripper," i.e., a generic "one of several." In its original form it denies that he is "*the* Ripper."

Towne was an obsolete form for *town* even in Victorian days. It is possible that the letters making up *towne* could be rearranged to be *not we* and inserted after *you*: "you, not we, can find" This would suggest that Druitt's murderers may have looked to see if the body had moved from the area toward the sea and had been unable to find it. Early after the drowning it would be unlikely to be near the surface with the rocks in Druitt's pockets weighting it down. Dodgson would no doubt have known that a body lightly weighted would tend to rise as decomposition took place.

Or, the reference to "we" could represent a taunting of the police, just as the entire poem was intended to be. Was Dodgson telling us that there *is* a reference to "Drewitt" in his diaries, and that the reference has to do with drink, Drewitt's reason for staying in the extra bed in his apartment? Or is he telling us that Druitt was losing control through drink? On numerous occasions in his diaries, Dodgson would note in the margin the dates of earlier entries on the same subject as the current entry; he knew where things were and frequently reread through them to locate past events and include them in current context. Is all of this just coincidence?

The only other connection I find with Druitt is through Bayne and what may have been his, but not Dodgson's, involvement in Rev. Samuel Barnett's mission to the East End. We know that Bayne was involved in 1890, that both Christ Church and New College were involved at least from 1885, when the Christ Church affiliate Toynbee Hall was formed. Both postdate Druitt's attendance at Oxford. Druitt would have to had worked as a volunteer alumnus, not as a student, to take him there.

Was Dodgson familiar with Blackheath? The answer is yes for he had a child friend who lived there, a Clare Turton. On 20 January 1879 he met her there at her home and brought her to see *Cinderella* at Drury Lane. [13]   He remained acquainted with her into the early 1880s as she visited him at the beach. Blackheath was a stop on the railway line.

Very tenuous connections. Or are they?

As we complete the analysis of a Dodgson/Druitt relationship, it is worth examining the suicide note found among Druitt's belongings. It read: "Since Friday I felt I was going to be like mother, and the best thing for me was to die." [14] These "words of Druitt" come from a local newspaper's report on the inquest proceedings held at Chiswick in which Montague's older brother William testified. As other writers do not give their sources, it must be assumed that this is their source also. Howells and Skinner indicate that the inquest records (at which the note was produced) are lost. Other writers' use of single quotations suggests that they were quoting from the original, but this may be just an editing error. Assuming that they did not, the newspaper precedes its quotation of the note thusly: " Witness. . . found a paper addressed to him (produced). The Coroner read the letter, which was to this effect: "Since Friday." [15]

To this effect can suggest in more modern usage that the material which follows is a summary statement. But in its more precise Victorian usage it would suggest that what follows is specific and that it specifies intent. If the source were the coroner's report itself, it would be safer to assume that the quote is correct and complete, evidence being placed into the record despite the fact that the letter would be attached as evidence in the file. Since all we have is a newspaper account, one can only infer that this quotation, the only one in the article that otherwise describes the testimony of witnesses without quotation, represents the full contents of the letter. This is also supported by the notion that this message represented the only hard evidence that the death was a suicide; they should, therefore, have quoted it completely.

The reason I pursue this so persistently is because its correctness is relevant to the following analysis. If the sentence constitutes the full note and is correctly quoted, it is structurally awkward for an Oxford graduate, although recognition certainly must be given to state-of-mind in the suicidal situation. *Since* implies "a continuation of," which makes *felt* inappropriate as it implies that the feeling had ended. *Feel* or *have felt* would have been better. The use of *was* in reference to dying implies that death is a past event when a suicide note logically references the future, particularly so in this case if a train ride to Hammersmith still had to be made. In essence, the note looks as though it were written after the suicide. This might not be an uncommon occurrence, however, as the suicidal person is writing for the after-the-fact audience and is sometimes in an after-the-fact state of mind when he communicates, already having committed *to* the act. Knight suggests that the notion that the author, if truly the Ripper, would only begin to think something was wrong "since Friday," which was at the end of November, is comic given the number of murders that had already taken place. [16]   Curiously, Rumbelow is the only writer to place the word *is* in place of *was*. Could this be an inadvertent error in transcription, an unconscious "cleansing" of the tense of the original, an unconscious awareness of its awkwardness?

Of course, the most obvious explanation may be that the sentence is in fact a summary which *is* describing a past event. But if so, why did the newspaper put it in quotations when no other direct testimony is presented that way? Why did they not paraphrase that message as they had all other testimony in the third person —that "he had felt that?"

In what I considered the most startling and unexpected finding in all of this research, although for some time I thought there might be a third person involved, I discovered an anagram from Druitt's message which makes better sentence sense than the original, remains in the first person, states that the message as provided is a lie, identifies Dodgson and Bayne as involved with him, has the same taunting tone as other Ripper messages, and references his own drowning, not as suicide, but as murder. It is bizarre, unexpected, and chilling for it also confirms the theme of the anagram derived from the poem above, "Up and down the goddam town. . ."

        I fib, idiots. I — we — are fine faggot killers. C.
Dodgson, T. Bayne threw me into the Thames.

Before objections are raised, *faggot* is a Victorian word of contempt for women and dates from the sixteenth century. Its reference to male homosexuals is twentieth century American. [17]

Is it possible that this was not a suicide note at all, but a fabrication to present to authorities exactly what they were hoping for, an explanation for an ending to the spree, a mind that snapped after the glut in Miller's Court? Is it possible that Montague Druitt intended to return from Hammersmith, that he had in fact gone there to meet someone who knew the rail system intimately and may even have suggested that he purchase a round-trip ticket? Or, did that person come prepared with his own return ticket to London to put in Druitt's pocket if necessary?

If we return to Dodgson's literature for a moment, in the search for the *Snark*, in addition to seeking it "with thimbles," the hunters "threatened its life with a railway-share." Is it possible that Dodgson was bringing this to life, too, just as he had the thimble, the refrain "Off with their heads!" and the slaying of the Jabberwock from the *Alice* works?

If Dodgson had left a time capsule with the verse on the board found in the nursery at Croft, not discovered until 1954, with no certainty that it would ever be found, one that declared his manifesto to the world in coded verse to: "Bluff a rough, sordid heathen world, and cheat death!" is it unreasonable to suggest that he might have left a clue with the body in the Thames, a body that might never surface, one which could very well have floated to the sea, never to be found?

Did Druitt become a victim because he played into Dodgson's mysterious "Rule 42 of the Code," whose origins, I believe, lie in that time capsule? There were forty-two students at the Blackheath school where Druitt taught. [18]

Was a fragile Montague Druitt being blackmailed, not for the money, but to push him further into his depression and increase his bizarre behavior? That would be possible because *no one* would believe a charge that "Lewis Carroll is Jack the Ripper." Were the checks found in his pockets payments to be made? Or did they represent termination pay from the school? Their denominations could suggest the latter, as the literature reflects. Just what role had he played in the murders, if any at all? Showing a remarkable physical resemblance to Prince Eddy, the Duke of Clarence, was his role part of a complex plot to disparage the monarchy by being seen in the slightest of disguises at certain times and places around the seamier parts of London? [19] Having the appearance of a "foreigner," was he a look-out in the heavily Jewish East

End? Was his fragility, his inability to control his emotions, becoming a problem that required his disposal or had it been planned early on?

Is it pure coincidence that Hammersmith — in addition to being on the Thames, in addition even to being where Dr. L. Forbes Winslow managed the asylum his father had founded — contains the ancestral home of none other than William Hogarth, who had been a member of the Masons and an early exposer of their secrets. [20] It was Hogarth's art Dodgson collected and whose renderings on the progression of cruelty ended on the vivisectionist's table with the "patient's" head depicted as held in place by a skull-screw and pulley known as a *Lewis*. [21] Is all this coincidence?

And finally, was *Hammersmith* itself chosen by the consummate word-game player as a phonetic cryptogram in its Cockney (silent "h") pronunciation for the first of the Ripper victims — Emma Smith. It was Smith whom authorities thought had been murdered by three or more "sailors" and whose murder, due to the qualitative differences in the crimes has been virtually excluded as a Ripper victim.   Was Emma Smith an early victim when they operated as a group of novices, a group which may have evolved into two, and then one, based on the instability of other members and the obsession of a perfectionist and loner? Was Dodgson not yet the "foreign skipper" while Bayne had fled to his vacation retreat on the continent, fearful that the police net might be closing?

Without a doubt, this twist in the story needs further exploration. Unable to pursue further investigation myself, I leave it to others to do so.   It is certainly not a critical piece in the overall case regarding Dodgson, although it may very well provide closure on what has been a conundrum from early on, if, indeed, we can believe it.

Returning to the Howells and Skinner thesis regarding the Apostles, I doubt that Dodgson especially would be involved with them, although he might very well have known of their existence. While his rage and its manifestation in sexual expression nearly blocks out his apparent and acknowledged homosexuality, which term did not exist in Dodgson's day but focused on gay prostitute-like behavior rather than inner orientation, [22] he appears to have lived his sexual life very much in secret. His world of fame and fortune as writer of "children's books" and his oh-so-necessary emotional, nearly daily involvement with the young girls would have ended if his orientation and activities had become known.   He was also a loner, really on the fringes of the "organizational" world, even at Oxford. Bayne had more of the organization in him, even if it were a role of "compliance" he was playing.

It is interesting that when one looks at the more modern history of the Cambridge Conversazione Society as presented by Howells and Skinner [23] one can see here, too, the incorporation of the same Masonic principles at the highest levels — i.e., that even murder and treason are not just tolerable, but might become necessary and desirable actions in the interest of the organization and its members. It is possible that Dodgson used what he perceived as the same Masonic hypocrisy to use Druitt, perhaps a fringe member of that society, for his own ends.

Chapter 16

A Conundrum

Perhaps unfairly so, I leave readers and future researchers with a conundrum whose primary purpose is to encourage further research into Dodgson's literature as a source of Ripper material. The following is an anagram, a reconstruction of a discrete piece of material published by Lewis Carroll after 1888 and which I leave for you to identify. I believe it is an accurate description of the murder spree, although it focuses only on the historically agreed-to five victims. Was it presented to be a full confirming confession up to a point in time? Or is it coincidence?

I strangled Nichols, Chapman, Stride, Eddowes. I gave each a moment to confess her gay sins. I cut the throats left ear to right and I removed uteri. Feisty whore Mary Ann Kelly flayed around. He and I mutilated her cunt. I mangled her face; I dismembered breasts, ears, heart, a thigh. We masturbated with glee on them. All victims' wounds were awfully messy __ a mushy, sticky slime.

Scotland Yard and Whitechapel police are no match for our sly foiling game.

I hate my mother; I stay mainly a yellow, selfish, sly, coy child.

He, Thomas Vere Bayne, I, Charles Lutwidge Dodgson, reign as Jack the Ripper.

Lewis Carroll

If the Rule of Three applies, is there at least a third anagram for this passage?

Chapter 17

To Be Done

This book is not intended to be in any way the definitive work on Jack the Ripper. It is intended to provide insights into an entirely new suspect that others with better access to sources and different investigatory techniques and insights can pursue, one that is a quite different direction than what has been taken historically.

My investigation has been limited by two things, which are in fact connected: resources and geography. This has been a difficult study to conduct based in the United States. The research trip to London was necessarily limited and was constrained by my then current state of knowledge. A "second trip" through some of the material and an investigation into areas never contemplated would no doubt prove valuable.

There are several areas of study that one could pursue which could either help confirm or refute the thesis presented. A brief listing follows:

Examination of the original Ripper letters with originals of the Dodgson letters currently in collections, potentially for fingerprint or other forensic evidence capable of analysis with modern techniques. I do not know the exact location of the Ripper originals, but they are most likely in the Black Museum, the limited access repository of crime memorabilia in London.

A search of the two-volume *Sylvie* works and *The Nursery "Alice"* for more anagrammatic material.

A more thorough search through Masonic records for evidence that either Dodgson or his father had been members. A previous study (date not known) concluded that the son was not, but a reopening of that study might prove differently.

An examination of records held in the Dodgson estate that might confirm or refute the existence of another family-rented house at Eastbourne during the summer of 1888.

An examination of the material excised from the diary manuscripts by family members prior to their publication might disclose a state-of-mind quite inconsistent with the image the family wished to have displayed in their presentation of the diaries, facts which might lend themselves to this investigation.

An examination of records of the City of London at Guildhall for evidence that a "C. L. Dodgson" rented a house or room during the period. If this had not been done in the clear, one could search for an anagram, but this might prove quite arbitrary as evidence unless the name found were clearly a construct and only appeared once.

A study of a possible connection between Dodgson and Bayne and the Apostles.

Confirmation of the extent to that Dodgson may have been involved along with Bayne with the East End mission at Toynbee Hall operated by the Reverend Samuel Barnett.

Confirmation of Druitt's involvement with that same mission, especially at the same time.

An examination of Oxford University records, especially of Common Room practices, that would confirm a connection between Bayne or Dodgson or both and Druitt.

Further investigation into other murders that might have represented preludes to the Ripper murders, especially those involving remains which showed signs of dissection.

An investigation of any diaries which Henry Parry Liddon may have kept for clues to his awareness of, if not involvement in, these crimes.

These are some of the areas which might prove fruitful to those skeptical of the extent to which rules of evidence have been stretched to limits which might be considered inappropriate.

Chapter 18

Conclusion

This is my story of Jack the Ripper; I believe it to be true. Some will not agree with me. But what is clear and undeniable in this work and *The Agony of Lewis Carroll* is that Charles Dodgson must be added to the suspect list, or better, be placed at the top of it.

It begins with a boy who lived under an extraordinarily coercive parenting environment, with a boy who became all that his parents wanted him to be, but who at the same time was retreating early and often into fantasy. What he met when he left home finally for public school at age twelve was totally beyond his experience, totally in conflict with all that he had been taught about loving and caring within the rigidly defined Christian upbringing of his family.

From what appears to have been a rather continuous homosexual assault on his person, he suffered what I originally thought might be a psychotic break from which he partially recovered. I now believe that he never recovered from it, but escaped totally into a world consumed by one goal and one goal only ― to gain revenge on his mother, father, and society, with hypocrisy the means to do so. The dream world in which he lived and focused all of his creative and destructive energies was one totally committed to securing the Jekyll facade created by the break and cultivating the hateful, spiteful, brooding Hyde which would later emerge in violent form.

Throughout this and my earlier work I have avoided using the labels of destruction, but he appears to have moved from performing rather benign antisocial acts in secret to being a full blown psychopathic killer, from writing for self titillation to cold-blooded, self-serving violence.

One might ask how anyone could take a sympathetic view of what in our gut we would call a monster, just as the papers of the day did. One could wonder where is the empathy for the poor, nameless women so callously murdered and mutilated for what looks like one man's misguided pleasure. It is difficult not to be judgmental. Without in any way justifying the atrocious adult behavior, one can have empathy for what must have happened to him, what cruelties and indignities he experienced as a youngster in his crucial formative years, day by day, bit by bit. Whatever it was, despite what gives every indication of being a life of some privilege, he was unable to overcome the early damage.

Just as I have tried to imagine the extent of assault that could cause a near total moral collapse of an already damaged boy, I have searched long and hard for the real origins of the mysterious number "42." One could wonder whether they go together, whether this bright, precocious, thin, effeminate, stuttering, naive boy with the high pitched voice counted one by one as a gang of forty-two older and wiser boys had their way with him in the unsupervised nighttime during that first year at Rugby, forty-two years before these murders began. Night-time became a hell for Dodgson; his references to it were frequent in his poems and letters. Just what it was he experienced will necessarily be left to the imagination. But one thing is certain: whatever happened was tolerated by the society in which he was raised as part of the toughening process, a process which *by its very nature* made its participants callous and indifferent to human suffering. This may have been one person who became toughened well beyond anyone's expectations.

I also depart from most if not all of the literature on the Ripper to suggest that these crimes began as a caper, fueled by rage, boredom, anti-establishment feelings, and emboldened by years of successfully hiding Victorian smut in his children's works. They then took on a life of their own in somewhat compulsive repetition and escalation.

The relevance for us today is not so much in perhaps solving these murders, but in understanding how people, especially young people, are destroyed internally by societal hypocrisy, some a little more, some a little less. For it is in the hypocritical double-standard between what is taught as right and just by our outwardly revered legal, economic, social, and religious institutions, the destruction of the family unit as the living model that such principles work, and finally the betrayal of those values by those most expected to provide an example, that young people learn that values are to be compromised *always* in the pursuit of self interest. In our betrayal of children we build a little psychopath in everyone, Judas style, then, when a few cannot contain the monster within, we wash our hands, Pilate style. It was betrayal and abandonment which I believe turned a loving Charles Dodgson into a rage consumed Jack the Ripper just as they turned his poor, alienated victims into street prostitutes.

Notes

Prologue

1. Stephen Knight, *Jack the Ripper: The Final Solution* (Chicago: Academy Chicago Publishers, 1986), 41.
2. Gordon Honeycombe, *The Murders of the Black Museum 1870 - 1970* (London: Mysterious Press, 1989).
3. Metropolitan Police Files (MEPO), microfilm records, Public Records Office, Kew, London, England, 3-141.
4. Honeycombe, *Murders of the Black Museum.*
5. Henrietta Octavia Barnett, *Canon Barnett, His Life, Works, and Friends* (London: John Murray, 1918).
6. Douglas G. Browne, *The Rise of Scotland Yard: A History of the Metropolitan Police* (London: George G. Harrap & Co. Ltd., 1956).
7. Donald Mc Cormick, *The Identity of Jack the Ripper* (London: Jarrolds, 1959), 52, quoting *Star*, 24 September 1888.

Chapter 1. The Murders

1. Martin Howells and Keith Skinner, *The Ripper Legacy* (London: The Penguin Group, 1987).
2. MEPO 3-140.
3. Howells and Skinner, *The Ripper Legacy.*
4. Francis E. Camps, *The Investigation of Murder* (London: Michael Joseph, 1966).
5. Ibid.
6. Donald Rumbelow, *Jack the Ripper* (Chicago: Contemporary Books, 1988).
7. Daniel Farson, *Jack the Ripper* (London: Michael Joseph, 1972).
8. MEPO 3-140, 19 September 1888.
9. Knight, *Jack the Ripper.*
10. Rumbelow, *Jack the Ripper.*
11. Knight, *Jack the Ripper.*
12. *Pall Mall Gazette*, 8 September 1888, 4.
13. Knight, *Jack the Ripper*, 55, quoting police report.
14. *Daily News*, 14 September 1888.

15. Farson, *Jack the Ripper*, quoting *Lancet*, 28.
16. *Daily News*, 10 September 1888, 4.
17. Camps, *The Investigation of Murder*.
18. *Star*, 24 September 1888.
19. George Buckle, ed., *The Letters of Queen Victoria: Volume 1, 1886 to 1890*. (London: John Murray, 1930).
20. *Daily News*, 1 October 1888, 4-5.
21. Colin Wilson and Robin Odell, *Jack the Ripper* (London: Transworld Publishers [Corgi Books], 1988), 62, quoting Harry Furniss.
22. Howells and Skinner, *The Ripper Legacy*.
23. Wilson and Odell, *Jack the Ripper*, 61.
24. Howells and Skinner, *The Ripper Legacy*.
25. Ibid.
26. *Daily News*, 10 November 1888.
27. Howells and Skinner, *The Ripper Legacy*.
28. Walter Dew, *I Caught Crippen: Memoirs of Ex-Chief Inspector Walter Dew, C.I.D. of Scotland Yard* (London: Blackie and Son, Limited, 1938).
29. Wilson and Odell, *Jack the Ripper*.
30. Ibid.
31. MEPO 3-140.
32. Rumbelow, *Jack the Ripper*.
33. Donald Mc Cormick, *The Identity of Jack the Ripper* (London: Jarrolds, 1959), 136.

Chapter 2. The Ripper Profile

1. Wilson and Odell, *Jack the Ripper*, 108-15.
2. Ibid., 75-76.
3. Wilson and Odell, *Jack the Ripper*, 109.
4. Wilson and Odell, *Jack the Ripper*, 110, quoting Dr. L. Forbes Winslow, *Recollections of Forty Years*.
5. Rumbelow, *Jack the Ripper*.
6. MEPO 3-141; see also Rumbelow, *Jack the Ripper*, 140-141.
7. Howells and Skinner, *The Ripper Legacy*.
8. Dew, *I Caught Crippin*, 86, 112.
9. Wilson and Odell, *Jack the Ripper*.
10. Howells and Skinner, *The Ripper Legacy*, 74, quoting Goodman from *Sala's Journal*.
11. Ibid., 74.
12. Rumbelow, *Jack the Ripper*.

13. Lieutenant Colonel Sir Henry Smith, *From Constable to Commissioner: The Story of Sixty Years Most of Them Misspent by...* (London: Chatto & Windus, 1906), 72.

14. Howells and Skinner, *The Ripper Legacy*.

15. Ibid.

16. Richard von Krafft-Ebing, *Psychopathia Sexualis, Contrary Sexual Instinct: A Medico-Legal Study* (London: F. J. Rebman, 1893).

17. Ibid.

18. Ibid.

19. William Blake, "The Four Zoas," "Night the Fifth," p. 337 (v. 241), closing line.

20. Arthur Evans, *The God of Ecstasy* (New York: St. Martin's Press, 1988), chapter 1.

21. Colin Wilson, *A Casebook of Murder* (London: Leslie Frewin, 1969), 135.

22. Ibid., 256.

23. Farson, *Jack the Ripper*.

24. Dr. Magnus Hirschfeld, *Sexual Anomalies and Perversions* (London: Encyclopoedia Press, 1938), 462.

25. Ibid., 462.

26. Eric Ambler, *The Ability to Kill* (London: Bodley Head, 1963), 156.

27. Manfred S. Guttmacher and Henry Weihoffen, *Psychiatry and the Law* (New York: W. W. Norton and Company, 1952), 394.

28. Ibid., 108.

29. Barnett, *Canon Barnett, His Life, Works, and Friends*.

30. Bernard Shaw, *Major Barbara*, act III, 440.

Chapter 3. A Life of Motive

1. Lewis Carroll, *Sylvie and Bruno* (New York: Dover Publications, 1988), 88.

2. Richard Wallace, *The Agony of Lewis Carroll* (Melrose, Massachusetts: Gemini Press, 1990), 26.

3. Lewis Carroll, *Sylvie and Bruno*, 332.

4. Wallace, *The Agony of Lewis Carroll*, 27.

5. Ibid., 59.

6. Sidney Halpern, "The Mother-killer," *Psychoanalytic Review* LII, Summer, 1965.

7. M. Masud R. Kahn, *Alienation in Perversions* (London: The Hogarth Press and the Institute of Psycho-Analysis, 1979). See appendix 2, *The Agony of Lewis Carroll*.

8. Wallace, *The Agony of Lewis Carroll*, 39, 33.

9. Derek Hudson, *Life of Lewis Carroll* (London: Constable and Company, 1954), 310.

10. Wallace, *The Agony of Lewis Carroll*, 40.

11. *The New York Times*, 22 October 1990, A19.

12. Stuart Collingwood, *The Life and Letters of Lewis Carroll* (London: The Century Company, 1898), 8.

13. Langford Reed, *The Life of Lewis Carroll* (London: W. & G. Foyle, Ltd., 1932).

14. Collingwood, *The Life and Letters of Lewis Carroll*, 8.

15. Wallace, *The Agony of Lewis Carroll*, 116.

16. Collingwood, *The Life and Letters of Lewis Carroll*, 23.

17. Wallace, *The Agony of Lewis Carroll*, 137.

18. Collingwood, *The Life and Letters of Lewis Carroll*.

19. Lewis Carroll, "The Valley of the Shadow of Death ," from Roger Green, ed., *The Works of Lewis Carroll* (London: Paul Hamlyn, 1965), 875.

20. Wallace, *The Agony of Lewis Carroll*, 152.

21. Hudson, *Life of Lewis Carroll*, 45-46, 66.

22. Lewis Carroll, *Useful and Instructive Poetry* (New York: Macmillan and Co., 1954; published by Frances Manella Dodgson), 44.

23. Wallace, *The Agony of Lewis Carroll*, 46.

24. Ibid., 236.

25. Lewis Carroll, from Roger Green, ed., *Alice's Adventures in Wonderland* and *Through the Looking-Glass* (New York, Oxford University Press, 1982), 6.

26. Wallace, *The Agony of Lewis Carroll*, 44.

27. Ibid., 54.

28. The sources for this detail are Anne Clark, *Lewis Carroll: A Biography* (New York: Schocken Books, 1979) and Phyllis Greenacre, *Swift and Carroll: A Psychoanalytic Study of Two Lives* (New York: International Universities Press, 1955.

29. Greenacre, *Swift and Carroll*.

30. William Shakespeare, *Hamlet*, act I, scene 2, lines 180-81.

31. Wallace, *The Agony of Lewis Carroll*, 191.

32. Wallace, *The Agony of Lewis Carroll*, 193 ff.; also Dominick A. Barbara, M.D., *The Psychodynamics of Stuttering* (Springfield, Ill.: Charles C. Thomas Publisher, 1982.

33. Roy J. Mathew, M.D., *Treatment of Migraine* (New York: SP Medical and Scientific Books, 1981), 57. See also Wallace, *The Agony*, 194ff.

34. Rollo May, *Man's Search for Himself* (New York: W. W. Norton, 1953. Reprint. New York: Dell Publishing, 1973.

35. Elizabeth Sewell, *The Field of Nonsense* (London: Chatto and Windus, 1952.

36. Wallace, *The Agony of Lewis Carroll*, 230.

37. Ibid., 230.

38. Ibid.

39. Simone de Beauvoir, "Must We Ban Sade?" reprinted in Aistryn Wainhouse and Richard Seaver, translators, *The Marquis de Sade, The 120 Days of Sodom and Other Writings* (New York: Grove Press, 1966), 9.

40. Ibid., 10.

Chapter 4. The Ripper Letters and Poems

1. Knight, *Jack the Ripper*.

2. Rumbelow, *Jack the Ripper*.

3. Knight, *Jack the Ripper*, 219.

4. Douglas G. Browne, *The Rise of Scotland Yard: A History of the Metropolitan Police* (London: George G. Harrap & Co. Ltd., 1956).

5. Camps, *The Investigation of Murder*.

6. Wilson and Odell, *Jack the Ripper*.

7. Wallace, *The Agony of Lewis Carroll*.

8. Rumbelow, *Jack the Ripper*.

9. Wallace, *The Agony of Lewis Carroll*, 137.

10. MEPO 3-140, frame 3153.

11. MEPO 3-142, frame 2.

12. Wilson and Odell, *Jack the Ripper*, 66.

13. Rumbelow, *Jack the Ripper*.

14. Thomas Vere Bayne, unpublished Diaries, Christ Church, Oxford University, Oxford, United Kingdom, August/October, 1888.

15. It is surprising to find the number of transcriptions of this letter that add the missing punctuation. It is clearly missing on the microfilm. Only Stephen Knight reproduces the capitalization and punctuation correctly. I have also reflected the line endings as they were written.

16. Morton N. Cohen, ed., *The Letters of Lewis Carroll* (New York: Oxford University Press, 1979), 717-18.

17. *Trials: for Murders, Robberies, Rapes, Sodomy, Coining, Frauds, and other Offences at the Sessions-House in the Old-Baily - Volume II* (London: L. Giliver, 1742), 136.

18. *Trials*, 136 ff. See also *Northampton Mercury*, 17 November 1724, Vol. V, No. 339, 979 ff.

19. From the photo-reproduction in Wilson and Odell, *Jack the Ripper*, 70.

20. Colin Wilson, *Origins of the Sexual Impulse* (London: Arthur Baker, Limited, 1963), 249.

21. Morton N. Cohen, ed., *Lewis Carroll Interviews and Recollections* (Iowa City: University of Iowa Press, 1989), 37 (quoting T. B. Strong, Bishop of Oxford in "Mr. Dodgson: Lewis Carroll at Oxford," *The Times*, 27 January 1932, pp. 11-12.)

22. Rumbelow, *Jack the Ripper*.

23. Wilson, *Origins of the Sexual Impulse*.

24. Lewis Carroll, *The Nursery "Alice"*, Martin Gardiner, ed. (New York: Dover Publications, 1966), 61.

25. Morton N. Cohen and Anita Gandolfo, *Lewis Carroll and the House of Macmillan* (Cambridge: Cambridge University Press, 1987), 242.

26. Reverend Frederic Farrar, *Eternal Hope* (New York: E. P. Dutton, 1878).

27. Ibid.

28. Ibid., 130-131.

29. Ibid., 136-151.

30. Ibid., 136-137.

31. "MK" (Rev. Samuel Minton), "Is the Doctrine of Everlasting Punishment Taught in the Scriptures?" *Revelation Against Rationalism* (London: James E. Hawkins, 1875).

32. MEPO 3-142, frame 166. I do not have a copy of that letter and there may be a transcription error in the first sentence.

33. Camps, *The Investigation of Murder*, 30.

34. Sugden, *The Complete History of Jack the Ripper*, (New York: Hyperion, 1994), 318.

35. MEPO 3-142, frame 235.

36. Rumbelow, *Jack the Ripper*.

37. Wilson and Odell, *Jack the Ripper*, 76.

38. Lewis Carroll, "A Game of Fives," in Roger Green, ed., *The Works of Lewis Carroll*, 803.

39. Rumbelow, *Jack the Ripper*.

40. Ronald Pearsall, *The Worm in the Bud: The World of Victorian Sexuality* (London: Weiodenfeld and Nicolson, 1969), 459.

41. *Cythera's Hymnal*, (publisher unknown, 1852), 36.

42. Ibid., 47.

43. Rumbelow, *Jack the Ripper*.

44. Wallace, *The Agony of Lewis Carroll*.

45. Charles Dodgson, *Diary Manuscripts*, 25 October 1874.

46. Wilson and Odell, *Jack the Ripper*, 75.

47. Ibid., 77.

Chapter 5. The Masonic Connection

1. Rumbelow, *Jack the Ripper*, 67.

2. Knight, *Jack the Ripper*.

3. Ibid., 177.

4. Paul Begg, *Jack the Ripper: The Uncensored Facts* (London: Robson Books, 1989). Whether *Juwes* was identified as a Masonic word by Knight for his own purposes or was used in Masonic oral tradition as an anti-Semitic word (blaming the Jews for the murder of Hiram Abiff as a parallel to the historical charge against Jews in the death of Christ) is uncertain. In any event, the word as having a Masonic connotation is not crucial to this presentation as there is considerably more near-Masonic symbolism evident.

5. Howells and Skinner, *The Ripper Legacy*.

6. *A Ritual and Illustrations of Freemasonry and the Orange and Odd Fellows Societies* (Shebbear, Devon, England: S. Thorne, 1851), xvi.

7. Ibid., 140-141.

8. Ibid., 93-94. See also Howells and Skinner, *The Ripper Legacy*, 79.

9. MEPO, 8 September 1888.

10. Knight, *Jack the Ripper*.

11. *Rituals*, 92.

12. Cohen, *Letters*, 706.

13. *Rituals*, 151.

14. John Fisher, ed., *The Magic of Lewis Carroll* (New York: Simon and Schuster, 1973), 214-17.

15. *Rituals*, 152.

16. Private communication, 17 April 1990, from K. A. McQuillan, Assistant Librarian, Library and Museum of the United Grand Lodge of England, London.

Chapter 6. The Vivisection Connection

1. William Gull, "The Ethics of Vivisection," *Nineteenth Century* Vol. II, 1882:456. Republished in *A Collection of the Published Writings of William Withey Gull*, Theodore Dyke Acland, ed. (London: The New Sydehalian Society, 1894), 177.

2. Charles Dodgson, Diary Manuscripts, British Library, London, United Kingdom, 12 February 1875.

3. Lewis Carroll, "Vivisection as a Sign of the Times," from Roger Green, ed., *The Works of Lewis Carroll* (London: Paul Hamlyn, 1965), 1089.

4. Theodore Acland, ed., *A Collection of the Published Writings of William Withey Gull* (London: The New Sydehalian Society, 1894), introduction.

5. Carroll, "Vivisection a Sign of the Times," 1091.

6. Coral Lansbury, *The Old Brown Dog* (Madison: University of Wisconsin Press, 1985), 115.

7. Lewis Carroll, "Some Popular Fallacies about Vivisection," from Roger Green, ed., *The Works of Lewis Carroll* (London: Paul Hamlyn, 1965), 1096.

8. Ibid., 1100.

9. Frances Cobbe, "The Woman and the Age" (1881), from *The Modern Rack* (publisher unknown, 1882), 4.

10. Ibid., 6.

11. Ibid., 11.

12. Frances Cobbe, "The Janus of Science," (1882) from *The Modern Rack* (publisher unknown, 1882), 118.

13. Gull, from Acland, *Collected Letters*, 176-177.

14. Acland, ibid., Introduction.

15. Knight, *Jack the Ripper*.

16. Gull, from Acland, *Collected Letters*, 177.

17. Wallace, *The Agony of Lewis Carroll*.

18. Wallace, *The Agony*, 228.   The original quotation is from Lewis Carroll, *Sylvie and Bruno*, XLIV-XLV.

Chapter 7. The Medical Connection

1. Sugden, Philip, *The Complete History of Jack the Ripper*, 441-466.

2. Wilson and Odell, *Jack the Ripper*.

3. *Daily News*, 9 September 1888, 4.

4. Howells and Skinner, *The Ripper Legacy*.

5. MEPO 3-141.

6. Wilson and Odell, *Jack the Ripper*.

7. Green, ed., *Diaries*.

8. Jeffrey Stern, ed, *Lewis Carroll's Library* (Washington, D.C.: The Lewis Carroll Society of North America, 1981), 66.

9. Bernard Taylor, *Cruelly Murdered: Constant Kent and the Killing at Road Hill House* (London: Souvenir Press, 1979).

10. J. W. Stapleton, *The Great Crime of 1860* (London: E. Marlborough & Co., 1861), 59-63.
11. Ibid., 292.
12. Green, *Diaries*, 133.

Chapter 8. The Urge to Tell

1. Stern, *Lewis Carroll's Library*.
2. Edgar Allen Poe, "The Imp of the Perverse" (From *The Unabridged Edgar Allen Poe*, Philadelphia: Running Press Book Publishers), 1056-61.
3. Ibid.
4. Wallace, *The Agony of Lewis Carroll*.
5. Carroll, *Sylvie and Bruno*, 22.

Chapter 9. The Nursery "Alice"

1. Lewis Carroll, *The Nursery "Alice"* with Introduction by Martin Gardner (New York: Dover Publications, Inc., 1966), vi.
2. Ibid.
3. Farson, *Jack the Ripper*, quoting *The Lancet*, 28.
4. Cohen, *Letters*.
5. Stern, *Lewis Carroll's Library*, 54.
6. See Knight, *Jack the Ripper*.
7. *Times*, 9 September 1888, 4.
8. Knight, *Jack the Ripper*.
9. *Times*, 9 September 1888, 4.
10. Wilson and Odell, *Jack the Ripper*.
11. Ibid.
12. Ibid.
13. Lewis Carroll, "Eight or Nine Wise Words about Letter-Writing," from Roger Green, ed., *The Works of Lewis Carroll* (London: Paul Hamlyn, 1965), 1075.
14. Sidney H. Williams, *The Lewis Carroll Handbook* (Folkstead, England: Dawson, 1979), 170. This work is an update of *The Lewis Carroll Handbook* by Sidney H. Williams, Falconer Madan, and Roger L. Green, eds.
15. Bayne, *Diariy Manuscripts*, 30 December 1888.
16. Farson, *Jack the Ripper*.
17. *Times*, 30 December 1888, 4.
18. Inquest Records, Guildhall, London, U.K., 4 October 1888.
19. Rumbelow, *Jack the Ripper*, 64.

20. Rumbelow, *Jack the Ripper*.
21. Ibid.
22. Ibid.
23. Ibid., 77.
24. Carroll, *Alice's Adventures in Wonderland*, 98.
25. Carroll, *The Nursery "Alice"*, chapter XIII, 49.
26. Wallace, *The Agony of Lewis Carroll*, 191.
27. Wilson, *A Casebook of Murder*.
28. Wilson and Odell, *Jack the Ripper*.

Chapter 10. Sylvie and Bruno

1. Wallace, *The Agony*, Chapter 5.
2. Carroll, *The Nursery "Alice"*, chapter X, 37.
3. See Greenacre, *Swift and Carroll*, Clark, *Lewis Carroll: A Biography*, and Wallace, *The Agony of Lewis Carroll*.
4. Carroll, *Sylvie and Bruno*, 79.
5. Mc Cormick, *The Identity of Jack the Ripper*, 52.
6. Barnett, *Canon Barnett*.
7. Clark, *Lewis Carroll*.
8. Rumbelow, *Jack the Ripper*.
9. Carroll, *Sylvie and Bruno*, 107.
10. Rumbelow, *Jack the Ripper*.
11. Wilson, *A Casebook of Murder*, 139.
12. Sugden, Philip, *The Complete History of Jack the Ripper*, 10.
13. Hirschfeld, *Sexual Anomalies and Perversions*, 462-63.
14. Cohen, *Letters*, 836.
15. Greenacre, *Swift and Carroll*, 168.
16. Wilson and Odell, *Jack the Ripper*.
17. Carroll, *Sylvie and Bruno Concluded*, 390.
18. Ibid., 390-391.
19. Ibid., 392.
20. Greenacre, *Swift and Carroll*.

Chapter 11. The Diaries

1. Clark, *Lewis Carroll: A Biography*, 262.
2. Wallace, *The Agony of Lewis Carroll*.
3. Ibid.
4. Lewis Carroll, "Isa's Visit to Oxford, 1888" in Green, *Diaries*, Volume II, appendix C, 557-561.
5. Carroll, *Diary Manuscripts*, 22 April 1877.

6. See Martin Gardner, "The Annotated Snark" in *Lewis Carroll's Hunting of the Snark* (Los Altos, Calif.: William Kaufmann, Inc., 1981).
7. Robert De Rosa, *Vicars of Christ* (New York: Crown Publishers, Inc., 1988).

Chapter 12. Handwriting Analysis

1. Rose Caterino, *Handwriting Analysis*, commissioned by the author, 26 January 1991.
2. Greenacre, *Swift and Carroll*.

Chapter 13. Dates, Names, and Numbers

1. *Encyclopaedia Britannica*, Volume 10, 1971, 776 ff.
2. Wilson and Odell, *Jack the Ripper*. Sugden, *The Complete History of Jack the Ripper*.
3. Wilson and Odell, *Jack the Ripper*.
4. Ibid.
5. H. W. Parke, *Festivals of the Athenians* (London: Thames and Hudson, 1977), 107-114.
6. R. Chambers, ed., *The Book of Days* (London: W. and R. Chambers, 1862-1863), 1864.
7. Pearsall, *The Worm in the Bud*, quoting letter written by Queen Victoria dated 7 January 1868.
8. Colin Gordon, *Beyond the Looking Glass: Reflections of Alice and Her Family* (San Diego: Harcourt Brace Jovanovich, 1982).
9. Chambers, *The Book of Days*, 1853.
10. Rumbelow, *Jack the Ripper*.
11. Chambers, *The Book of Days*.
12. Knight, *Jack the Ripper*.
13. Rumbelow, *Jack the Ripper*.
14. Cohen, ed., *Letters*.
15. Wallace, *The Agony of Lewis Carroll*, 47-48.

Chapter 14. Geography

1. Knight, *Jack the Ripper*.

Chapter 15. The Druitt Connection

1. Rumbelow, *Jack the Ripper*.

2. Howells and Skinner, *The Ripper Legacy*.
3. See Wallace, *The Agony of Lewis Carroll*, appendix 3, for a summary of historical thinking regarding the dynamics of homosexuality.
4. Howells and Skinner, *The Ripper Legacy*, 176.
5. Rumbelow, *Jack the Ripper*.
6. Howells and Skinner, *The Ripper Legacy*.
7. Knight, *Jack the Ripper*.
8. Howells and Skinner, *The Ripper Legacy*, 160.
9. Ibid., 161.
10. Ibid., 166.
11. Ibid.
12. Michael Harrison, *Clarence: Was He Jack the Ripper?* (New York: Drake Publishers Inc., 1972) 165-66.
13. Cohen, ed., *Letters*.
14. Howells and Skinner, *The Ripper Legacy*, 176 (quoting the *Acton, Chiswick and Turnham Green Gazette*, 5 June 1889).
15. Ibid.
16. Knight, *Jack the Ripper*.
17. *Oxford English Dictionary*, 1989.
18. Wilson and Odell, *Jack the Ripper*.
19. Ibid., facing page 192.
20. Knight, *Jack the Ripper*.
21. Ibid.
22. Wallace, *The Agony of Lewis Carroll*.
23. Howells and Skinner, *The Ripper Legacy*.

Bibliography

Abramamsen, David, M.D. *Murder & Madness: The Secret Life of Jack the Ripper*. New York: Donald I. Fine, Inc., 1992.

Acland, Theodore Dyke, M.D., ed. 1884. *A Collection of the Published Writings of William Withey Gull*. London: The New Sydenhanlian Society. Includes Gull's "The Ethics of Vivisection" from the *Nineteenth Century*, vol ii, 1882, p. 456.

Adam, Hargrave L. 1930. *The Trial of George Chapman*. London: William Hodge & Company, Limited. (Chapman was a Ripper suspect.)

Altick, Richard. 1970. *Victorian Studies in Scarlet*. New York: Norton. HV6535-G4A68.

Ambler, Eric. 1963. *The Ability to Kill*. London: Bodley Head.

Barbara, Dominick A., M.D. 1982. *The Psychodynamics of Stuttering*. Springfield, Illinois: Charles C. Thomas Publisher.

Barker, Richard H. 1947. *The Fatal Caress*. New York: Duell, Sloan, and Pearce.

Barnett, Henrietta Octavia. 1918. *Canon [Samuel Augustus] Barnett, His Life, Works, and Friends*. London: John Murray.

Bayne, Thomas Vere. The unpublished diaries of Thomas Vere Bayne, courtesy of Christ Church, Oxford University.

Begg, Paul. 1989. *Jack the Ripper: The Uncensored Facts*. London: Robson Books.

Bennett, Daphne. 1980. *Queen Victoria's Children*. New York: St. Martin's Press.

Blake, William. "The Four Zoas," Night the Fifth," p 327 (v. 241) (closing line). *The Poetry and Prose of William Blake*, edited by David Erdman. New York: Doubleday & Company, Inc., 1965.

Bloch, Ivan. 1938. *Sexual Life in England Past and Present*. London: Francis Aldor.

Boswell, John. 1980. *Christianity, Social Tolerance, and Homosexuality*. Chicago: The University of Chicago Press.

Browne, Douglas G. 1935. *The "Looking-Glass" Murders*. London: Methuen & Co.

_____ 1956. *The Rise of Scotland Yard: A History of the Metropolitan Police*. London: George G. Harrap & Co. Ltd.

Buckle, George Earle, ed. 1930. *The Letters of Queen Victoria: Volume 1, 1886 to 1890*. London: John Murray.

Bullough, Vern L. 1979. *Homosexuality: A History*. New York: New American Library.

Camps, Francis E. 1966. *The Investigation of Murder*. London: Michael Joseph.

Carroll, Lewis. 1867. "Bruno's Revenge." In *Aunt Judy's Magazine*, December, edited by Mrs. Alfred Gaddy. London: Bell and Daldy, p. 65-78.

_____. 1893. *Sylvie and Bruno Concluded*. London: Macmillan and Co.

_____. 1954. *Useful and Instructive Poetry*. Dodgson, Frances Menella, ed. New York: Macmillan and Co.

_____. 1958. *Symbolic Logic*. From: *Symbolic Logic and The Game of Logic*. New York: Dover Publications, Inc.

_____. 1960. *Alice's Adventures in Wonderland*. From Gardner, Martin. *The Anotated Alice*. New York: New American Library. See also Green, Roger L., ed. 1982. *Alice's Adventures in Wonderland and Through the Looking-Glass*. New York, Oxford University Press.

_____. 1965. *Alice's Adventures Underground*. New York: Dover Publications, Inc.

_____. 1966. *The Nursery "Alice"*. New York: Dover Publications, Inc.

_____. 1968. *Through the Looking-Glass and What Alice Found There*. From Gardner, Martin, ed. *The Anotated Alice*. New York: New American Library. See also Green, Roger L., ed. 1982. *Alice's Adventures in Wonderland and Through the Looking-Glass*. New York, Oxford University Press.

_____. 1981. *The Hunting of the Snark: An Agony in Eight Fits*. Tanis, James and Dooley, John, eds. *The Hunting of the Snark*. Los Altos: William Kaufman, Inc.

_____. 1988. *Sylvie and Bruno*. New York: Dover Publications, Inc. (This was produced as a facsimile copy and page numbers agree with the first edition.)

Caterino, Rose. 26 January 1991. *Handwriting Analysis*, commissioned by the author.

Chambers, R., ed. 1863-1864. *The Book of Days*. Edinburg: W. and R. Chambers.

Chesney, Kellow. 1970. *The Victorian Underworld*. London: Temple Smith.

Clark, Anne. 1979. *Lewis Carroll: A Biography*. New York: Schocken Books.

Cleckley, H. 1964. *The Mask of Sanity.* St. Louis: C. V. Mosby Company.

Cobb, Belton. 1956. *Critical Years at the Yard: The Career of Frederick Williamson of the Detective Department and the CID.* London: Faber and Faber.

Cobbe, Frances Power. 1876. Comments on the debate in House of Commons [on Vivisection Bill. She was at the time Hon Sec. Victoria St. Society for the Protection of Cruelty to Animals.

_____. 1882. *The Modern Rack.* A collection of her works and others, including articles in *Nineteenth Century* and *Fortnightly Review*, January and March 1882.

_____. 1889. *The Murderers Rack: Papers on Vivisection.* London: S. Sonnenschein and Co.

Cohen, Morton N., ed. 1979. *The Letters of Lewis Carroll.* New York: Oxford University Press. Referred to as "*Letters.*"

_____. 1989. *Lewis Carroll Interviews & Recollections.* Iowa City: University of Iowa Press.

_____. 1995. *Lewis Carroll: A Biography.* New York. Alfred A. Knopf.

_____ and Anita Gandolfo. 1987. *Lewis Carroll and the House of Macmillan.* Cambridge. Cambridge University Press.

Collingwood, Stuart Dodgson. 1898. *The Life and Letters of Lewis Carroll.* London: The Century Company.

Cowles, Virginia. 1956. *Gay Monarch: the Life and Pleasures of Edward VII.* New York: Harper.

Cullen, Tom. 1965. *Autumn of Terror: Jack the Ripper: His Crimes and Times.* London: Bodley Head.

Cythera's Hymnal. 1852. Claims publication by Oxford University Press but highly unlikely. Courtesy of British Library Private Collection.

De Rosa, Robert. 1988. *Vicars of Christ.* New York: Crown Publishers, Inc.

Dew, Walter. 1938. *I Caught Crippen: Memoirs of Ex-Chief Inspector Walter Dew, C.I.D. of Scotland Yard.* London: Blackie and Son, Limited.

Dodgson, Charles L. Diary Manuscripts. Courtesy of the British Library, Manuscript Collection, London, England.

_____. 1879. *Euclid and His Modern Rivals.* London: Macmillan and Co.

_____. 1888. *Curiosa Mathematica I - A New Theory of Parallels.* London: Macmillan.

_____. 1893. *Curiosa Mathematica II - Pillow Problems*. London: Macmillan.

Donaldson, Rev. Aug. B. 1902. *Five Great Oxford Leaders*. London: Rivingtons.

East, John M. 1967. *'Neath the Mask: The Story of the East Family*. London: George Allen and Unwin Ltd.

1811 Dictionary of the Vulgar Tongue: A Dictionary of Buckish Slang, University Wit and Pickpocket Eloquence. 1971. Chicago: Follet Publishing Co.

Evans, Arthur. 1988. *The God of Ecstasy*. New York: St. Martin's Press.

Farrar, Frederic, Reverend. 1878. *Eternal Hope*. New York: E. P. Dutton.

Farson, Daniel. 1972. *Jack the Ripper*. London: Michael Joseph.

Fisher, John, ed. 1973. *Magic of Lewis Carroll*. New York: Simon and Schuster.

Fraxi, Pisanus. 1877. *Index Librorum Prohibitorum*. British Library, no publisher. Courtesy of British Library Private Collection.

French, Richard D. 1975. *Anti-vivisection and Medical Science in Victorian Society*. Princeton, N.J.: Princeton Universisty Press.

Gardner, Martin. 1981. "The Annotated Snark." In *Lewis Caroll's Hunting of the Snark*. Los Altos, Calif.: William Kaufmann, Inc.

Gaunt, William. 1942. *The Pre-Raphaelite Tragedy*. London: Jonathen Cape.

Gernsheim, Helmut. 1949. *Lewis Carroll: Photographer*. London: Max Parrish & Co. Limited.

Gordon, C. A. 1888. "The Vivisection Controversy in Parliament: An answer to a speech delivered by Lyon Playfair in the House of Commons April 4, 1883." London: Williams and Nogate.

Gordon, Colin. 1982. *Beyond the Looking-Glass: Reflections of Alice and Her Family*. San Diego: Harcourt Brace Jovanovich, 1982.

Gordon, Richard. 1980. *Jack the Ripper*. New York: Atheneum.

Green, Roger L., ed. 1954. *The Diaries of Lewis Carroll*. New York: Oxford University Press. Referred to as "Diaries."

Green, Roger Lancelyn, ed. 1965. *The Works of Lewis Carroll*. London: Paul Hamlyn, Ltd.

Greenacre, Phyllis, M.D. 1955. *Swift and Carroll: A Psychoanalytic Study of Two Lives*. New York: International Universities Press.

Greene, Samuel D. 1870. *The Broken Seal, or, Personal Reminiscences of the Morgan Abduction and Murder.* Boston: H. H. and T. W. Carter.

Gull, William. 1882. "The Ethics of Vivisection." *Nineteenth Century* Vol. ii:456. Republished in *A Collection of the Published Writings of William Withey Gull*, Theodore Dyke Acland, ed. London: The New Sydehanlian Society, 1894.

Guttmacher, Manfred S., and Henry Weihoffen. 1952. *Psychiatry and the Law.* New York: W. W. Norton and Company, Inc.

Halpern, Sidney. 1965. "The Mother-killer." *Psychoanalytic Review* LII, Summer: 71-74.

Halsted, D. G. 1959. *Doctor in the Nineties.* London: Christopher Johnson.

Hannah, Walton. 1952. *Darkness Visible, A Revelation & Interpretation of Freemasonry.* London: Augustine Press.

Harlequin: Prince Cherrytop. Author unknown. Copy 8 of 300, privately published MDCCCCV by the Council of the Erotika Biblion Society. Courtesy of British Library Private Collection.

Harrison, Michael. 1972. *Clarence: Was He Jack the Ripper?* New York: Drake Publishers Inc.

Harrison, Shirley, Narrator. 1993. *The Diary of Jack the Ripper.* New York: Hyperion.

Heath, Peter. 1974. *The Philosopher's Alice.* New York: St. Martin's Press.

Hirshfeld, Dr. Magnus. 1938. *Sexual Anomalies and Perversions.* London: Encyclopedia Press.

Honeycombe, Gordon. 1989. *The Murders of the Black Museum 1870-1970.* London: Mysterious Press.

Howells, Martin and Keith Skinner. 1987. *The Ripper Legacy.* London: The Penquin Group.

Hudson, Derek. 1954. *Life of Lewis Carroll.* London: Constable and Company.

IATSV. 1881. Letter to Gladstone entitled "The Woman and the Age" by the International Association for the Total Supression of Vivisection. Easter, a free pamphlet.

Index Medicus. 1886. Report. Reflects licences and reporting required under Act 39 and 40 vict. p 77 Parliamentary Paper # 119 of session 1885. London: 1886. Hansen and Son. 12 p. fol.

Jonas, Gerard. 1977. *Stuttering: the Disorder of Many Theories.* New York: Farrar, Straus, and Giroux.

Khan, M. Masud R. 1979. *Alienation in Perversions.* London: The Hogarth Press and the Institute of Psycho-Analysis.

Knight, Stephen. 1985. *The Brotherhood: The Secret World of the Freemasons*. London: Grafton.

_____. 1986. *Jack the Ripper: The Final Solution*. Chicago: Academy Chicago Publishers.

Kohut, Heinz, M.D., and Ernest S. Wolf. 1978. "The Disorders of the Self and Their Treatment: an Outline." *Journal of Psycho-Analysis* 59:413-425.

Krafft-Ebing, Dr. R. von. 1893. *Psychopathia Sexualis, Contrary Sexual Instinct: A Medico-Legal Study*. London: F. J. Rebman.

Lansbury, Coral. 1985. *The Old Brown Dog*. Madison: University of Wisconsin Press.

Macnaghten, Sir Melville L. 1914. *Days of My Years*. London: Edward Arnold.

Marcus, Steven. 1964. *The Other Victorians: A Study of Sexuality and Pornography in Mid-Nineteenth-Century England*. New York: Basic Books, Inc.

Mathew, Roy J., M.D. 1981. *Treatment of Migraine*. New York: SP Medical and Scientific Books.

Matters, Leonard. 1964. *The Mystery of Jack the Ripper*. London: Arrow.

May, Rollo. 1953. *Man's Search for Himself*. New York: W. W. Norton. Reprint. New York: Dell Publishing, 1973.

McCormick, Donald. 1959. *The Identity of Jack the Ripper*. London: Jarrolds.

McQuillan, K. A., Assistant Librarian. 17 April 1990. Private communication from Library and Museum of the United Grand Lodge of England, Freemason's Hall, Great Queen Street, London WC2B 5AZ, U.K.

MEPO. Metropolitan Police microfilm reels 140-143. Records Office, Kew, London, UK.

Miller, Alice. 1981. *The Drama of the Gifted Child*. New York: Basic Books, Inc.

_____. 1983. *For Your Own Good: Hidden Cruelty in Child-Rearing and the Roots of Violence*. New York: Farrar, Straus, Giroux.

"M. K." 1875. "Is the Doctrine of Everlasting Punishment Taught in the Scriptures?" In *Revelation Against Rationalism*. London: James E. Hawkins.

Morgan, William. 1882. *Morgan's Freemasonry Exposed*: showing the origin, history, and nature of Masonry; its effects on the government, and the Christian religion, and containing a key to all the degrees of Fremasonry, giving a clear and correct view of the manner of conferring the different degrees, as practiced in all lodges throughout the globe, together with the means to be used by such as are not Masons to gain admission therin. The whole intended as a guide to the Craft and a light to the unenlightened. New York: L. Fitzgerald. Courtesy of The John J. Burns Library, Boston College, Chestnut Hill, MA 02167.

O'Donnell, Elliott. 1929. *Great Thames Mysteries.* London: Selwyn & Blount Lte.

Oxford English Dictionary. 1989. 2d ed. Oxford: Clarendon Press.

Oxford Latin Dictionary. 1968. London: Oxford at the Clarenden Press.

Parke, H. W. 1977. *Festivals of the Athenians.* London: Thames and Hudson.

Partridge, Eric. 1967. *A Dictionary of Slang and Unconventional English, 6th Edition.* New York: Macmillan Co.

Pearsall, Ronald. 1969. *The Worm in the Bud: The World of Victorian Sexuality.* London: Weiodenfeld and Nicolson.

Playfair, Sir Lyon. 1876. Speech delivered in the House of Commons on the second reading of Mr. Reid's bill for the total suppression of scientific experiments upon animals. April.

Poe, Edgar Allen. 1983. "The Imp of the Perverse." From *The Unabridged Edgar Allen Poe*, Philadelphia: Running Press Book Publishers.

Reed, Langford. 1932. *The Life of Lewis Carroll.* London: W. & G. Foyle, Ltd.

A Ritual and Illustrations of Freemasonry and the Orange and Odd Fellows Societies, also an account of the kidnapping and murder of William Morgan, who divulged the ridiculous and profane usages of the Freemasons. Abridged from American authors. Shebbear, Devon: S. Thorne. Avery Allyn. 1851. This is the work that was in the Carroll library sale. See notes and drawings. Courtesy of The John J. Burns Library, Boston College, Chestnut Hill, MA 02167.

Roche, Paul., trans. 1962. *The Orestes Plays of Aeschylus.* New York: Mentor Classic, New American Library.

Rose, Alfred. 1936. *Registrum Librorum Eroticorum.* British Library, no publisher. Contains five thousand entries of Victorian pornography.

Rowell, George. 1956. *The Victorian Theatre: A Survey.* New York: Oxford University Press.

Rumbelow, Donald. 1988. *Jack the Ripper.* Formerly *The Complete Jack the Ripper.* Chicago: Contemporary Books.

Sacks, Oliver, M.D. 1985. *Migraine: Understanding a Common Disorder.* Berkeley and Los Angeles: University of California Press.

Sermons by (39) Living Divines of the Church of England. 1840. London: Revington.

Sewell, Elizabeth. 1952. *The Field of Nonsense.* London: Chatto and Windus. Reprint. Norwood Editions, 1977.

Shaberman, R. B. 1978. "A Plum-Cake Lost and Found" An episode in the writings of Lewis Carroll and E.B.Wilcox, copy # 95 of 100, privately circulated.

Shakespeare, William. 1936 *The Tragedy of Hamlet, Prince of Denmark.* From *The Complete Works of William Shakespeare*, Cambridge Edition Text as edited by William Aldis Wright. 1936. Garden City, N. Y.: Doubleday & Co., Inc.

Shaw, Bernard. 1963. *Major Barbara.* From *Complete Plays with Prefaces* Volume I. New York: Dodd , Mead & Co.

_____. 1965. *Collected Letters 1874-1897.* Edited by Dan H. Laurence. London: Max Reinhardt.

Sims, George R. 1889. *How the Poor Live and Horrible London.* London: Chatto and Windus.

Sims, George R. 1906. *The Mysteries of Modern London.* London: C. Arthur Pearson Ltd.

Sitwell, Osbert and Margaret Barton, eds. 1930. *Sober Truth: Nineteenth Century Mysteries.* London: Duckworth.

Smith, Lieutenant Colonel Sir Henry. 1910. *From Constable to Commissioner: The Story of Sixty Years Most of Them Misspent by.* London: Chatto & Windus.

Smith, Sir William. 1853. *A Latin English Dictionary.* London: publisher not known.

Spiering, Frank. 1978. *Prince Jack.* New York: Doubleday.

Stapleton, J. W. 1861. *The Great Crime of 1860*: being a summary of the acts relating to the murder committed at Road. London: E. Marlborough & Co.

Stern, Jeffrey, ed. 1981. *Lewis Carroll's Library.* Washington, D.C.: The Lewis Carroll Society of North America.

Stevenson, Robert Louis. 1973. *Dr. Jekyll and Mr. Hyde.* New York: Interlyth.

Sugden, Philip. 1994. *The Complete History of Jack the Ripper.* New York: Carroll & Graf Publishers, Inc.

Symonds, John Addington. 1892. *A Problem in Modern Ethics being an Inquiry into the Phenomenon of Sexual Inverson.* No publisher, copy 87 of 100 printed privately.

Talbot, Rt. Rev. Bishop, et. al. 1929. *Henry Parry Liddon: 1829-1929, A Centenary Memoir.* London: A. R. Mowbray & Co. Ltd.

Taylor, Bernard. 1979. *Cruelly Murdered: Constance Kent and the Killing at Road Hill House.* London: Souvenir Press.

Trials: for Murders, Robberies, Rapes, Sodomy, Coining, Frauds, and other Offences at the Sessions-House in the Old-Baily. Volume II. 1742. London: L. Giliver.

Victoria, Queen of England and Barry Saint-John Nevill. 1984. *Life at the Court of Queen Victoria 1861-1901.* Exeter, England: Webb and Bower.

Wainhouse, Aistryn and Richard Seaver, trans. 1966. *The Marquis de Sade, The 120 Days of Sodom and Other Writings.* New York: Grove Press.

Wallace, Richard. 1990. *The Agony of Lewis Carroll.* Melrose, Mass: Gemini Press.

Walter. *My Secret Life.* 11 volume pornographic "autobiography." Courtesy of British Library Private Collection. Authorship and date of publication uncertain.

Wensley, Frederick Porter. 1931. *Detective Days: The Record of Forty-two Years' Service in the Criminal Investigation Department.* London: Cassell & Company, Ltd.

West, Pamela Elizabeth. 1987. *Yours truly, Jack the Ripper.* New York: St. Martin's Press.

Whittington-Egan, Richard. 1976. *A Casebook on Jack the Ripper.* London: Wildy.

Williams, Sidney H. 1979. *The Lewis Carroll Handbook.* (Update of *The Lewis Carroll Handbook,* by Sidney H. Williams and Falconer Madan, Roger L. Green, ed.) Folkstead, England: Dawson.

Wilson, Colin. 1963. *Origins of the Sexual Impulse.* London: Arthur Baker, Limited.

_____. 1969. *A Casebook of Murder.* London: Leslie Frewin.

_____. 1980. *The New Existentialism.* London: Wildwood House. Originally published as *Introduction to the New Existentialism* in 1966.

Wilson, Colin and Robin Odell. 1988. *Jack the Ripper.* London: Transworld Publishers (Corgi Books).

Index